SPARK'S SATIRE

'[Spark] has a receptive and wholly distinctive genius'
A.N. WILSON

'Spark is a natural, a paradigm of that rare sort of
artist from whom work of the highest quality flows as
elementally as a current through a circuit' NEW YORKER

'I consider Muriel Spark to be the most gifted and innovative
British novelist of her generation' DAVID LODGE

'A profoundly serious comic writer whose wit advances,
never undermines or diminishes, her ideas'
NEW YORK TIMES BOOK REVIEW

'Reading a blast of her prose every morning is a far more
restorative way to start a day than a shot of espresso'
DAILY TELEGRAPH

'There can be few novelists who command such
a formidable technique' *FINANCIAL TIMES*

'Delightful, laced with wry and witty observations'
DAILY

Muriel Spark

SPARK'S SATIRE

CANONGATE

Edinburgh · London

This Canons edition published in Great Britain in 2016
by Canongate Books Ltd, 14 High Street, Edinburgh EH1 1TE

www.canongate.tv

1

British Library Cataloguing-in-Publication Data
A catalogue record for this book is available on
request from the British Library

ISBN 978 1 78211 767 4

Typeset in Sabon MT by Canongate Books Ltd

Printed and bound in Great Britain by Clays Ltd, St Ives plc.

LONDON BOROUGH OF WANDSWORTH	
9030 00005 1718 8	
Askews & Holts	11-Aug-2016
AF	£10.99
	WW16006974

CONTENTS

ROBINSON

ROBINSON

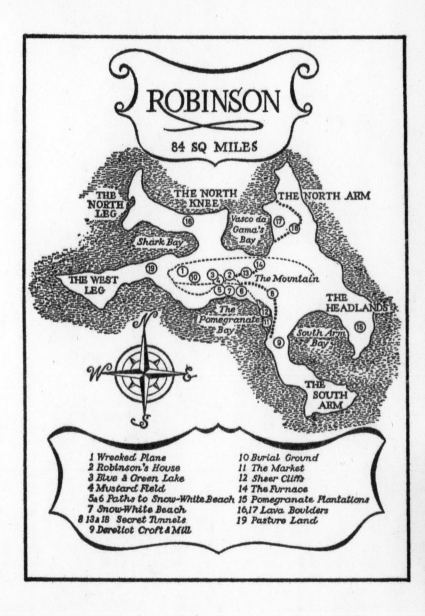

ROBINSON

84 SQ MILES

THE NORTH LEG

THE NORTH KNEE

THE NORTH ARM

Vasco da Gama's Bay

Shark Bay

THE WEST LEG

The Mountain

THE HEADLANDS

The Pomegranate Bay

South Arm Bay

THE SOUTH ARM

1 Wrecked Plane
2 Robinson's House
3 Blue & Green Lake
4 Mustard Field
5,6 Paths to Snow-White Beach
7 Snow-White Beach
8 13a 18 Secret Tunnels
9 Derelict Croft & Mill

10 Burial Ground
11 The Market
12 Sheer Cliffs
14 The Furnace
15 Pomegranate Plantations
16,17 Lava Boulders
19 Pasture Land

I

IF YOU ASK ME HOW I REMEMBER the island, what it was like to be stranded there by misadventure for nearly three months, I would answer that it was a time and landscape of the mind if I did not have the visible signs to summon its materiality: my journal, the cat, the newspaper-cuttings, the curiosity of my friends; and my sisters – how they always look at me, I think, as one returned from the dead.

You have read about the incident in the papers, and there were some aerial pictures of the island which, when I saw them later, were difficult to recognize as the scene of all I am going to tell you. Most of all, it is the journal that gives me my bearings. It fetches before me the play of thought and action hidden amongst the recorded facts. Through my journal I nearly came by my death.

Three of us were projected from the blazing plane when it crashed on Robinson's island. We were the only survivors of twenty-nine souls including the crew, and, as you know, we were presumed lost until we were found two months and twenty-nine days later. I had concussion and a dislocated left shoulder. Jimmie Waterford got off with a few cuts and bruises. Tom Wells had fractured ribs. I made a quick recovery, and had not been ten days on the island when I started my journal in a damp paper exercise book which Robinson gave me for the purpose. I see that I began by writing my name, the place, and the date, as follows:

January Marlow,
Robinson
May 20, 1954

My name is January, because I was born in January. I would like to state that I am never called Jan although some of the Sunday papers used that name on their headlines when the news came out that we had been picked up.

Robinson thought at the time that keeping a journal would be an occupation for my mind, and I fancied that I might later dress it up for a novel. That was most peculiar, as things transpired, for I did not then anticipate how the journal would turn upon me, so that, having survived the plane disaster, I should nearly meet my death through it.

Sometimes I am a little vague about the details of the day before yesterday until some word or thing, almost a sacramental, touches my memory, and then the past comes walking over me as we say an angel is walking over our grave, and I stand in the past as in the beam of a searchlight.

When I looked through my island journal again, quite recently, I came across the words, 'Robinson played Rossini to us on his gramophone.' I remembered then, not only Robinson's addiction to Rossini, but all that was in my mind on that evening. That was the twenty-fifth of June, not long before Robinson disappeared. I recall that night – it was my seventh week on the island – I left Robinson's house and climbed down the mountain track among the blue gum trees to the coast. It was a warm night, free from mist, full of moon. I had a desire to throw wide my arms and worship the moon. 'But,' I thought to myself, 'I am a Christian.' Still I had this sweet and dreadful urge towards the moon, and I went back indoors slightly disturbed.

Lying awake that night on my mattress I remembered that my grandmother from Hertfordshire used to recite a little rhyme to the new moon, no matter where, or in what busy street she might be. I saw her in my mind's eye, as I see her now, setting herself apart on the road, intent on the pale crescent against the deepening northern sky:

New Moon, New Moon, be good to me,
And bring me presents, one, two, three.

Then she would bow three times. 'One,' she repeated. 'Two. Three.' As a child it embarrassed me if I chanced to be out with her at new moon. I dreaded every moment that one of my school chums might come along and find me associated with this eccentric behaviour. I ramble on, for I am still a little intoxicated with the memory of my sudden wanting to worship the moon among the tall blue gums and sleeping bougainvillaea, with the sea at my ears. I was the only woman on the island, and it is said the pagan mind runs strong in women at any time, let alone on an island, and such an island. It is not only the moon, the incident, that I am thinking of. I consider now how my perceptions during that whole period were touched with a pre-ancestral quality, how there was an enchantment, a primitive blood-force which probably moved us all.

Sometimes people say to me, 'If only you hadn't undertaken that journey . . . ' 'What a pity you didn't catch an earlier plane . . . ' or 'To think that you nearly went by sea!'

I am inclined to reject the idea behind these remarks in the same way as I reject the idea that it is best to have never been born.

The plane crashed on the tenth of May, 1954. It had been bound for the Azores but missed the airport of Santa Maria in the fog. I woke by the side of a green and blue mountain lake, and immediately thought, 'The banana boat must have been wrecked.' I then went back into my coma.

It is true I had nearly taken a banana boat bound for the West Indies which called in at the Azores, but had been gradually dissuaded by my friends, after we had taken several looks at the Lascars, Danes, and Irish lolling round the East India Docks. And so, although I had finally taken the expensive Lisbon route by plane, still in my dreams it was the banana boat.

When I came round the second time it was in Robinson's house. I was lying on a mattress on the floor, and as I moved I felt my shoulder hurting very painfully. I could see, facing me through the misty sunlight of a partly open door, a corner of the blue and green lake. We seemed to be quite high on the side of a mountain.

I could hear someone moving in an inner room to my left. In a few moments I heard the voices of two men.

'I say!' I called out. The voices stopped. Then one murmured something.

Presently a door opened at my left. I tried to twist round, but this was painful, and I waited while a man entered the room and came to face me.

'Where am I?'

'Robinson,' he said.

'*Where?*'

'Robinson.'

He was short and square, with a brown face and greyish curly hair.

'Robinson,' he repeated. 'In the North Atlantic Ocean. How do you feel?'

'Who are you?'

'Robinson,' he said. 'How do you feel?'

'*Who*?'

'Robinson.'

'I think I must be suffering from concussion,' I said.

He said, 'I'm glad you think so, because it is true. To know you have concussion, when you have it, is one-third of the cure. I see you are intelligent.'

On hearing this I decided that I liked Robinson, and settled down to sleep. He shook me awake and placed at my lips a mug of warm tangy milk. While I gulped it, he said,

'Sleep is another third of the cure, and nourishment is the remaining third.'

'My shoulder hurts,' I said.

'Which shoulder?'

I touched my left shoulder. I found it stiff with bandages.

'Which shoulder?' he said.

'This one,' I said, 'it is bound up.'

'*Which* shoulder? Don't point. Think. Describe.'

I paused for light. Presently I said, 'My left shoulder.'

'That's true. You will soon recover.'

A little fluffy blue-grey cat came and sat in the open doorway, squinting at me as I fell asleep.

This was twenty hours after the crash. When I woke again it was dark and I was frightened.

'I say!' I called out.

No reply, and so, after a few minutes, I called out again,

'I say, Robinson!'

A soft living thing jumped on my chest. I screamed, I sat up despite the pain which the movement caused my shoulder. My hand touched soft fur as the cat sprang off the mattress.

Robinson came in with an oil lamp and peered down at me under its beam.

'I thought it was a rat,' I said, 'but it was the cat.'

He placed the lamp on a shiny table. 'Did you feel afraid?' he said.

'Oh, I'm quite tough. But first there was the darkness and then the cat. I thought it was a rat.'

He bent and stroked the cat which was arching around his legs. 'Her name's Bluebell,' he said and went out.

I heard him moving about, and presently he was back with some hot spicy soup. He looked tired, and sighed a little as he gave it to me.

'What is your name?' he said.

'January Marlow.'

'Think,' he said. 'Try to think.'

'Think of what?'

'Your name.'

'January Marlow,' I said, and placed the mug of soup on the floor beside me.

He lifted the mug and replaced it in my right hand.

'Sip it, and meanwhile think. You have told me the month and place of your birth. What is your name?'

I was rather pleased about his mistake, it gave me confidence.

'I am called by the unusual name of January because I was born in – '

Immediately he understood. 'Oh yes, I see.'

'You thought it was my concussion,' I said.

He smiled feebly.

Suddenly I said, 'There must have been an accident. I was on the Lisbon plane.'

I sipped the broth while I tried to elucidate what my statement had implied.

'Don't think too hard,' Robinson said, 'all at one time.'

'I remember the Lisbon plane,' I said.

'Were you with friends or relations?'

I knew the answer to that. 'No,' I said at once, rather loudly. Robinson stood still and sighed.

'But I must send a wire to London in the morning,' I said.

'There's no post office on Robinson. It is a very small island.' He added, since I suppose I looked startled, 'You are safe. I think you will be able to get up tomorrow. Then you shall see what's what.'

He took my empty cup, then sat down in a high wicker chair. The cat jumped on to his lap. 'Bluebell,' he murmured to it. I lay and stared, partly comatose, and it was difficult for me to collect a thought and place it into a sentence. Eventually I said,

'Would you mind telling me, is there a nurse, a woman anywhere about?'

He peered forward as if to compel my attention. 'That must be a difficulty for you. There is no woman on the island. But it is not difficult for me to nurse you. It will only be for a short while. Besides, it is necessary.' He put the cat off his lap. 'Regard me as a doctor or something like that.'

A man's voice called from the inner house.

'That's one of the other patients,' said Robinson.

'How many . . . the accident. How many?'

'I'll be back soon,' he said.

I thought he showed fatigue as he left my range of vision. Bluebell camelled her back, stalked on to my mattress, curled up, and began to purr.

We were a thousand miles from anywhere. I think the effects of the concussion were still upon me when I got up, the fourth morning after the crash. It was some time before I took in the details of Robinson's establishment, and not till a week later that I began to wonder at his curious isolation.

By that time there was no hope of our immediate rescue. Many of you will remember how the whole of the Atlantic had been notified, how military aircraft and commercial airlines searched for us, and all ships kept a look-out for survivors or portions of the wreck. Meantime, there we were on Robinson, with the wreck and the corpses. The island had been under mist when the first search party came over shortly after the crash. Robinson lit distress signals every night, but when, two nights later, the searchers returned, a torrent of rain had quenched the flares. On both occasions the plane had retreated quickly out of the mist, fearful of our mountain. There was nothing but to wait for the pomegranate boat in August.

My left arm ached in its sling when I rose dizzily from my couch on the floor, but dazed as I was, Robinson sent me immediately to nurse Tom Wells who lay with broken ribs encased in a tight jacket which Robinson had contrived, made of canvas strips bound diagonally from back to front, the layers overlapping each other by two-thirds. Robinson explained the principle of this jacket very carefully before telling me that in any case I mustn't remove it from the patient. My hours of duty were from eight in the morning until three in the afternoon, when Robinson relieved me.

A long thin man, with his head bound in a proper bandage, did night shifts, and I believe Robinson took over from him also, during the night, so that someone was always ready to attend to Tom Wells.

Robinson had introduced me to the tall man; I recollect his naming me 'Miss January', but I did not catch the man's name, although he seemed familiar to me. I asked Robinson several times in those first days, 'Who is the other nurse? What's his name?' but it was a full week before the name had sunk in, Jimmie Waterford. This Jimmie was very friendly to me, as if we were previously acquainted. It was some time before I remembered having met him on the Lisbon plane. The monosyllabic 'Tom Wells', however, stuck in my mind right away.

About this time I became aware of a small lean boy, about nine years old, very brown and large-eyed. I had seen him when I first got up, but did not really notice him for several days. He followed Robinson everywhere. He had certain duties, like fetching small consignments of firewood into the house and making tea. His name was Miguel.

In the mornings Robinson would give me instructions. I followed them with meticulous care, as one dazed and unable to exercise curiosity. Meanwhile Robinson and the tall man would go off together for two or three hours at a time.

Tom Wells, besides being the most seriously injured, was a difficult patient. He moaned or made noises nearly all day, although Robinson gave him injections. He seemed to have grasped our situation and was, in fact, more conscious than I was at that time. I have always been against nurses who won't stand nonsense from their patients, but I found myself becoming snappy and sharp with Tom Wells, as to the manner born. Robinson would smile in his weary manner, when he overheard me telling the man, 'Stop that noise', 'Pull yourself together', 'Drink this', and so on. All this, before I had in any way got my new environment into focus. I knew, with an inhuman indifference, that there had been an accident. I accepted the situation of being simply in a place, that Robinson was in charge, and that I was to look after Tom Wells at certain fixed times.

Exactly a week after the accident, Robinson said to me at breakfast, 'Try to eat as little as you can. Most of our food is tinned, and I had not counted on guests.'

It was only then that I realized I was eating at all. Robinson had produced meals, and I now presumed I had been eating them. I looked at my plate on the round, pale-wood table. I had just finished a portion of yellowish beans. Beside my plate was half a hard thick dry biscuit, of a type which I now recalled having dipped into strong warm tea during the past few days.

After that, I noticed the place more closely. When I began that day to act independently of Robinson, he seemed relieved. It was two days later that he gave me the exercise book for my journal.

I wanted to be at home again, giggling with Agnes and Julia when they came to tea on cold afternoons. Giggling over childhood anecdotes was the main thing with my sisters, and how, afterwards, I would wonder at my own childishness!

And yet, at those moments, I enjoyed the silly sessions. There had been a time, after my elopement as a schoolgirl, the birth of my son, and my widowhood that same year, when I was estranged from my sisters. From Agnes, because she was the eldest: lumpy, unmarried, and resenting my adventure. Agnes kept house for our grandmother. When Grandmother died, Agnes married the doctor; she married after all. We became friends, up to the point where it is possible to be friends with Agnes, who eats noisily, for one thing.

My younger sister, Julia, was still at school when I ran away from it to marry. Six months later my husband was dead. I tried to take an interest in Julia, with her tall prettiness. But she was considered a loose girl; I thought so too. 'It's nothing but men, men, men, with Julia,' I said once to Agnes.

'Oh, shut up,' said Agnes.

Years later, Julia married a bookie. They were married in a register office. I was not invited. I saw the bookie at Grandmother's funeral; I mistook him for the undertaker at first.

'I mistook him for the undertaker,' I whispered to Agnes.

'Oh, shut up,' said Agnes. She did not tell me then that she planned to marry the doctor within a month.

After that, when we began to be reconciled, Julia and Agnes would come to tea with me, though I rarely visited them. Agnes lived at Chiswick and Julia at Wimbledon, and it is a bother to get to those places from Chelsea. We soon found the only common ground between us – our childhood. We would giggle till about six o'clock when my son Brian would come in, rosy-cheeked from his school games. My sisters would never leave without seeing him. I fancied they envied me Brian, for the years went on and both were childless.

When I had run away as a schoolgirl, and Brian was born, Agnes had shown no interest in the child. Her curiosity was in my direction. 'You're far too young for this sort of caper,' she said from her privileged position as a visitor in a nursing-home – she perpendicular, I horizontal. 'I thought you were supposed to have brains,' she said.

But when they saw Brian in later years, both my sisters were, I think, surprised at his lack of blight; they had somehow expected the child of such a young girl to grow up peculiar.

'Goodness,' said Julia after the funeral, 'look at January's boy. Isn't he a real *boy*!'

But they had yet to discover Brian's extraordinary social skill, for that side of his personality had already, in his middle teens, advanced beyond his age.

'Goodness,' said Julia, 'hasn't he got *charm*!'

I often wondered if Agnes and Julia really came to visit Brian, not me; trailing all that way from Chiswick and Wimbledon on cold afternoons. Even during the first phase of my religious conversion, when I took to lecturing my sisters, they continued to come.

Journal, May 20, 1954 – The area of Robinson is only a little over 84 square miles, if you can call them square that run in such strange directions. Robinson bought the island fifteen years ago from a Portuguese and settled here after the war. Its former name was Ferreira. Robinson showed me a map. If you hold it east-upmost it resembles a human shape. There are several peninsulas which Robinson calls the North Arm and the South Arm of the island, the North Leg and the West Leg. Robinson's house is on a plateau nearly a thousand feet above the sea. It is a volcanic mountain, only cinders and lava at the top, but he says the descent passes through the range of known climates. R. once sprained his ankle up there, when he tripped on a patch of ling. In July the upper third of the mountain is covered with flowering thyme. I have these facts from Robinson. He has given me this notebook. He said, 'Keep to facts, that will be the healthiest course.' I am always tired.

Now, as I look at the crinkled page of my first journal entry, I recall that it was Robinson's idea to write very small, to make no paragraphs, to save the paper. Even so, the exercise book did not last out my time on the island; I had later to use some loose writing paper which I found on Robinson's desk.

I recall that Robinson had advised more than once, 'Stick to facts.' He had advised strongly against gazing at the sea in the hope of a boat or at the sky for a plane – a depressing habit, he said. I could scarcely keep my eyes from the sea and sky in those first weeks, although the boat which would bring Robinson's provisions and take away his pomegranates was not due at the south coast until the second week of August. I had been pressing Robinson about the possibility of constructing a radio transmitter. He said there were no means. I thought as I wrote my first journal, 'By now Brian will believe me to be dead.' But I did not write this down, as I did not know it for a fact.

II

ROBINSON'S HOUSE WAS AN EARLY nineteenth-century
building in an earlier Spanish style. It was a stone bungalow
set on a wide natural terrace of the mountain. Around it ran
a low wall, and over this, from my room, I could see the blue
and green lake on mornings when there was no mist. I did not
go beyond the great arched wrought-iron gates in the first two
weeks. Instead, when my confusion had dissipated, and when I
had time off from nursing Tom Wells, I wandered in the small
neglected garden or sat in the neglected patio, stroking my
injured shoulder and watching the fountain that did not play.

Most of the rooms had been out of use, apparently for
some months. I swept them out. Three rooms and the big
stone kitchen served as Robinson's living quarters. Miguel
slept in a small room amongst a great amount of fishing
equipment. The other rooms were curiously furnished, each
one with three floor-beds, mere pallets stuffed with a silky
material made out of a local fern, a wicker chair and a polished wood table. Each one had a carved crucifix on the wall.
As soon as I had my wits more alert I questioned Robinson
about these rooms.

'Who sleeps there, usually?'

'The pomegranate men,' he answered. 'They are plantation
workers who arrive every August by the boat. They remain
for three or four weeks working on the pomegranate orchard

17

up at the Headlands and gathering in the fruit, while the boat does business at the Canaries and the west coast of Africa.'

'And the rest of the year you live alone on the island?'

'Yes.'

'With Miguel,' I added, pumping him for a clue about the boy.

'Miguel has been with me five years. He is to go to school later this year, and then I will be alone with myself again.'

Certainly I did inquire: 'Whose child is Miguel?'

'You do like to get everything straight,' Robinson said mysteriously.

I was silent then. I was not so concussed that I failed to gather that Robinson was leading me on in some way to express my suspicions. It then flashed upon me that Miguel was not, as in fact I had suspected, Robinson's own child, probably illegitimate.

'Quite a mystery, isn't it?' said Robinson, quite eager for me to agree.

'I see no mystery. I can guess his origin,' I said, meantime wondering what I myself meant, quite.

'What is it then? What's your guess?'

'He's an orphan of one of the pomegranate men who died, and you've adopted him,' I said for some reason.

Robinson said: 'You must have heard it from Waterford.'

'I've never been to Waterford.'

'Jimmie Waterford,' he said. 'The tall fair man who was on the plane with you. He must have told you about my adopting Miguel. He knows a little of my affairs.' He seemed to accuse me as he spoke.

'No,' I said, 'it was a guess. I thought it likely.'

He seemed relieved. 'You know,' he said, 'I expected you to place the paternity on me.'

'No, that would not be likely,' I said.

'Good gracious me,' said Robinson, looking at me. 'Women,' he said, 'do come out with things.'

Journal, Sunday, 23rd May – This is the end of our second week on Robinson. My shoulder hurts. I suppose it will need electrical treatment when I get home, if ever. I am sitting in the doorway of my room. J[immie] W[aterford] has just returned, and is milking the goat. Robinson is absent. I know now where they have been in the day-time while I have been nursing Tom Wells. First they buried the dead. Next they started examining the wreck, and they are now salvaging from it. Miguel fishes in the stream all morning. Robinson has a list of the dead. There are twenty-six items, and only four names of which he is certain. The others are described by anything which happened to be attached to the corpse, such as a metal watch-band dangling, I suppose, on the charred wrist, a ring on a finger-bone, or a lucky charm worn under the shirt. Robinson has been very efficient. I have seen the list. I am free to walk about on the island now that the dead are buried. Jimmie is singing as he milks the goat, I think a Dutch song. He is partly Dutch, his name was not always Waterford. I remember, now, that I met him on the plane before we crashed. His pronunciation of English is quite good, and his vocabulary most unusual. I think R. is worried about Jimmie, in a personal way, as if he were not a stranger. Jimmie looks slightly like Robinson, about the nose. This is a suspicion. Robinson advised, stick to facts, write facts. All right, there is the fact about Tom Wells, his behaviour to me this morning. I shall have to complain to Robinson.

On that morning I had carried to Tom Wells at noon a bowl of cream of tomato soup which we had opened for him. It was set on a tray with some of our hard, thick biscuits. I balanced it in my right hand, my left still being in its sling.

Tom Wells was propped up; for the past week his health had been improving. As I approached his bed, which was a real bed, not, like mine, a mattress on the floor, he said, 'Have they all been interred?'

'Yes.'

He put out his hand and touched me.

'You're a nice piece of homework,' he said.

I think I could have saved the soup. Really, I do not know, maybe I deliberately let go of the tray. The soup tipped over him, down the front of his shirt and over the sheets, like blood in a Technicolor film.

Leaving him in this plight I returned to the kitchen, where Robinson was carving a duck-like bird which he had roasted. Jimmie had his back to the door, and when I entered he was speaking rapidly and softly in his Dutch language. Robinson saw me and said to Jimmie in an open voice:

'Miss January is here.'

The scene with Tom Wells had unnerved me.

'My name is not *Miss* January. I am Mrs Marlow.'

'Well, well,' said Robinson.

I said, 'I have spilt the soup over Tom Wells.'

Robinson went out, returning presently for another bowl of soup. I sat at the kitchen table and ate the meal, staring glumly.

Jimmie Waterford, with his long arms, reached in front of me for the bread. His blond head was out of bandages now.

When Robinson joined us Jimmie addressed me:

'Ha!' he said. 'No man is an island.'

'Some are,' I said. 'Their only ground of meeting is concealed under the sea. If words mean anything, and islands exist, then some people are islands.'

'That's a point,' said Robinson.

'Is so,' said Jimmie, 'mayhaps.'

That afternoon I wrote the journal entry and in the evening I said to Robinson,

'You must make other arrangements about Wells. I won't nurse him.'

'I am not obliged to make any arrangements for anyone,' he said. 'Have sense,' he added, mimicking Jimmie who used often to say, 'Have sense.'

'I will not be left alone with that man in this house.'

'Be reasonable,' said Robinson.

'You must speak to him,' I said. 'Warn him. Threaten.'

'I shall say you wear a knife in your stocking.'

Of course I had no stockings. I was lucky to have legs.

'Listen to the frogs,' I said, for I had calmed down, and the frogs were howling among the rushes in the mountain lake.

'How long have you been married?'

'I'm a widow,' I said, 'and a journalist' – I thought this was understating the case, but it provided an approximate category to poet, critic, and general articulator of ideas. Now that my head was clear I was a little tired of hearing Robinson's advice, 'Keep up your journal. Stick to facts. Describe the scenery', as if, in the normal way, I could not put words together.

Robinson remarked, 'Those are two conditions of life which make for resourcefulness. You can handle Wells yourself. Try to hide your dislike of him.'

'Oh, I've nothing against him, apart from his conduct this morning.'

'Why, of course you have,' said Robinson.

It occurred to me that Robinson resembled, in appearance, my brother-in-law, Ian Brodie, the doctor whom Agnes had married. It was not a strong resemblance – a matter only of the shape of the head, but I wished that it did not exist, seeing that I should have to live with Robinson till August.

III

'HELP YOURSELF TO ANY of my books,' Robinson said.

Now, he had a large library behind glass bookcases. I should not, myself, put books behind glass. Here at home the books are not neat. Robinson's library was well bound and groomed. I observed that some were uncut first editions. I am addicted to a form of snobbery which will hardly keep a first edition on its shelves. To think of a man keeping uncut first editions on an island gave me a snobbish sort of amusement.

Although my married life had lasted only six months, my husband had conditioned many of my tastes. When I ran away from school to marry him he was fifty-eight, a Classics professor whose mother was connected by marriage to my grandmother. Until he met me he had led a retired life. It was a shock to me to discover he had married me for a bet. Sometimes, when I wondered how it would have been had he lived, and I came to realize how old he would have been – seventy-four at the time of my stay on the island, I shuddered, thinking absurdly of the wrinkled hands of old men. In spite of that, and although my tastes did no longer exactly incline to the scholarly type of man, such as I had married, my taste in books was largely a perpetuation of his. Inside the cover of all Robinson's books was a bookplate marked with the words:

Ex Libris
Miles Mary Robinson

below which was a fairly dreadful woodcut representing a book open on a table lectern, a quill pen, and an old-fashioned lamp on the table. Beneath this, in gothic lettering, was the motto *Nunquam minus solus quam cum solus*.

Jimmie Waterford came to find me, very shortly after the incident with Tom Wells and the soup. I was teaching the cat to play ping-pong in a corner of the patio, while brown Miguel looked on, silent and very contemptuous of this occupation.

'One thing,' said Jimmie, 'I tell.'

'Hallo, Jimmie,' I said.

Jimmie squatted down and I put the ping-pong ball in my pocket for the next lesson.

'Please to go make tea for Mr Tom Wells,' he said to Miguel.

I realized he wanted to talk to me privately, and so I settled myself beside him.

'Is this,' he said. 'To tell you Robinson isn't man for the ladies. I am not a stranger to Robinson.'

I knew already that he was familiar with Robinson. And there was the likeness about the nose which now caused me to think they might be related.

I had taken rather a liking to Jimmie on the Lisbon plane. This was partly because of his peculiar idiom of English speech which I later learned had been acquired, first from a Swiss uncle, using Shakespeare and some seventeenth-century poets as textbooks, and Fowler's *Modern English Usage* as a guide, and secondly from contact with Allied forces during the war. And, on the plane, I had taken to Jimmie also because of his seeming unpremeditation in talking to me in the first place.

23

'Is bad weather to fly.'

'Now, is it?' I said.

'You like a drink? Lo!'

He screwed the cap off his leather and silver flask, and removed the flat cup from its base.

'I don't think so, thanks,' I said by way of form.

'You take the cup, I swig from the vessel,' he said, handing me the cup half-filled with brandy.

Just then a member of the crew with his head bent and brown chin sunk into his neck walked rapidly aft. Within a few seconds he walked quickly back again and disappeared from sight. That was the first and last I saw of the crew of our plane. In the meantime Jimmie was telling me,

'I think I want my head examined. Mayhaps you think I come on a holiday. Oh no, oh no. Do you make holiday?'

'No, business,' I said. 'Lovely brandy,' I said, 'it makes me feel more normal.'

There were clouds molten in the setting sun beneath us and we were going into cloud, climb as we might.

'I think you are not a business-woman,' said Jimmie, taking a pull from his flask.

'Thanks,' I said.

'Is a compliment,' Jimmie pointed out.

'I see,' I said amiably. 'Thanks.'

'I furnish you with a little more hooch.'

'No, thanks. I've had enough. It was nice.'

None the less, he poured some more brandy into my cup which I sipped appreciatively. I find that, when travelling abroad alone, it is wise and actually discreet to take up with one well-chosen man on the journey. Otherwise, one is likely to be approached by numerous chance pesterers all along the line. One must, of course, discriminate, but it is a thing one learns by experience, how to know the sort of man who is not likely to press for future commitments. I felt I was lucky to meet with Jimmie. In fact, I had more or less picked on him at the airport, out of a need for protection from a broad-faced English commercial man with a loud voice and a lot of luggage who had been looking much my way. There were also a couple of Spaniards, who when I failed to recognize their separate salutations, had teamed up with each other.

While I sipped Jimmie's brandy, I heard the broad-faced Englishman's voice from several yards to the fore, engaged in conversation with an American couple.

'Just let me open the brief-case,' he was saying. 'I'll show you the article. I tell you, the pattern dates back to the time of the Druids.' He fished into his case and produced a circular badge of white metal about three inches in diameter. I could not make out the interior design but it looked like a gnome sitting on a bar within the circle.

'It's infallible, I can tell you,' said the Englishman. 'It brings the owner *the* most incredible luck. You see, the shape and pattern is a replica to an nth, an *nth* of an inch, of an ancient Druid charm discovered on the moors of Devonshire, England, only fifty-seven years ago. It is a magic charm. *How* it works, or why, I don't pretend to know. But it works.'

'Well, now,' said the American lady.

'Well, now,' said her husband.

'We unloaded five hundred thousand the last half of last year to New Zealand alone,' said the Englishman.

'Well, now.'

'If you ask me,' Jimmie said softly to me, 'for my part I imagine perchance he wants his head examined.'

I sipped the brandy and nodded agreeably.

'Hey, there,' said the Englishman so that his voice carried all up the saloon, and the Americans looked abashed. 'I've been ringing for you, my dear boy,' he said, as the suntanned steward appeared. 'I fancy a whisky – and what about my friends here?'

'Lemon squash,' said the American lady.

'Tonic,' said her husband.

'You need something stronger than that. You stopping at Santa Maria? It's damp there, I can tell you.'

'Well, now,' said the American lady. 'A squash.'

'Whisky and tonic,' said her husband.

'Going home to the States?'

'Well, now, Bermuda first,' said the American lady, her eyes glued to the magic charm which the Englishman was holding between finger and thumb.

Jimmie remarked to me, 'That man is holding converse in a loud key.'

'I did see this chappie at the airport,' said Jimmie, 'and in the moment I behold him I perceive he is not a superior type of bugger. I say to myself, Lo! this one is not a gentleman.'

'Really?' I said.

'I have the instinct for the gentlemen,' said Jimmie, 'as likewise for the ladies.'

I thought, 'He is a most amusing companion', and meanwhile the plane began to bump through the weather to the Azores. Jimmie's face was long and fine; his nose turned up slightly at the bridge giving him a humorous expression; his hair was very light; I judged his age to be in the early thirties.

'You cross the Atlantic Ocean?' he said.

'I'm stopping at the Azores.'

'Myself likewise. And in the long run,' he said, 'I proceed southward by the sea to another island.'

'Which island is that? I'm rather interested in islands.'

'Is not on the map. Is too small.'

The man with the lucky charms was asking his friends, 'You know your future?'

'Pardon?' said the American lady.

'The magazine *Your Future*?'

'Well, now, I don't.'

'I own it *and* I run it,' said the man.

I noticed that the sun had set.

When, at the end of my second week on Robinson, I began to recognize Jimmie, I was immensely cheered up by the memory of our conversation on the plane. The tall fair man with his head in bandages regained in my eyes the shape and status of my amusing travelling companion.

When he squatted on the patio repeating, 'Robinson is not man for the ladies. I know Robinson from the past', I was not at all surprised. I had already noticed that he was familiar with Robinson, and had gathered that, in fact, Robinson had been that ultimate destination to which he had referred in the plane.

'Robinson is not man for the ladies.'

That, too, I knew already. There is easily discernible in some men a certain indifference, not to women precisely but to the feminine element in women, which might be interpreted in a number of ways. In Robinson I had detected something more than indifference: a kind of armed neutrality. So much for his attitude to me. And I thought it likely that he could be positively hostile to the idea of women in general.

'Look here,' I said to Jimmie, 'I wasn't born yesterday.'

'Is so?' said Jimmie gallantly.

'And in any case,' I said, 'Robinson is not my style.'

'Do not become rattled,' said Jimmie, 'in consequence of what I say.'

'You can tell Robinson from me – '

'Ah me!' said Jimmie, 'I am not messenger from Robinson. I tell you this from my own heart.'

That put a different complexion on things. I was quite charmed by Jimmie. He appealed to a quality in my mind which I considered the most advanced I possessed, and which was also slightly masculine.

'You like this?' said Jimmie.

He held out to me a little shining lipstick case. I took it and opened it. The lipstick inside was almost unused, but not quite. There was a little blunt smear at the end. Suddenly I threw it with a clink into the dry fountain.

'It is salvage,' I said. I was not only repelled by the idea of using a dead woman's lipstick, I was furious at Jimmie's implication that I might entertain a romantic interest in Robinson.

'Is true,' he said.

Having buried the dead, they had been gathering from the environs of the burnt-out plane everything that remained a recognizable object. It was surprising, the sort of things they had picked up several hundred yards from the wreckage. Among them were my reading glasses intact in their case, with my name and address in Chelsea on the inside. I had said, when Robinson handed them to me,

'I'd rather have my make-up case. I can read without the glasses.'

'Can't you read without the make-up?'

'I don't feel quite myself without make-up.' This was true. And I was not made any happier by the condition of my dress and coat, though I had patched them up since the accident.

And so, when Jimmie offered me this gruesome lipstick, I felt sure that Robinson had repeated my complaint. I darkly discerned they had been discussing me considerably as a female problem. I left Jimmie sitting on the patio, and thinking how I must keep my end up, I helped myself to a couple of Robinson's cigarettes above my allotted ration. I was the only other smoker besides Robinson on the island, and he had generously, though with an air of resignation, agreed to share with me, strictly fifty-fifty, his total supply for the duration of our stay. This gave us nine cigarettes a day each. As a result of his discussing me with Jimmie, and the incident of the lipstick, I had eleven cigarettes that day, while Robinson had only seven. I felt that this course was preferable to nurturing a grudge.

IV

AT THE END OF THE THIRD WEEK Tom Wells was able to get up. He still wore the canvas contrivance in which Robinson had, with good success, encased his broken ribs which seemed to be knitting together nicely. This left me free from my nursing duties, and all the afternoons were my own. And now that the dead were buried I was free to wander about the island.

'If you're going for a walk,' said Robinson, 'take this raincoat. The weather is a woman in this island.' It was my first excursion, a sunny day, the sixth of June, the Feast of Pentecost.

I already had one arm in the garment when I peeled it off and threw it on the ground as if it were teeming with maggots. The violent action hurt my left arm which was just out of its sling.

'It is salvage,' I said.

Robinson sighed and picked it up. 'Borrow mine,' he said.

Robinson's waterproof was not much too big for me. For my first walk, he advised the path down the mountain to the south coast of the island, along the white beach, and returning by a second mountain path which was visible from the villa on clear days. Robinson pointed out the whole route from his gateway, for there was no mist.

The descent did not start immediately from Robinson's villa. The house was built on a flat shoulder wide enough to contain the blue and green lake and a patch of ground the size of a field which was visible from the patio. Robinson had planted this field with mustard which was now in bloom so that I was almost dazzled by its shimmering yellow. Placed so near the lake, the field was a startling sight. 'I planted mustard for the effect,' he said. Apart from the pomegranates, which he cultivated on an eastern part of the island as a business, he did not grow any of his own food. No runner beans, potatoes, onions, spinach, rhubarb, no tomato frames nor currant bushes, nor peaches and plums. A large storehouse behind the house held his quantities of tinned supplies and grain. I thought this odd, since the ground on the plateau surrounding the villa was fertile and the sun blazing hot, and the mists gentle and frequent.

This was the first day since the accident that I had been alone with myself. I planned eventually to explore the whole island. Robinson had told us of a lava-landscape on the other side of the mountain which, he said, was like moon scenery. There was also an active crater. This excited me. But Robinson warned me against wandering further than the south beach on this my first excursion.

The gradient was irregular, gentle and steep by turns. At one point I had to scramble down over old lava flows. Here I took my foothold on tough beds of thyme and ling about four inches high, and eventually came to a grassy woodland and a clump of blue gum trees which, from Robinson's villa, had looked like dwarf vegetation.

I must say that throughout my stay on the island I was more observant of my surroundings than I had ever been before, or have been since. I had often, previously, been accustomed to topographical observations, but that had been according to rule, deliberate. Now, without any effort of will, my eye recorded the territory, as if my eyes were an independent and aboriginal body, taking precautions against unknown eventualities. Instinctively I looked for routes of escape, positions of concealment, protective rocks; instinctively I looked for edible vegetation. In fact, I must have been afraid. And whereas, on my previous travels, I had been scenery and landscape-minded, had been botanically inclined, had been geologically enchanted, had known the luxury of anthropological speculations, I found myself now noting the practical shelter to be obtained from small craters and gulches and lava caverns. Fissures, cracks and holes attracted me for their contents of nettles and fungus, possibly edible. One could keep a fire alight more easily at a level above the mist-belt; one could, if necessary, survive, and bed down on bracken from these lower woodlands. Fresh-water streams were frequent. One night spent on the sphagnum moors of the cloud-belt would be fatal. On the other side of the mountain, where Robinson used to disappear for several hours on end, there was plenty of game, as I knew from his occasional reappearance with woodcock, partridge and sometimes snipe; or sometimes he brought back a rabbit. I now wished I had learned to use a gun. I had been told of a fresh-water stream from which Miguel was clever at getting trout. I wondered in what part of the island this stream could be. And then I wondered what all the panic was about. I had apparently nothing to fear.

As I climbed down the pathway among the last of the lava rocks to the coast I saw Miguel approaching along the beach. I waved. He saw me, but did not respond. Miguel was not hostile exactly, but he was difficult to please. I think in those first four weeks he was jealous of our having appeared out of the skies and drawn off all Robinson's attention.

He had spent the greater part of his childhood with Robinson, with whom he spoke good English. His mother having died in his infancy, the father had attached himself to a trading boat and become one of Robinson's pomegranate men. Miguel had always accompanied his father on his working periods on Robinson, and, when the father had died, Robinson adopted the child. Robinson spoke often of Miguel's forthcoming departure for school in Lisbon, as if it were a great but inevitable misfortune. He had not yet fixed on any particular school, so strong was his disinclination to part with Miguel.

Of course I had attempted to strike up a friendship with Miguel but so far there was nothing doing. Jimmie had also failed in this respect. A sort of competition had developed between us for the child's attention, let alone affection. Tom Wells, who was only now risen from his sick-bed, had so far been too taken up with his own discomfort to notice him, but Jimmie and I had been disconcerted to find, on Tom Wells's first afternoon out of bed, when he had been sat up with blankets on the patio, that Miguel had hung shyly round the man, who did not attempt to encourage the child, particularly. The next day, Robinson, with an air of omnipotent indulgence, brought to Tom Wells his own brief-case which had happened to be among the salvage – it having presumably been clutched in Wells's hands at the time of his projection from the plane. As Tom Wells seized on this with delight and began to examine the contents, Miguel had approached without further hesitation, and thrust his brown hand into the interior.

'Let me see,' he said, snuggling up to Wells, 'what you've got there.'

He was overjoyed when Tom Wells produced one of his sample Druid emblems.

Jimmie and I were quite put out. My attempts to teach the cat Bluebell to play ping-pong were partly inspired by a desire to impress Miguel. He seemed to think it was an unworthy idea. Jimmie, who had been suffering from delayed shock, although his physical injuries had been slight, went so far as to attempt a cart-wheel on the patio, and suffered a nasty nose-bleed as a result. Miguel was indifferent. I fetched the great cold key from the kitchen and put it down Jimmie's back. Miguel watched uppishly and without comment. 'That youngster doesn't even bloody laugh at my great sorrow,' said Jimmie, dabbing his nose.

And so I was not surprised when Miguel did not wave back to me from the beach, although I saw him look up. He had certainly seen me. I decided to amble along the beach towards him. The sand was extremely fine, and less white than it had looked from a distance against the black lava rocks. Up against the cliffs some pink star-shaped flowers were opening out of the very sand. A few yards away from where the cliff path joined the beach, the ribs of a small sailing vessel lay half-buried, and farther along was the wreck of an old clipper, its leonine figurehead still intact and pointing skyward. I cleared a space among the weed on the mouldering forepart and sat there to rest, leaning on the bowsprit and rubbing my painful left arm.

When he saw me sitting there, Miguel stopped self-consciously. He lifted a pebble and threw it into the curling sea. At this coast the sea was two miles deep and the currents were dangerous. Robinson had warned us not to bathe in the sea, for even where the currents were safe the sharks were not. The blue-green lake was the island bathing-pool.

From the map of Robinson which he had shown me I knew that this stretch of beach lay in the small of the back. I could not help thinking of the island in this anatomical way, because of Robinson's constant references to the Arms and Legs.

Miguel continued to throw pebbles, and I watched the sea, in case he should be embarrassed by my watching him.

There was a special fascination about the sea surrounding Robinson, stretching for a thousand miles to the nearest post office. It was only a few seconds later that I realized Miguel had stopped chucking pebbles, and I fancied he must be approaching. I looked along the beach but could see no sign of him, although I had a view of the whole stretch. A small strip of vegetation grew against the black cliffs, but this was too low to hide Miguel unless he lay flat. I decided he must be lying flat, and set off along the beach, examining the base of the cliffs very closely. I reached the end of the beach, where the black rock rose sheer out of the sea, without having found any trace of Miguel. I was bewildered, then frightened. I could see no place where he could be concealed except the sea. I scanned the sea fearfully, hoping I should not see a head bobbing far out of my reach, but I saw nothing but the waves chopping with the undercurrents, which might have concealed anything. I did not really think he could have jumped into the sea in the few moments that my eyes had been turned from him. I did not really think he would be so foolish. I was sure Miguel was somewhere safe but I was disturbed by having no reason for this certainty. For a moment I thought perhaps they had never existed, that Robinson and his household were a dead woman's dream, that I was indeed dead as my family believed and the newspapers had by now reported. In view of these ideas, I thought the most necessary course of action was to return to Robinson's house by the shortest route and report the disappearance of Miguel.

The quickest route led from the end of the beach where I now stood, although it was not exactly the shortest. It zigzagged up the mountain, a gentler gradient than that of the path I had used on my downward journey. I had been tacking up this path for twenty minutes when I came upon a derelict croft-house and watermill on a small plateau overhanging a stream which trickled down a small ravine. It now struck me that Robinson's predecessors, hermits though they might be, had made efforts to cultivate every green spot on the island. Later, when I saw the rich pasture-lands of the West Leg and South Arm, I felt a sort of outrage that their work was falling to waste. I saw by the croft-house a number of mango trees still bearing fruit, but they were bedraggled and untended. It was from here that Robinson must have gathered the poor specimens of mango which we ate for breakfast. I did not suppose the trees would bear much longer.

Many times, during my climb, I had turned to scan the beach below and the surrounding mountain scrub for some sign of Miguel. I began to worry seriously, mainly because I had every obvious reason to worry. When I came up to the deserted croft I took a last look round, for above this plateau the cloud-belt was forming as it usually did in the late afternoon, and this made it impossible to see the coastline from where I stood.

I decided to rest from my climb for ten minutes on this plateau, and I ambled about, walking round the cottage, looking through the gaping windows. I tried the door. It was open. I entered, and saw Miguel by the crumbling hearth laying twigs for a fire. He had a can of water and a tin of coffee.

'Hallo,' I said. 'How did you get here?'

He looked pleased with this question, and so, to please him more, I said,

'I saw you on the beach. I looked away for a moment, and when I looked again you were gone.'

He even laughed at this.

'How did you do it?' I said. If he had climbed the mountain I must have seen him. But he must have climbed the mountain and I did not see him.

'There's a secret cave,' said Miguel, 'with a tunnel.'

'Where? I should like to see it.'

He shook his head.

'Does Robinson know the secret cave?'

'Yes. But he won't show it.'

He handed me a tin mug of his hot black coffee brew.

'Robinson won't show you the caves. He only shows me.'

'Oh, is there more than one?'

He did not answer, having already let slip too much.

'This is lovely stuff,' I said, and lest I should seem patronizing, I added, 'but it needs some sugar.'

He fished into the inside pocket of his lumber jacket and brought out a paper screw of sugar. This he opened and emptied into my mug, stirring it with a twig. We sat on the hearthstone and sipped. Meantime I was wishing I was at home.

'I'm off now,' said Miguel.

'I'm coming too,' I said.

'No, you wait a short time.'

I thought he wanted to go to some other secret caves and didn't want me to discover the way, so I said,

'All right. Let's say about ten minutes. Will that do?'

'Well,' he said, 'you wait till it stops raining.'

I noticed that it was raining, not very heavily.

'Oh, is that all?' I said. 'Well, I don't mind the rain.'

'Robinson's raincoat will get wet,' the boy pointed out.

I could not deny it. I waited till the shower was over, then emerged to catch sight of Miguel making his nimble way home through the thicket above me.

V

'I WISH,' SAID JIMMIE, 'I stay at home. I commence to think I want my head examined for making this dangerous journey.'

'Same here,' I said, without really meaning it.

I did wish to go home, but not that I had never come away. If I had stayed at home, there might have been a fire in the house, or I might have been run over, or murdered, or have committed a mortal sin. There is no absolute method of judging whether one course of action is less dangerous than another.

'Same here,' I said, simply to convey agreement that our situation might be better than it was.

We had brought a picnic and were settled on the banks of the blue and green lake. In front of us was a lumpy patch of goat meadow leaning down towards the cliff, and below, since there was no mist, was the sea. To our right was the vivid yellow mustard field. The effect was fairly Arcadian, if only one could relax and enjoy it.

'Why did you come?' I said. I was curious to know where Jimmie had come from, why he had taken the Lisbon plane to the Azores with the purpose of finding his way to Robinson, how long he had known Robinson, and at the same time was irritated by this curiosity of mine which did so indicate that these people were becoming part of my world. I had rather regarded them as travelling companions – as one might take

up with a man on a plane. I like to be in a position to choose,
I like to be in control of my relationships with people.

On the sixth of June I had written in my journal:

I feel that we were all unwelcome on the island. The
emergency is over. Tom Wells is now able to get about.
I am beginning to use my left arm. Jimmie, who received
only a small cut in the head, and in fact had not even lost
consciousness at the time of the crash, is suffering from
nerves. Robinson seems rather irritated by all of us.

'Why did you come?' I said to Jimmie.

'Is Robinson's vast properties,' he replied. 'Robinson's
family beseech me, "Go and bring back Robinson to his
birthright. Begone, we shall foot the bill." Thus, I came. But
is first I should reside at marvellous Azores and next is pleasant ocean voyage to the island of Robinson which I envisage,
and to behold my kinsman old Robinson. Mayhaps a month I
should reside here, or two. I should say, "Robinson, return!"
He should say, "Not me, chum." I should say to him, "Is
properties, Robinson. The old uncle has died and, behold,
the properties fall to neglect." Robinson should reply, "So
what?" and I should say, "Who is to administer these great
estates?" He should tell me, "Not me, chum. Is all yours."
And I figure, six months should elapse before I return my
steps towards the family of Robinson to reveal to them I
fail in my great mission. As I have planned, I should say to
them, "I fail." They say to me, "Alas." They pay the bill. So
I have had six months' merry voyaging and they should pay
up. Whereafter they should say, "Now who shall administer
these properties?" I say, "Robinson desires this post to me."
But,' said Jimmie, 'this destiny has not come to pass. Is fizzle
out, and I fall from the sky. I languish.'

'I don't see,' I said, 'how your plans are changed at all. You can still return within six months and take over Robinson's affairs for him.'

'All is changed,' said Jimmie, 'since I am cast from the heavens. Is numerous dead. Robinson is cross. I lose my nerves. Robinson takes no care for the honour of his family.'

I began to reflect on Robinson's lordly estates.

'Where are these properties?' I inquired.

'In Tangier,' said Jimmie.

'Do his family live in Tangier?'

'No, in Gibraltar. They possess abundant cash. I am but the poor kinsman.'

'What sort of lands do they possess in Tangier?'

'Is not lands. Is motor-scooters. Is vast import business. For my part, I tell you, I should have been fine and dandy a managing director. But I lose my nerves.'

'Never mind,' I said. 'They will come back.'

'Is multitudinous prospects for motor-scooters in the north of Africa. In the course of time I should create many factories. But all is lost. In point of fact I consider how I want my head examined.'

'Perhaps in any case Robinson will return to his family.'

'Nevermore,' said Jimmie. 'I am acquainted with Robinson from the days of my youth, and is for cert he chuck the world.'

To teach a cat to play ping-pong you have first to win the confidence and approval of the cat. Bluebell was the second cat I had undertaken to teach; I found her more amenable than the first, which had been a male.

Ping-pong with a cat is a simplified and more individualistic form of the proper game. You play it close to the ground, and you imagine the net.

Gaining a cat's confidence is different from gaining the confidence of any other animal. Food is not the simple answer. You have to be prepared to play with it for as long as two hours on end. To gain the initial interest of a cat, I always place a piece of paper over my head and face and utter miaows and other cat noises. This is irresistible to most cats, who come nosing up to see what is going on behind the paper. The next phase involves soft whispering alternately with the whistling of high-pitched tunes.

I thought *Bluebells of Scotland* would be appropriate to Bluebell. She was enchanted. It made her purr and rise on her hind legs to paw my shoulder as I crouched on the patio whistling to her in the early afternoons.

After that I began daily to play with her, sometimes throwing the ping-pong ball in the air. She often leapt beautifully and caught it in her forepaws. By the second week in June I had so far won her confidence and approval as to be able to make fierce growling noises at her. She liked these very much, and would crouch menacingly before me, springing suddenly at me in a mock attack. Sometimes I would stalk her, one slow step after another, bent double, and with glaring eyes. She loved this wildly, making flying leaps at my downthrust head.

'You'll get a nasty scratch one day,' said Robinson.

'Oh, I understand cats,' I said.

'She understands cats,' said Jimmie unnecessarily.

Robinson walked away.

Having worked round Bluebell to a stage where she would let me do nearly anything with her and play rough-house as I pleased, I got an old carton out of Robinson's storehouse and set it on end against the patio wall. Bluebell immediately sat herself inside this little three-walled house. Then the first ping-pong lesson began. I knelt down two yards away from her and placed the ball in front of me. She crouched in readiness as if it were an ordinary ball game. With my middle finger and thumb I pinged the ball into Bluebell's box. It bounced against the walls. The cat sprang at it and batted it back. I sent it over again to Bluebell. This time she caught it in her forepaws and curled up on the ground, biting it and kicking it with her silver hind pads. However, for a first lesson her style was not bad. Within a week Bluebell had got the ping-pong idea. Four times out of ten she would send the ball back to me, sometimes batting it with her hind leg most comically, so that even Miguel had to laugh. On the other occasions she would appropriate the ball for herself, either dribbling it right across the patio, or patting it under her body and then sitting on it. Sometimes she would pat the ball only a little way in front of her, waiting for me, with her huge green eyes, to come and retrieve it.

The cat quickly discovered that the setting up of her carton on the patio was the start of the ping-pong game, and she was always waiting for me at that spot after lunch. She was an encouraging pupil, an enthusiast. One day when she was doing particularly well, and I was encouraging her with my lion growl to her great excitement, I heard Robinson's voice from the back of the house.

'Bluebell! Pussy-puss Bluebell. Nice puss. Come on!'

Her ear twitched very slightly in response, but she was at the ball and patting it over to me, it seemed in one movement. I cracked it back, and she forth again.

'Bluebell! – Where's the cat?' said Robinson, appearing on the patio just as I was growling more. 'There's a mouse in the storehouse. Do you *mind*?' he said to me.

The cat had her eyes on my hand which held the ball. I picked her up and handed her to Robinson. Bluebell struggled to free herself and go for the ball. I thought this funny and giggled accordingly. But Bluebell was borne reluctantly away by solemn Robinson, with Miguel following like a righteous little retainer.

Jimmie grinned. Something about Jimmie's grin and Robinson's bearing embarrassed me. I began to wonder if Robinson felt intensely about incidents like this. I should not myself have thought of the affair as an 'incident' at all. It was a great bore.

I could see that Robinson was making an effort to form some communal life for the period of our waiting on the island. I could see he conceived this a duty, and found it a nuisance. It had been different in the first few weeks, when we were impaired by the crash. Then Robinson had met the occasion. So, too, had Jimmie, who was now suffering belatedly; he kept insisting he had lost his nerves.

Robinson rose at five, we at six, by which time our plateau was flooded with the early sun, and not far below was the white mist, swathing the mountain right down to the coast. It seemed that the whole sky was beneath us and we on a sunny platform in space, with our house, mustard field, blue and green lake, the goat meadow before us and the mountain rising behind.

At this hour Robinson would go to the goat in its pen with a quantity of three-leaved plants, like large, leaved clover. These he had sprinkled with a considerable handful of salt.

'Why do you salt its food, Robinson?'

'It works up a thirst, and so increases the milk. Besides, it gives the milk a good salt flavour.'

It was one of the few bits of husbandry I saw Robinson practise. For the most part he made shift as easily as possible with tins and the derelict orchards of the croft.

I cooked the breakfast. Having found a sack of good oats in the storehouse I now made porridge every morning.

Previously he and Miguel had eaten a mango or half pawpaw from one of the old croft orchards with a tin of baked beans. My institution of the porridge was designed to eke out the beans, for I saw that the stores were not large.

'Oh, when we've finished the beans we would go on to something else,' said Robinson; 'there are other tinned things.'

It was not only a matter of what was and was not proper for breakfast:

'Are you *sure* the pomegranate boat will come in August?'

'Quite sure.'

I did not care for the thought of its omitting to come and leaving the five of us tinless and starving. I did think Robinson might have grown something. The climate was suitable for maize, which is not troublesome. Fresh vegetables would have been no trouble. I decided to search the island for roots or berry-bushes which could be transplanted into Robinson's plateau. I was moody whenever I thought of the kitchen garden that Robinson did not have.

It is true that, with Robinson's makeshift system, the place was easy to run. As Tom Wells regained his health, our chores were finished by eleven in the morning. We took turns to prepare meals. The rest of the day we were free. We frequently quarrelled.

To my surprise, when we were sufficiently recovered and organized, and first sat down to meals together, Robinson said a prayer for grace. Despite the crucifixes on the walls of each room, I had not thought Robinson was a religious man; and I had vaguely supposed that the crucifixes had belonged to the previous owner, Robinson not troubling to remove them. I was even more surprised to observe that the form of grace he said was that used by Roman Catholics, 'Bless us, O Lord, and these Thy gifts. . . . In the name of the Father, the Son. . . . ' And when we had finished he gave thanks according to the form used by

English Catholics, following it with that usual prayer for the faithful departed which frequently suggests to my mind that we have eaten them.

I had entered the Catholic Church the previous year, I wondered if Robinson really was a member of the Church. But I do not care to ask people this question. I assumed, meantime, that he was so, and I wondered really why he chose to live so separated from the Sacraments; but that was his business.

After supper Robinson had us all into his sitting-room. This was a strain. It never seemed to be the simple and normal thing for us to do. And I felt he did not so much invite as have us in, as one's headmistress would have one in to tea; an obligation on both sides.

Robinson encouraged a certain formality among us. We were as yet ignorant of each other's antecedents. Robinson did not ask any questions or lead us to talk about the circumstances which had brought us on the Lisbon plane, our homes, and destinations. I gathered from this that he was anxious to regard our intrusion into his life as temporary: once you know some facts about a person you are in some way involved with them. Evidently Robinson wished to avoid this. So did I. At first this reserve gave an illusion of natural growth to our relationships.

But of course the decent gulfs did not last. Sometimes it seemed that Robinson did not so much desire to preserve distance between us as to prevent intimacy; he seemed more anxious that we should not be friends than that we should not intrude upon each other. And, for many reasons, I did not want Robinson to know what Jimmie had told me about him.

In other ways, as I saw my companions day by day, I did begin to feel curiosity about them.

Sometimes in those evenings we would play chess. Robinson and I were more interested in chess than were

45

Jimmie and Tom Wells who approached it as if it were some therapeutic task set by Robinson. They would talk too much.

'Look here,' Wells said one evening, 'where does this get us, anyway?'

'Is question you ask,' said Jimmie.

Robinson said pleasantly, 'Chess is good for the mind.'

'Look here,' Wells said, 'who are *you* to say what's good for my mind?'

I thought this reasonable enough. But I simply did not like Tom Wells. So I said, 'Oh, don't be difficult,' without looking up from the board where Robinson's King's Bishop, his only remaining protection, would threaten my Queen, should I move my King's Knight as I desired.

'Would you like to hear some music?' Robinson said.

He put a record on his gramophone. It was the first of six, a whole opera of Rossini, *La Cenerentola*.

I felt that Robinson was determined to keep control. He was fixed on controlling himself, us, and his island. He was not prepared to permit any bickering to bind us together and shatter the detachment which he prized.

Jimmie started to relax and listen politely. I did the same, though I felt a difficult mood begin to overtake me. I don't think Tom Wells had any intention of rudeness, it was only that he had never thought of music as anything but a background to talk. And more, not even a background; according to his notion, you had some music to take away the silence and then you continued talking, but in a louder voice.

'Ah, now,' said Wells, looking genially round the company, 'naturally this is a strain on us all, but we're lucky to be alive.'

He often said 'We're lucky to be alive' for no apparent reason save that he was pining to chew over and over our advent on the island, and thus for us all to get to grips with each other. 'It's unnatural living like this alone with Nature,' he would say, 'but we're lucky to be alive.' And sometimes he would bring out this phrase after he had spent half an hour calculating how much he was out of pocket through the plane mishap.

Perhaps there was nothing really objectionable about his 'lucky to be alive'. You must understand that I did not like Tom Wells.

'Amazing lucky shave,' said Wells. 'It's a remarkable thing, only that morning when I got my plane ticket at the Bureau I said – '

'Do you like Rossini?' said Robinson. He handed us glasses of rum for which I was most grateful at that moment.

'I hope this won't make me remiss,' said Tom Wells, holding his glass up to the lamp for some reason, and squinting at it with one eye. He said to me, 'Do you like cabaret?'

Robinson smiled weakly and sighed. At the sound of his sigh I suddenly decided to annoy him too.

'I love cabaret,' I said, 'if it's good.'

'A jolly good floor show,' said Tom Wells.

'Extremely nice,' I said. 'Do you know the Caribee Club in Duke Street?'

'Naturally,' said Wells.

'And the Daub and Wattle? They do a nice floor show there.'

'My word,' said Wells, 'we've got a lot in common, you and I.'

Robinson sat with his music, affronted. Serve you right, I thought, for your inflexible pose. Give you something, I thought, to exercise detachment upon.

'If I had the right music and a decent dress,' I said, 'I could perform a floor show all on my own.' It is true that I can do a rather effective song-and-dance turn, and often do, to amuse my intimate friends.

47

'Got any jazz?' Tom Wells said to Robinson, who was putting Rossini on the other side of the record.

He didn't answer.

Jimmie raised his eyebrows, and looked wise.

'You and I must have a chat,' said Wells to me.

Miguel was reclining on the hearth. He looked to one and the other of us, not following our actual conversation, but feeling out for himself how things stood between us all.

Jimmie sat like three wise monkeys, taking an occasional sip from his glass. It struck me he was secretly happy that Robinson was being slightly challenged and things were pepping up.

Presently Jimmie winked at Robinson who made no response, sitting vigilant by his gramophone, winding the handle every now and again, and replacing the records of his Rossini.

I left them, and went for a walk. My moods are not stable at the best of times. It was on this occasion I experienced that desire to worship the moon, and I thought, how remarkable, since I was a Christian: I thought of my grandmother bowing in the roadway, 'New Moon, New Moon, be good to me.'

After that, of course, I had difficulty in shaking off Tom Wells. He followed me about, as far as he was physically able. This was not very far; he was still fairly weak and still bound in his tight corset of canvas strips. He resented a great deal his injuries being more severe than Jimmie's or mine.

'You two were lucky,' he would say, 'That Robinson,' he would say, 'has no feelings or he wouldn't expect me to move about in my condition. It's not natural; I ought to be taking things easy.'

'You need exercise to avoid complications, Robinson says.'

'*Robinson says*! *Robinson says*! – Haven't you any guts?'

'It's his island.'

Robinson said to me, 'He seems to want jazz music. I haven't any jazz.'

'He thinks you very unnatural,' I said, 'not having a wireless.'

'I can't please everybody,' Robinson said.

'I wish he would stop following me.'

'Your own fault,' said Robinson. 'You have to keep a man like that at a distance.'

'He has his funny side,' I said. 'Have you seen the stuff he keeps in that brief-case?'

It was in the heat of the day. I was peaceably watching Robinson cleaning a gun. He stood in the cool stone room with his back to a vaulted window which blazed with light. When I mentioned Tom Wells he stopped cleaning the gun. He said, 'I've told him that we are none of us interested in the contents of his bag.'

'I am,' I said, 'very interested.'

'Not while you're on this island, you aren't,' said Robinson.

I had been sitting by a high table lolling with my elbows on it, but I stood up quickly. Robinson flung his rag on to the table and hanging up the gun on the wall, took down another.

'Try to conceal your anger,' said Robinson.

'I take an interest in what I please,' I said.

'Not while you're on this island.'

I left him, and went out to find Jimmie. On the way I took two cigarettes from the box on Robinson's desk. Thinking it over, I made some allowances for Robinson's behaviour, for he had recently been harassed by Wells. Only the previous day I had witnessed a scene between them, when Tom Wells had made a dreadful fuss about some documents which he said were missing from his brief-case.

'I say, Robinson, was this case open when you found it?'

'No, it was tight shut.'

'It must have been open,' said Wells. 'Some papers must have fallen out. Some important confidential documents. They're missing.'

'The bag was not open,' Robinson said steadily. 'It was lying about thirty yards from the plane near the spot where I picked you up.'

'The papers were in the case before the plane crashed. Now they're gone. How d'you explain that?'

'I am not an occulist,' Robinson said.

I found Jimmie on the patio reclining in a deck-chair beside Tom Wells. Miguel was hovering near Tom Wells's chair, and I could not at first see what they were doing.

As I approached Wells looked round.

'Robinson there?' he said.

'No, he's cleaning the guns.'

'Makes no odds, really,' said Tom Wells. 'Only Robinson doesn't seem to care for these articles. He's a cranky bird if you like.'

I lit one of Robinson's cigarettes and felt in a position to defend him.

'That's a nice thing,' I said pompously, 'to say about your benefactor.'

'Look, Janey,' he said, 'all right, so what, let's put it at the maximum. O.K., Robinson saved my life. Does that give him the right to boss me around for three months?'

'It's Robinson's island,' I said.

Miguel gazed at us both, back and forth. Meantime I noticed, spread out on the flat of Tom Wells's bag, a number of small shining objects of curious shapes.

'I commence to think,' said Jimmie, 'that Robinson is becoming exceedingly cheesed.'

'*Pas devant*,' said Tom Wells, casting his eyes towards the child.

'Is not clandestine remark,' said Jimmie. 'I declare to Robinson's face the same.'

I began to scrutinize the curious objects of silver metal spread out on Tom Wells's bag. Miguel kept fingering them with delight.

'See,' said the boy to me, 'Mr Tom has given me one of his jewels.' It was a four-leaved clover, done in metal, attached to a chain. Miguel slung it round his neck.

'That will bring you luck,' said Tom Wells.

'What is luck?' said the boy, for although his pronunciation of English was good, his vocabulary was limited to what he had learned from Robinson.

Jimmie laughed. 'Is very humorous,' he said, 'that the youngster should ask what is luck. Robinson does not speak that word, he does not accord with the idea luck.'

'You seem to know a lot about Robinson,' Tom Wells observed.

'Is so,' said Jimmie genially. He had not confided to Tom Wells anything of a past association with Robinson, but I could see Wells suspected this. I imagined, and rightly, that Robinson had advised Jimmie not to talk much about himself.

'You would think to hear you,' said Wells, 'that Robinson was an old friend of yours, and you'd just dropped in.'

Tom Wells was more transparent than I was in his curiosity to know the story of Robinson's life. In time, I felt, bit by bit, the story would simply come to me. Jimmie would talk, Robinson would let fall; and so I asked few questions.

Tom Wells was constantly pestering us with questions. For my part, I was as close as Robinson. In fact, one of the few grounds on which I understood Robinson was the fear of over-familiarity which I shared with him. The less

I said about my past life, the better, to Tom Wells, and on an island.

'It will bring me luck. What's luck?' Miguel was saying. He took the metal clover in his brown hands, raised it to his wide lips, and kissed it. 'What's luck?'

Jimmie and I were searching the air for a definition when 'Long life and happiness,' said Tom Wells.

'Now come over here, sonny, and I'll show you the signs of the Zodiac. When were you born?'

Miguel looked blank.

'What month?' said Tom. 'You don't have to give date and year. I shan't give you a comprehensive horoscope reading unless you're prepared to pay money for it, see? Got any money on you?'

I suppose he had a way with children.

Miguel fondled his clover charm, and giggled with delight.

'What month were you born?'

'Don't know.'

'When's your birthday, you daftie?'

'Next year.'

'What month? January, February, March, April . . . ? Come along – you pay your money and you take your choice.'

'January,' said Miguel, as if he were choosing a colour.

'Before or after the twenty-first?'

'Eh?'

'What date in January? First, second, third, fourth . . . ? Make up your mind.'

'First,' said Miguel.

'That's my birthday,' I said.

'No it is not,' said Miguel, 'it's mine.'

Jimmie said, 'Is humorous.'

'Look here,' said Wells to me, 'you can't have his birthday. His birthday's the first of January, see?'

Miguel danced round Wells, and picked up the glittering trinkets, one by one. Wells regarded him with the greatest benevolence. At that moment I realized that Tom Wells bore a strong resemblance to my brother-in-law, the bookie, Curly Lonsdale. He was about the same age as Curly, about fifty. Like Curly, Tom Wells had a loose mouth in a square puffy face, and would gesture continually with his square hands, fingers outspread. The over-intimate gurgle in the voice was the same as Curly's.

The first I had heard of Curly was when my sister Agnes wrote to me 'Julia has married such a common little man. He's a Turf Accountant. He looks like one of those that seduce landladies' daughters in their braces. Julia is of course lucky to marry anyone. . . . '

Years later, after my grandmother's funeral, I met Curly. I was not surprised to find him fairly frightful, but I was enormously surprised, on this occasion and subsequently, to see how my son took to him. Brian delighted to go spinning off with Curly in his three-year-old Jaguar to the pictures on a Saturday afternoon. The first time, Brian was brought back at half-past eight, brimming with the exotic new world which he had tasted. 'Curly was carrying seven hundred and fifty on him, he showed me, great bundles of fivers . . . and after the pictures we had fish and chips in a pretty nice restaurant at Leicester Square, and after that we went to a house to meet a lot of Curly's friends. They were all playing cards, and there were piles and piles of cigarette ends in the ashtrays and fivers all over the place. And the chaps were terribly keen on the game, they had their coats off – '

'Sitting in their braces,' I said.

'That's right. And Curly's going to take me to the races when the season starts.'

'Did they give you anything to drink?' I said.

'Oh yes. There was ginger ale. Sam – that's one of Curly's friends – gave Curly a snifter – that's brandy, you see, and I think he was pouring out one for me, but Curly said, "Something soft for the youngster, Sam, else his old woman's going to create." That was awfully funny, because Curly winked at me; and he looked awfully funny.'

'Were there any ladies?'

'No,' said Brian. 'No dames. But there was a photo of a smasher on the grand piano.'

'Do you really like Curly?' I said.

'He's the best man in our family,' said Brian, as if there were dozens to choose from. Apart from Curly Lonsdale the only other man in our family was Agnes's husband, the doctor, Ian Brodie. From any point of view, it seemed to me, Curly was preferable to Ian. One of the things that worried me, as I sat on the patio watching Tom Wells, so like my brother-in-law Curly, winning his way with Miguel, was who had taken charge of Brian since I had been presumed dead; Agnes and Ian Brodie, or Julia and Curly? On the whole, I hoped it was Curly, whom I could never, myself, take to.

'This is Ethel of the Well,' said Tom Wells, picking out one of his trinkets. It was a large-headed female figure. Its mouth was cut wide from ear to ear, its arms stuck flat against its metal sides, and from under the lines of its long straight skirt protruded the representation of a pair of thick curling boots. 'The original Ethel,' said Wells, 'was found in a well in Somerset. She dates back to the sixth century. Ethel has terrific properties as a luck bringer; I could show you hundreds of letters from people whose life has been changed by Ethel.'

Miguel let the four-leaved clover drop on his breast and made a dive at Ethel of the Well. 'When I think,' said Tom Wells, 'of the business I'm losing. There's the magazine also, who's taken it over? I've got the proofs of the June number here. Well, we're lucky to be alive.' He fumbled in his bag. 'Listen to this letter from a satisfied customer: "Dear Mr Wells, My wife and I would like to tell you that we have had incredible luck since you sent us Ethel of the Well. Ethel is certainly the tops. My wife was dogged by ill health for twelve years. Now I have got a better job, and we certainly swear by Ethel. Wishing you congrats and all the best from my wife and I, Yours faithfully, Mr & Mrs Harper." That's only one out of hundreds from simple ordinary folk. I get a lot of confidences, too. People must open their hearts to someone, mustn't they? I know thousands of secrets – some of them would open your eyes. Rich and poor alike, they write to Tom Wells.'

'Ethel!' said Miguel in hushed awe.

'Then there's Natty the Gnome,' said Wells.

'Show me Natty,' said Miguel.

'To Natty,' said Wells, 'I owe the fact that I am here to tell the tale. Mind you, it isn't the first time Natty has saved a life in an accident. I wish I had the letter here – '

'It would have been luckier if there had been no accident,' I said.

'There must have been a Jonah on the plane. You are powerless when there's a Jonah.'

'Show me Natty,' said Miguel.

Wells selected from his wares a small charm and handed it to the child. 'You can keep that,' he said, 'I've got others.' It was a dwarf-like figure with a peaked cap sitting cross-legged. 'Thank God for Natty,' he said. 'I've always had faith in Natty. We must be losing thousands of orders.'

I could see Jimmie was as envious as I was of Tom Wells's salvage. All our possessions had been burnt up in the plane, and we had no form of competition for the attention of Miguel.

'There was to be a full-page ad for Natty in the June number of *Your Future*,' said Wells.

'Show me the Future,' said Miguel.

'Letters pour in daily from every part of the world from thousands of men and women of all ages,' Wells said, 'in praise of Natty the Gnome and affiliated products.'

'Mayhaps they now shall cease to write,' said Jimmie, 'when they hear of your bad luck which has befallen.'

'What bad luck?' said Wells aggressively.

'Show me the Future,' said Miguel, apparently under the impression it was one of the metal charms.

'Let him see the magazine,' I said.

Wells carefully placed his range of lucky charms on the patio floor; he fished emotionally into his bag and produced a paste-up proof of his magazine, which he held sorrowfully before his eyes.

'What's going to happen about *Your Future*, I don't know,' he said. 'The June number won't appear, naturally, because this here in my hand is the June number. I prepared it while on tour, and I intended to mail it from Santa Maria to our offices in Paddington. What they are doing at Paddington, I don't know, I dare not think.'

'Mayhaps they all pack up,' said Jimmie.

'They won't,' said Wells, 'not while I'm alive they won't.'

'By now you must be presumed dead,' I said, 'like the rest of us.'

'*They* will know,' said Wells. 'Trust them. They know I'm alive, you can be sure.'

'They know all about Mr Tom,' said Miguel, who seemed to feel that his friend was under attack.

'You see,' said Tom, 'I have friends among the Occult. There's no getting away from it; they know what's going on in the world. I'm not talking about a lot of ignorant fortune-tellers, mind you; these are scientists of every description and in every sense of the word. Some of them have letters after their names. They are people that have devoted their lives to the study of the unknown. I am not an adherent, mind you, of any particular group. There are countless methods of probing the mysteries of the universe. I number among my acquaintances distinguished psychometrists, clairvoyants, Karma interpreters, astrologers, yoga spiritualists, divine healers, astral radiesthetists, saliva prognosticators, and so on and so on. They are men and women of vision. It's the quality of the medium that counts, naturally. I go in for quality. All my friends are of high esoteric quality.'

He lapsed into a sigh of exhaustion, content merely to spread his square hands palm-up before him, as if they spoke for his cause.

'Mr Tom's friends know,' said Miguel.

'Listen to the innocent child,' said Tom Wells. 'He's got the right ideas, that boy.'

'Is this the Future?' said Miguel, holding up a medallion with cabbalistic signs in red enamel round its perimeter.

'That's the Chaldean Contact Medallion, sonny. You've picked a winner there. Real enamel lettering. Astounding potency, and puts an end to ill health, exhaustion, fatigue, insomnia, et cetera. It is also an infallible aid to joyous achievement. You can also keep that one, I've got plenty.'

'Show him the magazine,' I said, 'that's what he's asking for.'

Tom Wells frowned surreptitiously at me. 'It's a bit beyond him,' he whispered. '*Your Future* is mainly for those who have passed through the early talismanic stages of spiritual attainment.' He tapped his sheaf of papers. 'We have serious articles here,' he said, 'by professors.'

'Give me *Your Future*,' said Miguel.

'Give him *Your Future*,' I said.

'It's only in proof form,' said Wells. 'He won't understand it. It's my only copy. He has the charms, that's sufficient.'

Miguel seemed to feel a sense of deprivation.

'I want *Your Future*,' he observed to me.

'For shame,' said Jimmie, 'withholding these documents from the little child.'

'He can have it to look at,' said Wells, 'but I want it back, mind, and I don't mean maybe.'

Miguel grabbed the pasted-up proofs and started turning the pages. He seemed to be attracted by the pictures in the advertisements, but did not waste time on the text.

'I told you,' said Wells, 'it wouldn't interest the child.'

Miguel sensed that his treasure was about to be removed. He clutched it to his chest and said, 'It's mine.'

'No,' said Wells, 'give it back.'

'Is cruelty,' said Jimmie, 'to give to a child and then with-draw.'

At that moment Robinson appeared. Miguel hastily grabbed from the step where he had laid them his three lucky charms, and clutched them fiercely, together with *Your Future*.

'What the hell's going on here?' said Robinson. He was looking at the litter of lucky charms on the floor of the patio around Tom Wells where he had laid them out.

Tom Wells placed a hand on his ribs to indicate pain.

'This is Mr Wells's range of samples,' I said. 'They are all vibrating with luck.'

'I was decent enough to hand over that rubbish to you,' Robinson said to Wells, 'on condition you kept it to yourself.'

Tom Wells closed his eyes and rubbed his ribs.

I picked up one of the charms. 'This one is Ethel of the Well,' I said, 'guaranteed to – '

'What have you got there?' Robinson was looking at Miguel. The boy handed over the proofs, keeping the charms clenched in his other hand.

Robinson tore the proofs several times across. We all gasped.

Eventually Wells said, 'That's an actionable offence. If there wasn't a lady present I'd tell you what I think of you. That's my property you've destroyed. And while we're on the subject I'd like to know what's happened to the papers that are missing from my case. They were top secret.'

Robinson said to Miguel, 'What have you got there?'

The child opened his hand and showed him the charms.

'Give them back to Mr Tom,' said Robinson, quite nicely.

'They're mine,' said Miguel.

'They are harmless things,' I said.

'They bring you luck,' said the boy.

'Listen to me, Miguel: these are evil things,' said Robinson, 'you must give them back.'

Miguel said, 'It's cruelty to give to a child and then with-draw.'

'Is humorous,' said Jimmie.

Robinson looked round at us and said, 'You are clearly in the wrong, as my guests, to alienate the child.'

'Give those articles to Mr Tom like a most noble youth,' said Jimmie to Miguel.

The child began to cry at this first sign of desertion.

'Give them back to me for the meantime,' said Wells. 'I'll keep them for you.'

'You must not subject the boy to trickery,' said Robinson. 'He must know I don't permit him to have them at all.'

Wells tried again, 'Give the lucky charms to Robinson,' he said, 'and they may bring him some luck.'

Miguel cheered up. 'Robinson can have one of them,' he said. 'Robinson can have the medal for luck, I'll keep Ethel and Natty and I don't mean maybe.'

'I shall not keep it for luck,' said Robinson ruthlessly. 'I shall throw it into the Furnace over the mountain. You see,

Miguel, these bits of metal are full of harm.' As he looked at them lying in the boy's palm, I caught an expression of nausea on Robinson's face. I thought to myself, 'He really believes they have evil properties.'

'Miguel,' I said, 'give them all back to Mr Tom, and presently we shall give you something better to make up.' I wondered desperately what we could give him.

'You must not mislead,' said Robinson. 'The fact is, you have nothing to give him. Apart from this rubbish of Wells's, and the clothes you wear, you are all, for the time being, destitute.'

The boy was mildly weeping again. I said, 'You ought not to torment him with all this argument.'

'Well,' said Robinson, 'I shall not take the things from him by force. In any case, I wouldn't care to handle them.'

'That's rather superstitious of you,' I said.

I could see that Robinson was furious. As if retorting to a challenge, he lifted up a few of the charms from the patio and examined them. He really hated handling them.

Suddenly he poured them into Wells's lap and said, 'Bella is sick, Miguel. Come and have a look at her.' Bella was the goat. 'Bella,' said Miguel. He followed Robinson, putting the amulets in his pocket.

'There's something wrong with that man,' said Tom Wells.

'It's Robinson's island,' I said.

'I'm a British citizen,' said Wells. 'He has destroyed my property. Those are the simple facts; I'll take it up with the authorities when we get home.'

He started picking up the pieces of his magazine. This was difficult owing to his encased ribs. Jimmie and I scrambled round trying to help him. When we had gathered all the bits I had an idea, and obtained some transparent sticky tape from Robinson's desk.

I brought this out to the patio and set about piecing the torn pages together like a jigsaw. Like Miguel, I found the advertisement section with its supporting photographs the most alluring. There was an intense turbanned Indian, a scholarly fellow in horn-rimmed glasses, a motherly soul, a good-looking young man in a monk's cowl, a wild-eyed girl resembling Emily Brontë, all accompanied by appropriate announcements, which also fascinated me.

BARI SAWIMI can provide Tactile Regeneration. Send fragment of Personal Garb, cloth 3" x 7" for immediate postal reply & satisfaction. P.O. 37s. 6d. no cheques to 'Bari Sawimi', Box 957 *Your Future*.

MURIEL THE MARVEL with her X-ray eyes. *Can read your very soul.* Scores of satisfied clients. . . .

CONSULT BROTHER DEREK. Troubled? Anxious? Is that well-paid job just out of your reach? Write to Brother Derek. . . .

I discovered in one of the pictures a touched-up likeness of Wells himself, entitled Dr Benignus.

Trust DR BENIGNUS. Treat him as your Father. FREE advice to all readers of *Your Future* and members of the Dr Benignus Magic Circle of Friendship. Financial, Matrimonial, and Moral Problems treated in Strictest Confidence. Dr Benignus has brought Consolation and Happiness to Thousands. . . .

At last I had the proofs complete, though ragged.
'That's sweet of you, honey,' said Wells.

'Is not to call Miss January honey,' said Jimmie, 'as if she was a trumpet, and any – '

'You mean strumpet,' I said.

'Strumpet,' said Jimmie, 'and any indignities vented upon this lady, I black your eye full sore.'

Tom Wells clasped his ribs, closed his eyes, and addressed me: 'To be serious for a moment, there's an article in this issue that will appeal to you. See page twelve. It's called "Are We Fulfilling the Prediction of the Apocalypse?"'

'Is serious,' said Jimmie.

'Naturally,' said Wells, 'it's extremely serious.'

'I mean, that I black your eye,' said Jimmie.

VI

TO REACH THE OTHER SIDE of the island there was no way but over the mountain. From our plateau it rose steeply, but the path wound to east and north-east, cutting off the higher reaches, and descending through stretches of squelchy moss on the lava rocks, through juniper woods to a green plain at the North Arm. At some points on the path where the clumps of juniper lay above, and only a thin white sunlight penetrated the clouds, the scene was sharp, its dark and light the texture of a woodcut. In direct sunlight a variety of greens twinkled suddenly, glimpses of mossy craters. Curious red lights appeared, which I later discovered were caused by vapours rising from the soil like rusty dew. To the west of this route the mountain was pitted with deep wide craters. The shallower pits were filled with iridescent blue and green pools. This was the moonish landscape of which Robinson had spoken. The feel of the earth underfoot, the colours, even the air, were strange.

I have never seen so many mountain springs. Robinson said these little brooks were constantly appearing, so that every time he crossed the mountain, which was about every month, he would notice some two or three new springs. At a point just above our plateau, where the rock was uncovered and the sun particularly strong, I saw a small cactus type of plant, and, from the wedge of rock where the cactus had taken root, and as if from the plant itself, a small stream bubbling with force. This was on the occasion of my first crossing the mountain. I was with Robinson, who was bound for a certain mineral spring which contained strong healing properties; he thought it might cure his sick goat. Robinson was very taken by the sight of the water apparently gushing from the cactus. 'That's a new spring,' he said. He left me there and went back to the house to get his camera. I still have the print of the photograph. It looks a fake, the cactus opening its thick lips, like a carved fountain gryphon, to disgorge a stream of water.

Robinson walked ahead. He addressed me over his shoulder, 'Are you keeping up your journal?'

'No, I've lost interest lately.'

'You should write it up every day.'

'I don't care for it. I may continue later.'

'You should care for it. I thought you were a writer.'

'You don't catch me writing anything unless it suits me,' I said.

'Ah,' he said, 'I see. You write for pleasure. Taken to its logical conclusion your attitude – '

'Look at the mimosa clump,' I said. There was a coppice on a plateau below us, and at its edge about six mimosa trees. I am always angered when people say to me, 'Taken to its logical conclusion your attitude . . . '

'Keep up your journal,' he said. 'It will take your mind off Jimmie.'

'I don't see that I want to keep my mind off Jimmie,' I said.

Of course, working over this conversation later, in my fury, I regretted not having replied, 'You are insolent', or something like that.

Jimmie and I had been planning an expedition over the mountain, and after some hesitation we had consulted Robinson about the route. I had, in fact, attempted to pump Miguel as to the best way across the mountain, but 'Ask Robinson,' he said.

'I don't suppose there's anything worth seeing on the mountain,' I said purposely.

Miguel laughed, and then to give me something to think about he said,

'There are three secret tunnels.'

'I'll believe them when I see them,' I said.

'Ask Robinson,' he said.

Jimmie and I did not particularly want to ask Robinson. We would have preferred to set out on our own, for we felt that Robinson would somehow contrive not to take us both together. As it transpired, this was true. Robinson had made it clear that he was not in favour of my friendship with Jimmie. Now it is true that I was becoming rather attached to Jimmie, mostly because of our situation on the island, and the qualities of the island, the colours and the atmospherics and mists, and that sort of thing.

One afternoon when Tom Wells was sleeping, Robinson and Miguel fishing in one of the streams above our plateau, I said to Jimmie, 'Let's get out of this.'

'Whither?' said Jimmie.

'Over the mountain, perhaps?'

He shook his head. 'I know not the mountain.'

'What other parts of the island do you know?' I said.

'The burial ground,' he said.

Robinson had promised to show us all of the island. It was now our eighth week. My only excursion had been that to the beach by the southern path. Tom Wells, partly because of his injury and partly because of a lazy incuriosity, did not attempt to explore very much; I thought he seemed to wish to reproduce about himself as far as possible the environment of his magazine office at Paddington. Robinson had put a desk in his room, where he had his papers spread before him and wrote articles for forthcoming numbers of *Your Future* on paper sadly provided by Robinson. Sometimes he read such of Robinson's books as would hold his attention. He complained much of the food, the climate, and the money he was losing by his incarceration on the island – that is how he expressed it. 'This enforced incarceration,' he said every day, along with other often repeated phrases such as 'My wife's gone over to her sister's, I dare say', 'We're lucky to be alive', and 'There's something unnatural about that Robinson'. He complained, too, of Robinson's having wheedled the trinkets out of Miguel and cast them in a live crater known as the Furnace: 'That Robinson's a religious maniac', or 'That man goes crazy if you give the child a kind look'.

On one occasion when Robinson had been particularly irritated by my winning Miguel's praise for a very fine ping-pong match with Bluebell, it occurred to me that I, compared with Robinson, Jimmie, and Tom Wells, was bearing up pretty well in the circumstances. Having mused thus, I immediately helped myself to four of Robinson's share of the cigarettes, to safeguard my soul against the deadly sin of pride. It is really mortifying to do a small mean injury to someone; but a theologian once told me that this is not sound doctrine.

Jimmie observed my theft, and while I lit up and luxuriously puffed one of the plundered cigarettes I explained the motive to Jimmie. It was then, it being the early afternoon and Tom Wells being asleep, that I said, 'Let's get out of this.' We planned an excursion for the following day. Jimmie led the way to the burial ground which lay slightly to the north-west of our plateau, less than a mile from the house. We had a short steep climb; after that the downward slope was easy. On the western side of the mountain there were a few lava pits, but not nearly so many as I subsequently saw on my north-eastern crossing with Robinson. I was surprised to see that the plane had been wrecked, not on one of the hefty cliff faces of our mountain, but on a gentle green hillside, merging into downland. Here, on the night of the crash, Robinson had found us, Jimmie wandering in a daze with blood running down his face, I unconscious and lying still as death on my side, Tom Wells groaning and twisting by the light of the blazing plane. Eventually, as dawn broke, and Jimmie was calmed, he and Robinson had carried us to the shore of the green and blue lake.

Quite nearby, in a flat-bottomed hollow, Jimmie and Robinson had buried the dead, and lest the graves were not deep enough – since two grave-diggers for the remains of twenty-six dead are too few for deep digging – they had unsettled a number of rock boulders and lava lumps from the sides of the mound surrounding the hollow, rolling them down into the graveyard. These newly uprooted rocks, some a sort of porous red and some black lava, littered the hollow, protecting the burial ground from disturbances of mist and rain, until the pomegranate men should arrive in August and perhaps be persuaded to work over the graves, thus to give the bodies more security.

Sometimes, on the plateau where Robinson's house stood, when the wind was from the north or east, a curious smell of burning would pervade the atmosphere, penetrating the rooms. It was sulphurous. Robinson said it came from a bubbling eruption still lively on the mountain, which he called the Furnace.

'I should like to see the Furnace,' I said.

'I will take you there, one day.'

Whenever the wind was north-east, bringing the burning sulphur smell, I had reminded him of his promise.

Sitting with Jimmie above the burial ground I noticed a burnt-out smell, although there was no wind.

'There must be a molten lava pit nearby,' I said.

'Is the odours of the aeroplane which you smell,' said Jimmie. He rose and beckoned to me. I followed him down the hill and there, to our left, lay the wreck of the plane, reclining on its grassy slope, and still, after eight weeks, giving off a smell of burning as a dead fire-eating dragon might smell in its decay.

When I saw the wreck I started to cry. Jimmie said, 'Ah me! Partake of a drop of brandy.' Even so, I could not stop crying, even though I giggled at Jimmie's words, and even though I had already, many times since my recovery from the accident, pictured to my mind the scene of the wreck, attempting to realize it as an exercise for pity, since pity is an emotion which does not come easily in the bewilderment and first fears of a very strange environment.

I do not know whether it was for pity that I wept at the sight of the wreck, only that I could not stop crying. We walked on until both the wreck and the burial ground were concealed behind a grassy hump, and we settled, watching the sea shimmering below us, but still I went on crying.

We had a picnic pack with us – two guavas, some banana cream biscuits, and a bottle filled with the pale yellow mineral water which Robinson and Miguel frequently brought from the mountain. Jimmie opened the pack and poured out a drink for me into an enamel mug. Although I was crying hard I thought it looked yellower than usual, and when I tasted it, I said, 'What have you put in it?' recognizing the taste and glow of brandy.

'Where did you get the brandy?' I said, at the same time weeping away.

Jimmie took his leather and silver flask from his jacket pocket and held it to my nose. 'I give you a drop more should you desire.'

'Where did you get it?'

'Is personal gift which I have received from a kinsman. When I am salvaged from the aeroplane, so also is my worthy flask.'

I did remember Jimmie's flask in the plane, and his sharing his brandy with me there. I said, dabbing my eyes, 'Where did you get the brandy – I know that the flask is yours, but where did you get the brandy?' For, on the plane, Jimmie and I had emptied his flask between us.

Jimmie looked lovingly at the flask, smelt it, and then, placing it next his ear, swilled it round to hear the splash of liquor.

'Is salvage,' he said. 'Alas, drink up and weep no more.'

I knew it was not salvage from the plane. The few battered bits of luggage that had been found in the vicinity of the wreck had been examined and labelled by Robinson, and some of the clothes distributed to Tom Wells and Jimmie for their present needs, I refusing such creepy garments. Certainly, there was no liquor intact in those far-flung battered and pathetic suitcases.

'Salvage from where?' I said, with my simply physical tears streaming. 'From Robinson?' I said.

And I said, 'Look here, Jimmie, this is Robinson's brandy. You shouldn't take Robinson's brandy.'

'Is in order to mortify my immortal soul, I help myself,' said Jimmie, 'like you have declared to me. And after all, bloody hell, a little of that which you fancy does good things to one.' He took a spotted silk scarf from his neck and gave it over to me to use for a handkerchief, since my own was wet with my crying. He poured himself out a portion of new brandy. I did not notice at the time, but realized later that the scarf was salvage. Meantime, I used it to cry into.

Jimmie lay back on his elbows and sipped.

'Many times past when Robinson has been old buddy of mine – ' But he stopped, and presently he said,

'Robinson approaches.'

I looked up, and saw Robinson's head bobbing behind a hill some distance away, then, after a space, his head and shoulders behind a nearer mound, until gradually he wholly appeared, climbing up to our picnic place.

'What are you crying for?' he said, looking from me to Jimmie and then back at me.

I giggled, without stopping crying, at his suspicious look. I did quite like Robinson, but lately in his anxiety to keep order on his island he had seemed to me rather quaint.

'She laments for the aeroplane disaster, I guess,' said Jimmie leaning still on his elbows and sipping the brandy.

It did not sound quite convincing, which caused me to giggle again. At this Robinson looked hard at me, and then he said, 'Take some brandy.' And still looking closely at me he addressed Jimmie, 'Give her some brandy.' This surprised us both, for he had not seemed to have observed the flask cup in Jimmie's hand, far less that it contained brandy.

'I have some here,' I said, holding up the enamel mug.

Robinson put his nose inside.

'What's that mixture?'

'Mineral water and a dash of – '

'Not my *best* brandy?' said Robinson.

'Is so, naturally. Have sense,' said Jimmie.

'Do you mean to say,' said Robinson, 'that you have put my best brandy into mineral water? No wonder January is crying.'

I understood that he was making this fuss about his best brandy to save us the embarrassment of the question why we had his brandy at all, and I thought it rather nice of him.

'It tastes very good with mineral water,' I said.

The tears continued to pour from my eyes.

'Is woeful,' said Jimmie.

Robinson sat down beside us. He said to Jimmie:

'Any left in the flask?'

'Plenty.'

Jimmie handed him the flask. Robinson passed it to me and told me to take a good swig, which I did.

The brandy glow, almost like an emotion itself, began to spread within me. I felt it was demanded that I should say something about my crying. I did not know what to say. I thought of saying 'I feel such a fool,' but stopped myself, reflecting that women usually say this when they cry. I said, 'Oh dear, I don't know what to say.' But this sounded to me the depth of inanity.

'Try a cigarette,' said Robinson, and offered me his open cigarette case.

'No,' I said, '*you* have one of *mine*.' I fished into our picnic pack and brought out the envelope in which I kept my cigarettes.

'All right, I *will*,' said Robinson. '*Many* thanks.' Not that I cared much, I was too absorbed in my crying.

It stopped for a bit, while I smoked the cigarette.

'I wish I had some make-up for my face,' I said, trying to think up and utter some concrete complaint. And it was true that while I was on the island I greatly missed my make-up; I do not care to go about with nothing on my face so that everyone can see what is written on it. One of the day-dream fantasies that came to me like homesickness when I was on the island, was a make-up session. In my mind, I would be in my bedroom at home, performing the smoothing and creaming and painting of my face, going through the whole ritual of smoothing and patting, down to the last touch of mascara, taking my leisure, one hour, two hours. Whereas in reality, at home, I make up my face rather quickly, and only when, rarely, the idea seizes me, do I make a morning of it.

'We have some stuff among the salvage,' said Robinson. 'You could use that, if you feel it absolutely necessary.'

'No fear,' I said, and started to cry again.

'It isn't absolutely necessary,' said Robinson.

'Is essential,' said Jimmie, 'for a lady that she adorn her visage with a bit of paint.'

'Simply and factually it isn't essential,' said Robinson, 'but I have no objection to it.'

How it annoyed me when Robinson stated what he had or hadn't objections to! I stopped crying. I said, 'Your objections aren't in question.' I started to pack our bag as a sign that the picnic was over. It was not the first time that Robinson had intruded when Jimmie and I were out picnicking.

Robinson, as if he knew what was in my mind, said to Jimmie, 'I came to tell you about Bella. She's been vomiting. Milk her as usual but throw away the milk in case it is infected.'

He hurried on ahead while Jimmie and I followed. We stopped to watch the mist as it began to form, swirling like curdled milk below us.

It was the afternoon of the next day that I crossed the mountain with Robinson to procure mineral water for the goat. Jimmie had wanted to accompany us but Robinson had found an emergency to prevent him: dampness in the storehouse. All the packages had to be moved, and the piping behind one of the walls replaced.

'Keep up your journal; it will keep your mind off Jimmie.'

To which, of course, I should have replied, 'You are insolent.'

And while I answered, 'I don't see that I want to keep my mind off Jimmie', I was wondering how best, during the five

weeks remaining to me on the island, to preserve some freedom from Robinson's interference in the matter of Jimmie,
while retaining his protection from Wells.

Robinson inquired: 'Has Jimmie told you much about
himself?'

I said, 'Jimmie has told me a lot about you.'

'What has Jimmie told you?' I expected that question.
Looking round, I saw Miguel above and behind us, following.
Watching him, I sorted out my few sensations, and noted, one,
that Miguel must have approached subterraneously, and, two,
that I felt rather sorry for Robinson. It is hard for a recluse,
and such an upright one, to feel his seclusion threatened by
others' knowing a little about him.

'Here comes Miguel,' I said.

Robinson made an effort to look interested in Miguel's
approach, then he casually repeated, 'What has Jimmie told
you?' He gave an amused chuckle, as if to say, whatever he
has told you isn't to be taken seriously.

'Hallo there, Miguel,' I shouted. The truth is, I have a
sharp tongue when I am annoyed, and it is better to say anything beside the point rather than what I might say, at such
moments, pointedly.

Miguel was grinning happily as he clambered behind us.

'You came by a secret tunnel,' I observed to him.

Robinson looked surprised for a second, then defeated, as
if his last friend had betrayed him. It is always the same with
people who make a fetish of self-control: they strike the most
histrionic attitudes. How was I to know that the existence of
the underground channels was supposed to be a secret?

Fortunately Miguel did not seem embarrassed by my remark.

'From this point,' said Robinson, who was a little way
above me, 'you get a sight of the sea on both sides: Vasco da

Gama's Bay on the north, and our Pomegranate Bay on the south. I call it the Pomegranate Bay because that's where the pomegranate boat puts in.'

It was, very much, a splendid sight. I was prepared to say no more on the troublesome subject of the underground caves, but Miguel devilishly put in, 'I know all the secret tunnels on the island.'

'I should like to see them,' I said.

'They are nothing much,' said Robinson, 'they are slimy holes in the mountain. In one of them there's a point where you have to crawl on your stomach. And they are, of course, no longer secret.'

'She doesn't *know* them,' said Miguel.

'I only know of them,' I said.

'She doesn't know the secret tunnels,' said Miguel again with delight.

'I can smell the Furnace,' I said. I could also hear the rumbling, and presently I saw the red earthy smoke rising in puffs on the far side of a hill.

On the side of the crater from which we approached, the slope leading to its pit was fairly gradual, covered with tropical foliage, plants thick as ox tongues, but green from the numerous rivulets that scored this bank. As these streams of water reached the bottom of the crater they sizzled and steamed, this sound and vapour mixing with the rumble and sulphurous clouds of the eruption. The far wall of the crater was steep and sheer, and it was against this cliff that the breakers of red cloud beat and dispersed so that we could stand on the lip of the crater at our side watching the bubbling opposite, without much discomfort. From where we stood it would have been easy to walk down or slide into the bottom. But from the opposite edge it was a sheer drop.

'How awful to fall in,' I said. 'No one would survive it.'

Robinson said, 'The body would be sucked under immediately. There is a continuous action of suction and rejection going on down there.' He added, 'Curiously, if you throw in anything sizeable the eruption gives out a sort of scream. There must be a narrow tubular shaft leading down from the pit of the crater, and the suction action through this narrow pipe causes the sound, do you see?' I didn't see but I lifted the biggest stone I could manage, and sent it rolling into the milling mud. It gave out a very dreadful scream.

'Sometimes,' said Robinson, 'without provocation it sighs.'

'I should like to hear it sigh,' I said.

Miguel was half-way down the bank, picking some large-petalled flowers which seemed to have been by their original nature blue, but through the constant activity of red vapour had evolved to streaky mauve.

'Don't go too far, Miguel,' Robinson called. 'It's slippery farther down, and you might find yourself sliding in. We shan't come and drag you back.'

Miguel laughed. He said, 'The flowers are for Mr Tom.'

On the way back, Robinson once more referred to my journal.

'Keep it up. You will be glad of the notes later on. After all, you did intend to write about islands.'

'Not this island,' I said.

'Man proposes and God disposes,' he said.

I thought, There's something in that, and a pity you don't keep it in mind when your own scheme of things is upset.

I had been commissioned to write about islands in a series which included books about threes of everything. Three rivers, three lakes, and threes of mountains, courtesans, battles, poets, old country houses. I was supposed to be doing Three Islands. Two of my chosen islands I already knew well: Zanzibar and Tiree. I had thought one of the Azores would

complete an attractive trio. Someone else, now, has written
the book on Three Islands. I believe someone has added to
the series Three Men in My Life.

Robinson continued to harp on the advantages of my
keeping a journal. My anger had dwindled to nothing at the
sight of the Furnace, and in a more congenial humour I said,
'Oh well, I'll see.'

'Stick to facts,' said Robinson. 'There's the Furnace for
one. And there are so many curious things on the island –
the moths, have you noticed? And those very long lizards,
the trees, those miniature jumpers in the stunted part of the
mountain, the ferns.'

I thought, 'And the derelict croft, the lack of cultivation.'
As if I had said it, he continued,
'You have not seen my pomegranate orchard.'
'No,' I said. 'Perhaps you'll take us there.'
He was silent for the rest of the journey home.

VII

BLUEBELL WAS CHASING BUTTERFLIES on the patio. Tom Wells was indoors sitting in his braces. Jimmie was with Robinson repairing the leaky pipe behind the storehouse. Miguel was sitting at the kitchen table doing his arithmetic. I sat in the sun, extremely tired in my bones after the crossing of the mountain on the previous day. I was making an entry in my journal:

Wednesday, 30th June – Robinson was born at Gibraltar in 1903, of a wealthy military family. He was educated in England and France. Then, about the age of twenty-four he entered an Irish seminary to study for the priesthood. This was highly regarded by his widowed mother, a Catholic, whose only child Robinson was. His father had been killed in 1917.

After a period in the seminary, and just before he was due to become a Deacon, Robinson refused to be ordained. He travelled in Spain, Italy, and South America, making observations of Catholic practices, and at the end of a year he left the Church on account of what he considered its superstitious character. In particular he objected to the advancing wave of devotion to the Blessed Virgin, and to this effect he wrote many letters to Catholic papers and articles later collected into a book entitled *The Dangers of*

Marian Doctrine. Still professing the Catholic faith himself, Robinson maintained that the Church had fallen into
heresy.

Robinson fought with the Republicans in Spain, but
suffered a revulsion and deserted after six months. He
then retired to Mexico, where he lived on a deserted ranch
for some ten years.

In 1946 Robinson's mother died. He returned to bury
her. He entrusted his considerable fortune to an uncle res-
ident in Gibraltar with interests in Tangier. He bought this
island which was then called Ferreira, from a Portuguese
called Ferreira. He has been living here ever since.

His full name is Miles Mary Robinson. For some reason not clear to me one does not call him Mr Robinson,
nor imagine anyone calling him Miles.

I sat limply in the cane chair, exhausted by this assembling of
facts. I had enjoyed the small catty task – since by his 'stick to
facts' Robinson had not meant facts about himself – and now
obtained satisfaction from the thought, 'He has got what he
asked for', but I could not rest in this simple thought. I was
not even certain at this time whether all these facts were true.
I had got them from Jimmie.

I was wondering again which of my sisters would consider herself Brian's guardian. He had recently gone away to
school, and it was a question whether, when the summer holidays started, he would reside in the home of Curly Lonsdale
or Ian Brodie.

I had seen, lying on Robinson's desk, his publication *The
Dangers of Marian Doctrine*, with pages of pencilled adden-
da on which he was apparently still working.

My brother-in-law Ian, a Catholic from the time of his
birth, and rather aggressive about his religion, was always

using that word, danger, in connection with Our Blessed Lady, though for my part I did not see the connection. On returning from his continental holidays Ian frequently wrote to the Catholic newspapers letters of concern about the Marian excesses he had witnessed at feast-day processions in Italy or Spain, and their danger. What, he once demanded of me, were the bishops thinking of to permit these dangerous extravagances?

'I don't know, Ian,' I said, 'what bishops think of, for I don't know any bishops.'

'Any good Catholic,' said Ian, 'should be horrified to see the Mother of God worshipped as if she were a pagan goddess.'

'Do you believe in pagan goddesses?' I said. 'Do you believe they exist, have power?'

'Well, in the psychological sense – '

'I mean, in the real substantial sense.'

'No, not exactly.'

'Then I don't see the danger. Prayers addressed to the Blessed Virgin are not likely to be received by pagan goddesses.'

'There's a question of distortion of doctrine,' said Ian. 'These people make more fuss of the Blessed Virgin than of Jesus Christ. *That's* dangerous. And it's becoming prevalent all over the world. I've just written a letter – '

'I don't see that devotions to the Blessed Virgin are likely to be rewarded with the gift of corrupt doctrine.'

'It puts people off the Faith,' said Ian.

'What people?'

'Non-Catholics, lapsed Catholics, respectable Christians. . . . '

'There's always a stumbling-block. If it isn't one thing it's another.' I was thinking of Ian himself, and how for years I was put off the Catholic Church because he was a member, and carping exponent, of it.

'I said in my letter,' Ian continued, 'it is time these dangerous impurities were purged – '

After that I seldom argued with Ian lest he should win the argument. He could support himself with a range of theological reference unknown to me, and which I simply did not trust him to handle rightly. Moreover, he was a Catholic by birth, and I but a convert; those hereditary Catholics cannot bear to be opposed by newcomers. And again, perhaps most important, I was partly afraid of Ian Brodie, obscurely endangered by him.

Agnes had told me once that her husband was sexually impotent. She had no right to tell me any such thing, but I felt she was not telling me anything that I did not really already know. To this day, I vaguely feel that Ian's impotence is in some way bound up with his suspicions of the Blessed Virgin, which he termed jealousy for the True Faith – a phrase which I noticed Robinson had used in his publication.

During these first weeks on the island I was increasingly struck by similarities between Robinson and Ian Brodie. At the time I exaggerated them, but still, tenuously, they existed. Robinson, short, muscular, and dark-skinned, did not at casual sight look anything like long seedy Ian Brodie; only a likeness between the shape of their heads came to me at odd times. But Robinson was far more intelligent and more controlled.

Again, Robinson's anti-Marian fervour was far more interesting to me than Ian's, for with Robinson it was an obsession of such size that he had left the Church because of it; he had formed for himself a system bound by a simple chain of identities: Mariology was identified with Earth mythology, both were identified with superstition, and superstition with evil. Sterile notion as it seemed to me, still it was a system and he had written it up in his book. Ian Brodie, on the other hand, was dark with inarticulate emotions about religion, which his spasmodic rationalizations failed to satisfy; he was mean by temperament, was a miserable minimist, and was for ever demonstrating how far he could go against the Church without being excommunicated.

And whereas I could never really dislike Robinson, I hated Ian Brodie's guts.

But when Robinson showed his anxiety to keep authority on his island, to know what was going on between us, to prevent our quarrelling or behaving other than impersonally, and to prevent our making friends with Miguel, and, most of all, to detect any possibility of a love affair between Jimmie and me, I was reminded of Ian Brodie, and noticed very much the shape of Robinson's head. I was reminded of instances of Ian Brodie's extraordinary urge to ferret into my private life, and in particular of a morning towards the end of the Easter holidays when I said to my son Brian, 'Let's get out of this.' I telephoned to Agnes, who had arranged to come to tea next day, to tell her I was going abroad for a couple of days.

We went to Dieppe, then caught a bus to Rouen. I was sitting alone outside a café looking at a tower with a big clock, Brian having gone for a walk round about. I half-noticed an English car passing. I was feeling too agreeable with life to be on the alert for anything whatsoever. The car passed again. Brian returned to announce he had found a pastry-cook's owned by a man by the name of Marcel Proust, and this seemed to us both excessively funny. The English car passed again. I saw immediately that it was Ian Brodie's Singer, and that Ian was driving.

'I thought he was in Germany,' said Brian. So did I think he was in Germany. I felt sure he had followed us. I was wrong, but he deserved to be the victim of my suspicions, because of the suspicious way he was driving round and round, past the café where I had been sitting alone. I was not wrong in this, that having caught sight of me alone in Rouen, he had determined to find out who my companion was. He was always inexhaustible in trying to catch me in an illicit love affair, but he never succeeded; and whether this was because I never, in fact, had a lover, or whether I had, but effectively concealed the fact, you may be sure Ian Brodie is still guessing. It was my plan, from the time I became aware of his absorption in this question, to keep him guessing; and always, should his horrible curiosity about my private life appear to flag, I revived it quickly by some careful chance reference which, on his greedy investigation, led him nowhere.

That time in Rouen, when he had noticed that we had recognized him, it was too late for him to stop with any show of innocence. However, in about ten minutes he passed again, this time going through the motions of recognition.

'I could hardly believe my eyes. What are you doing here?' I should have replied, 'What are *you* doing here?' But I said, 'Oh, just looking round,' while Brian said, 'Taking the air.'

'Oh,' he said, looking from one to the other of us. 'Well, no wonder you're always hard up.'

'Will you have some coffee?' said Brian.

Robinson appeared on the patio carrying three packing cases bound together by string. I shut my notebook guiltily; he noticed this, and I thought, Now he has guessed that I've been writing about him. I was coming to terms with this slightly disturbing thought, when he said,

'I ought to have a mule. I've always resisted having a mule because the nuisance of keeping animals on the island sometimes exceeds their usefulness.' I wondered if this was some obscure reference to me, then immediately decided it wasn't. Sometimes I had to resist a tendency to read deep nasty meanings into Robinson's words.

'A mule would be useful for crossing the mountain,' I observed.

'Exactly,' said Robinson. 'I have to take all these packages over the mountain on foot.'

Jimmie came round from the storehouse with two bundles of cartons. They seemed to be heavy.

Tom Wells emerged from the house in his braces, stretching his arms and yawning. 'What's afoot?' he said.

Jimmie pointed to the cartons. 'Is commodities gone to rot.'

'Which, what?' said Wells. He had obviously been deeply sleeping.

Robinson said, 'A certain amount of my tinned food is inconsumable. It has to be disposed of quickly.'

'We open these big tins,' said Jimmie, 'we look, we look away; we look again, and look away.'

There were high stacks of tinned food in the storehouse, great six-pounders as well as the small grocer's-shop kind.

'What about the rest of them?' I said.

'They are all right,' said Robinson. 'It is only part of the last consignment that is damaged.'

Jimmie, anxious to console him, said, 'We dump them in the ocean.'

'We dump them in the Furnace,' said Robinson wearily, 'and I wish I had a mule.'

'Look,' said Wells, 'you don't want to cart that muck over the mountain.'

I said, 'Chuck them over the cliff, then follow them down to the sea.'

'Chuck them over the cliff and keep following them down,' said Jimmie.

'They must go into the Furnace,' said Robinson. 'The food is bad. The tins are opened. The sea will throw them up

83

again, and I can't have my beach littered with rank meat. The Furnace is final.'

'The sharks will demolish them,' I said.

'Not in tins,' said Robinson. 'They draw the line at tins.'

It seemed to me that Robinson was particularly perverse. He heaved the first pack on to his shoulder by its rope and set off for the mountain. Jimmie wanted to accompany him. Robinson firmly refused his help. 'Be a decent chap and stack up the stuff in the store. Put down plenty of disinfectant. The place stinks.'

The smell of the two remaining packs of cartons was fairly fierce. I prepared to accompany Jimmie to the storehouse with buckets of Jeyes' Fluid, while Tom Wells clutched his ribs. 'I hope all the rest of the food is in good condition. There's five weeks to go. We could easily starve,' he said.

'Is in good condition,' said Jimmie; 'we have put to the test the samples of all commodities.'

An hour later Robinson returned for the next package. He looked terribly exhausted. So were Jimmie and I after our exertions in the storehouse. I had made tea, thinking meanwhile at least Tom Wells could have done as much. We sat floppily in the big stone kitchen.

'You've put sugar in my tea,' said Wells. 'I don't take sugar.'

I had done it deliberately. I said:

'Oh, I'll pour another cup for you.'

This I made very watery, but he did not complain about it. However, he said, 'I'm sick and tired of drinking tea without milk.' Our tinned milk was running low.

I said, 'We ought to have lemons. Lemon tea is nice. I am sure lemons could be cultivated here.'

'They couldn't,' said Robinson.

I thought. 'Not if the job was left to you', for the lack of cultivation on the island was a continual irritation to me.

It was not simply that it offended some instinct for economy and reproduction. It was more; it offended my aesthetic sense. If you choose the sort of life which has no conventional pattern you have to try to make an art of it, or it is a mess.

I said, 'I think lemons would grow at the foot of the slopes on the South Arm.'

No one paid attention to this remark.

'What with the lack of make-up and the tinned food,' I said, 'my skin is getting very dry.'

'Lemon wouldn't help that condition,' Robinson said.

'Here we are,' said Wells, looking round with a flourish, 'wrecked on a desert island, and January harps about her skin.'

'Is my intention,' said Jimmie to Wells, 'to cast this beverage upon your face in the event that you do not keep your bloody hair on. Is monstrous to declare such offensive insults when a lady is in plight with regard to her complexion on an island.'

Robinson got up. 'Two more trips,' he said.

'Leave them till tomorrow,' said Wells.

'I can't leave them stinking out there on the patio.'

'Dump them on the mountainside for tonight,' I said. 'No need to trek all that way to the Furnace.'

And Jimmie pointed out, in support, 'The mist descends.'

'All right,' said Robinson surprisingly, for he hardly ever accepted any of our advice.

This time he also accepted Jimmie's help in carrying the heavy weights to the mountainside. As they set off I noticed again a look of exhaustion in Robinson, not only in his face but in the droop of his arms and the way he carried himself.

Next day Robinson and Jimmie set off to pick up the packages they had left a short distance up the mountain and carry them to the crater. This was Jimmie's first visit to the Furnace.

'They scream,' he said to me, on his return. 'We have shoved these stinking bundles into the crater. First they roll, then they run, and lo! when they enter this cauldron, is a scream.'

Mr Wells, who had overheard him, said, 'You know, old chap, being stuck on this island is bound to have a psychological effect on one. I feel it myself. It isn't natural to live alone with Nature. I should guard against hallucinations, if I were you. A course of meditation – '

'The Furnace does scream when you throw anything into it,' I said.

Jimmie said to him, 'I like to see you descend into that mighty Furnace. Then is two screams – one is of the Furnace and one is of Mr Wells.'

In the evenings, however, we did not bicker quite so much. The evening after turning out the storehouse, when we were settled in Robinson's room, some drinking rum, some brandy, we were tired and relaxed with each other so far as to speculate how it would be when we were rescued, how surprised everyone would be.

'I hope to God my wife's gone over to her sister's,' said Wells. 'There's a brother of mine, he's a bachelor, he fancies my wife. I shouldn't be surprised if they haven't got married, me presumed dead. If so, that's just too bad, I'm still the husband – what d'you say, Robinson?'

'You are still the husband,' Robinson said, 'and in any case I think you can't be presumed dead till after seven years.' He spoke very slowly, for he was worn out after his two mountain journeys.

'Is definite that you remain the husband of the wife,' said Jimmie amiably, 'and in the event your brother is an honourable type of bastard, he will not marry your wife. In the contrary event, is manifest that you are bound to black that rotter his eye.'

'I reckon I might do him in,' mused Wells.

'Is to go too far,' said Jimmie. 'No, no. Is better to disfigure his countenance. Is only justice to your wife.'

'I'd give *her* a piece of my mind,' said Wells.

'No, no, please,' said Jimmie. 'Is not nice to give a lady a piece of your mind.'

'Ah well, we're lucky to be alive.'

'The goat must go,' Robinson said.

'Poor Bella, is she very sick?'

'Yes, and suffering.'

'You kill her?' said Jimmie.

'Oh yes, I'll have to shoot her.'

'Is better to slay such a beast with a knife,' said Jimmie.

'Not better,' said Robinson, 'only more traditional.'

'I miss the milk,' said Wells. 'I must say, just as I was getting used to it.'

'Yes, we do miss the milk.'

'Ah well, we're lucky to be alive.'

I recall that evening as the most pleasant few hours I spent on the island. A heavy rainstorm had left the atmosphere moist and cool. Robinson talked, as he sometimes did, of the history and legends of the island. It was a traditional hermits' home. In the fourteenth century, five hermits living on different parts of the island had been attacked by a band of pirates, only one surviving to tell the tale. The island had always been privately owned. It had passed through the hands of a line of Portuguese. Vasco da Gama, on one of his voyages, put in at the island between the North Arm and the North Leg, at a point which was now called Vasco da Gama's Bay. Pirates and smugglers used the island considerably, often without the knowledge of the inhabitants, for there was a cave in the sheer cliffs of the South Arm known as the Market, which was accessible only from the sea, and even then was dangerous to approach, owing to the numerous rocks and a particular whirlpool at its mouth. At the Market, however, the pirates would meet and barter their plunder, so it was said.

From a long crack in the wall of Robinson's room the flying ants were squirming out, spreading their wings and fluttering about. Tom Wells had fallen asleep. I, too, was giving but a drowsy ear to Robinson's voice. I had taken a red cashmere tablecloth from a drawer in the dining-room to use as a shawl which I wore as an Indian sari pinned up over a shirt borrowed from Robinson. This enabled me to wash and repair my shabby green dress, and the change of dress in a way contributed to my peace of mind.

Robinson and Jimmie were arranging to examine a disused ship's boat which lay at the West Leg Bay, with a view to repairing it.

I was so reluctant to disrupt our peace that I put off telling Robinson I had found one of my possessions which I thought had been lost at the time of the crash.

This possession was my rosary. It had been in the pocket of my coat at the time of the crash, and later, when I had recovered, I was not really surprised to have lost it, for although the other contents of the pocket were intact – a handkerchief and a packet of matches – these were comparatively light, and less likely to fly out of my pocket when I was thrown clear of the plane than was my rosary.

I found the rosary in a drawer in Robinson's desk.

I had once casually mentioned to Robinson that my rosary might be somewhere in the vicinity of the wreck, where the salvage had been picked up. 'An antique one,' I said, 'made of rosewood and silver, quite valuable.' Even then I must have sensed that he would be best induced to hand over the rosary if he thought I valued it mainly for its antiquity, rosewood and silver. And it was indeed a very attractive object.

I found it quite unexpectedly in Robinson's desk. It is true I had no business to open the drawers and examine his papers and read the letters. I suppose I desired to find out to what extent he resembled Ian Brodie, and I suppose I hoped to discover something bearing on his relationship with Jimmie and his family: so far I had only Jimmie's version, which was most engaging, and invited further investigation. Anyway, I went to his desk in the first place to borrow the pencil-sharpener, and was waylaid by curiosity. And anyway, I found my rosary at the back of the second right-hand drawer. I took it away with me and lest I should judge Robinson too hard I also took a cigarette.

Two days later I was busy in the kitchen preparing to cook some nettles I had got Jimmie to gather. I had remembered reading about the vitamin properties of nettles, and I felt our diet needed improvement.

From the open lattice I saw Robinson leading the very sick goat from its pen. It occurred to me he might kill the goat there in front of the window.

I called out, 'Robinson! Don't kill it here. I can't bear the sight of blood.'

'I'm going to take her up the mountain near the Furnace,' he said.

A picture of Bella's corpse sliding into the Furnace and screaming came to my mind. I ran out and stroked the creature which stood in a weary stupor. Miguel ran up and hugged her, almost knocking her down, for she was thin and frail.

Miguel was crying.

I said, 'Never mind, Miguel. I have something to show you.'

Robinson said quickly, 'If you mean the rosary, I do not want the boy to see it.'

Miguel looked interested. 'Show me Rosie.'

This was the first sign that Robinson had discovered the absence of the rosary from his desk.

'I intended to tell you that I had found it,' I said.

'What's it like?' said Miguel.

'Rather nice. Silver and rosewood.'

'Show me Rosewood,' said Miguel.

'I simply don't want the child to see it,' Robinson said. 'He's extremely susceptible to that sort of thing.'

I stroked poor Bella, and tried to interest her in her bucket of water, but she would not touch it.

'That sort of thing can easily corrupt the Faith,' Robinson said.

'What bloody rot,' I said with a vehemence intended more for Ian Brodie than for Robinson. 'What a fuss to make about a rosary.'

'Let's see the rosary,' said Miguel.

Robinson led the drooping goat away through the gate to the mountain path. Miguel followed him, but he was sent back within twenty minutes.

'Robinson wouldn't let me stop and watch Bella die.'

'Robinson is quite right,' I said snappily.

'Show me – '

'Make yourself scarce for half an hour, because I'm busy,' I said.

The sound of a shot bounded down from the mountain.

'Poor old Bella,' said Miguel. 'Will she be dead now?'

'Yes.'

'Perhaps she won't die first shot.'

'Robinson's a careful shot,' I said.

'Will there be blood?'

'Not much.'

Ian Brodie used to return from the Continent having gone out of his way to feed his fury by witnessing all the religious processions and festivals.

'Awful old crones hobbling along after the statues, clinking their rosaries, mumbling their Hail Marys, as if their lives depended on it. And the sickening thing, young people, people in their prime, caught up in the mob hysteria. That sort of thing corrupts the Faith.' Ian Brodie would almost foam at the mouth in these denunciations. And sometimes, both repelled and attracted, I could not keep my eyes off him – Ian, mouthing his contempt, looked positively lustful.

'Why do you go near the shrines? Why do you watch the festivals if they upset you?' I said. 'Surely you must be tired of being so upset.'

'You can't avoid them in Italy,' he said.

'Why not go to Iceland for your holidays?' I said.

'You would find them there,' spluttered Ian. 'You find these fanatics everywhere.'

'That's true,' I said, looking hard at him.

'You never seem to realize the materialistic implication of all these demonstrations,' said Ian. 'You don't understand the gravity of what's going on in those orgies and processions you go in for.'

'I don't go in for them,' I said.

'All this Mariolatry is eating the Christian heart out of the Catholic faith,' said Ian. 'It is a materialistic heresy.'

'What bloody rot,' I said. And if there was one thing against which I did feel strongly at that moment, it was Ian Brodie, with his offensive way of looking at a woman. I thought: no wonder Agnes vows she will never become a Catholic.

I held Ian in such contempt that from time to time I wished to do him a wrong, and to rid myself of the self-righteous feelings he provoked. My most effective method of hurting Ian was to tell him that I had won money on a horse, even if I hadn't. This served to injure him in two ways: one, he was reminded that he had no influence over me – for he was morally against betting; and two, the mere suggestion that anyone but himself had received a sum of money, let alone money for nothing, really upset him, really gave him a pain.

Looking forward to going home, I was necessarily looking backward. Ian Brodie had been loud against me leaving home for so long a period. Brian went away to school; he liked the idea. Therefore so did I. And I thought it would be good for him to have a change from Curly Lonsdale's company. Ian Brodie's suspicion was that I had a lover whom I proposed to meet abroad, in term-time, returning prim and replenished to my chaste widowhood for the summer holidays: I was indebted to Agnes for this information.

Looking forward to my going home, my return from the dead, my intrusion into whatever new arrangements had been made, I had often in mind my past encounters with Ian. I liked to picture the effect if I arrived with Jimmie in my wake. For Jimmie was always saying, 'If I give my candid opinion, is providential that you are not consumed in the aeroplane so as to marry me.'

Ian usually got into a state of horrible excitement if he had cause to suspect that I might get married. At the same time as I let my mind wander round the possibilities of Jimmie – possibilities like his threatening to black Ian's eye – I was calculating the price of this tempting form of entertainment. And when I tell you that I have another category of acquaintance, certain dry-eyed poets and drifters dear to my heart, you may see the extent of my temptation in the matter of accepting Jimmie. For many a time did I sit on the banks of the blue and green lake reflecting how highly these intelligent loafers, whose regard I valued, would regard me, should I fetch into captivity so exceptional and well-spoken a bird as Jimmie. They would have him along to Soho. They would have delight for at least half a year.

Journal, Thursday, 1st July – Jimmie Waterford was born in 1919. He is a second cousin of Robinson, having been brought up in Gibraltar by Robinson's mother, his father being dead, his mother having disappeared.

The circumstances of Jimmie's mother's disappearance were this. Soon after her widowhood she went on a visit to her parents in Namur, leaving Jimmie with his nurse in Holland. In her father's household was a chef of whom he was very proud. He set so much store by his chef's cooking that he would not permit his family to season their food according to taste. Few guests came to his table, lest they should require salt and pepper, and then only those who understood and acquiesced in their host's rule, for this father held that the food was excellent without additional seasoning, but with it all would be ruined, the chef insulted.

Invariably, however, the ancient silver cruets were caused to appear on the table, for form's sake. Regularly, they were emptied and refilled, any laxity in this respect being a high domestic crime.

On the first evening of her visit, Jimmie's mother casually reached for the great heavy salt, and ignoring the choking cries which proceeded from her father's throat, ignoring his bulging eyes and her mother's fluttering hands, she placed a little salt on the side of her plate. The father turned her out of the house that very hour. She was not impoverished, she went to an inn for the night, and might well have returned to her home in the north of Holland the next day. But the being turned out on the streets with all her baggage seemed to give her the idea, and she remained on the streets for the rest of her known life.

To this day, I don't know whether this particular story is true. There was just enough of the element of rootless European frivolity in Jimmie to make any yarn about his connections seem possible, or, on the other hand, to make suspect his stories; and this may have been part of his wooing, he may have sensed that I am a pushover for a story, that I would far rather have a present of a good story than, say, a bunch of flowers, and will more or less always take kindly to the raconteur type.

I was able to substantiate some of his tales later on, when I found the evidence among Robinson's papers. Certainly he was related to Robinson and had been brought up in Gibraltar by Robinson's mother. I think it possible that Jimmie was an illegitimate child of Robinson's father, and so a half-brother to Robinson. The facts he had given me concerning Robinson were apparently correct, for I found letters addressed to Mexico, and many touching on the theological problems which had engaged him then, and on the question of his leaving the Church. But where Jimmie himself was concerned, his life and adventures, I doubted as much as I was amused.

When, up to our seventh week on the island, he sat beside me in the afternoons, between the blue and green lake and the mustard field, and embarked on his memories: 'Along about the time that the hostilities were declared . . . ' I felt sure that Jimmie was the most delightful man I had ever met, not in the least without wondering whether he had, in fact, taken such a part in the Resistance, had escaped with a pair of Gestapo trousers as a memento, had rescued the Polish countess – she in the hollow sideboard, he disguised as a furniture remover. About these and other exploits I shall never quite know. Of course, it is possible they are true; I myself once attended the Derby disguised as a gypsy, and there waylaid Ian Brodie who refused to cross my palm with silver, though I importuned him somewhat, he being present not to bet or to watch the races, but on business which he called sociological research – in reality to lacerate himself with the loathsome spectacle of an hysterical nation. I got away with it: Ian never knew that I know what he is like when solicited by a gypsy. And so perhaps I am wrong to doubt the adventures of Jimmie.

Later that day I added to my journal of 1st July:

> The uncle who was entrusted with Robinson's future died at the beginning of this year. The money is mostly in the motor-scooter business, and one of the reasons for Jimmie's concern about it is this. He is the next beneficiary after Robinson, and is Robinson's heir. So far Robinson has been indifferent to Jimmie's arguments, refuses to return, or in any way to consolidate the motor-scooter concern.
>
> Tom Wells is still making a fuss about the papers which he says are missing from his case. He has even been to the scene of the crash to search for them. He swears that he saw the papers in his bag in the plane just before the crash. Robinson maintains that the papers could not have escaped from the bag, since it was firmly shut when he found it.

The next day, Friday, the second of July, I discovered that my rosary was missing again, from the pocket of my coat where I had put it. For the rosary devotion a chain of rosary beads is not strictly necessary, you can say the rosary on your fingers. The reasons for my distress were, one, that it was my only material possession apart from the clothes I had been wearing at the time of the accident; two, although you can say the rosary on your fingers, there is nothing quite like the actual thing; three, this was a beautiful object, unique and, unlike my clothes, intact; four, I had intended to show it to Miguel, and so win his attention; five, and most pressing, to lose my rosary so soon after having found it gave me a sense of fatal misgiving, and I realized that I had attached to its discovery an important mystique. Then there was a sixth reason, the mystery of its disappearance. Last thing at night it had been in the pocket of my coat hanging up behind the door of my room. First thing in the morning it had gone. The rosary had been removed from my pocket during the night. I decided to make a fuss, and went to look for Robinson.

He had left the house, and there was no sign either of Jimmie or Miguel. I remembered then that they had arranged to leave early on their expedition to the West Leg Bay to examine the old ship's boat.

I found Tom Wells out on the patio shaving, a sight which usually I could not bear. Tom Wells would wash and dress all over the house and grounds, rubbing his face with a towel as he walked along the corridors, putting on his shirt as he came into breakfast; and although I think Robinson did not like it, he put up with it.

As I approached, Wells said, 'Pardon me shaving out here. The light's better.'

I said, 'Have you seen my rosary? I've lost it.'

'Pardon?'

I repeated my question.

He said, 'Didn't know you had a rosary. What's it like?'

I said, 'A chain of rosewood beads with a silver crucifix at the end.'

He said, 'Oh, one of those R.C. items.'

'Have you seen it anywhere?'

'No, lovey.'

'It was in the pocket of my coat last night. This morning it was gone.'

He said, 'I heard Robinson up and about during the night. They all left early.'

'If Robinson has taken it,' I said, 'I'll murder him.'

'Could be Robinson,' he said. 'He's R.C., isn't he?'

'I don't know about that,' I said. 'The point is, he has no right to take my possessions.'

'True enough,' said Wells. He put away the shaving things neatly in Robinson's fitted box. 'And I should like to know what's happened to my papers. Now listen, while we're on the subject, dear. I want to talk to you.'

'I must look for my rosary,' I said. 'I must make sure I haven't dropped it somewhere.' I was still prepared to make a fuss.

'Wait a minute, dear.'

'You're ready for breakfast,' I said. 'I'll go and make the coffee.'

But, over our coffee with tinned milk and hard biscuits, he said, 'What d'you make of Robinson?'

'If I find that he came to my room while I was asleep and took my rosary there will be hell to pay.'

Wells laughed. 'He wouldn't come to your room for anything else, my dear, I can tell you that much. He's not a lady's man, I can tell you.'

'Oh, I was not suggesting – '

'I bet you aren't. There's your boy-friend too. *He's* another.'

'Another?'

'Queer.'

'What?'

'Homosexuals, both of them. Disgusting. Unnatural.' He pushed away his plate violently as if that too were disgusting and unnatural.

I have come across men before who imagine that every other man who does not rapidly make physical contact with his female prey is a homosexual. And some who I know regard all celibates as homosexuals.

'Mind you,' said Tom Wells, 'your boy-friend has looks, I don't deny. And of course I don't deny that Robinson is a fine chap in his way. To hear him talk is an education in itself. But what I'm telling you is for your own sake, sweetie; these homos can be spiteful, so just watch yourself.'

I said, 'I prefer not to discuss the subject, for I don't think you understand it.' I did not at all feel that I could convey the temperamental shades of Robinson and Jimmie to Tom Wells. I did not feel called to do so.

It was true that sometimes a sort of tendresse was evident between them, that Jimmie would crinkle between his third and index finger the light waves of his hair, that Robinson was not 'a lady's man'. I felt incapable of convincing Tom Wells that such things were not conclusive, not even unusual in men. For he would have repeated, as I had heard Curly Lonsdale say, 'Do you think I don't know a man when I see one?' – as if the whole world consisted of the class of society with which they were familiar. But in any case I did not feel obliged to explain anything to Tom Wells. 'In any case,' I said, 'it is not our business.'

But Tom Wells gave me a look that might be described as 'knowing' except for the fact that it was also calculating. He winked knowingly at me, and I detected the calculation in the other eye. It was at this moment that the idea first came to me that Wells was a blackmailer. I had no clear reason for retaining the idea, but certain propositions came clearly to my mind. One, it was probable that Wells believed a homosexual relationship to exist between Robinson and Jimmie; two, whether this was true or not was irrelevant to Wells; three, his purpose in speaking of it to me was not, as he had said, to warn me, but to establish it as a fact in my mind; four, he was capable of saying anything about anyone if it served his own ends.

Miguel came rushing in dangling a dead hare by its ears. He ran to show it to Tom Wells, his enchanter.

I inquired of Robinson that afternoon about my rosary. He neither admitted nor denied having taken it.

'If you came into my room while I was asleep and searched my pocket, that was very wrong,' I said, using my best moral tone, since, after all, he set himself up as our moral organizer.

'Whose room?' he said.

'Mine,' I said.

'Really?' he said. 'Yours?'

I could tell by this rather mean defence that Robinson felt himself to be in the wrong.

'I should like to have my rosary,' I said.

'Will you promise not to teach Miguel to recite it?'

'I'll promise nothing. Give me my property.'

'I am thinking of Miguel,' he said. 'I wish him to grow up free from superstition.'

'To hell with you,' I said. 'There's nothing superstitious about the rosary. It's a Christian devotion, not a magic charm.'

'All those Hail Marys,' he said.

I realized suddenly that Robinson was not speaking in the normal course of argument, not stating his objections to my request, or putting his point of view against mine. He knew very well the contents of the rosary meditations, and he was probably less ignorant of their nature than I was. It struck me for the first time that he was not simply attempting to make small difficulties, or to exercise his authority on the island simply from a need for power, but that he was constitutionally afraid of any material manifestation of Grace.

'Oh well,' I said, 'I can do without it.'

I was not surprised that, late that night when I was going to bed, Tom Wells stood in my path to tell me that his brief-case containing his samples of lucky charms, all his proofs of *Your Future*, and the articles he had been writing, had disappeared.

VIII

NEXT MORNING, SATURDAY THE THIRD of July, Robinson
was gone. It was nothing for him to have gone out before the
rest of us were up, but he had always returned before elev-
en o'clock. We had breakfast and proceeded with our usual
chores. At noon we asked each other where Robinson could
be. At one o'clock Miguel began to cry.

Robinson's bed was made, his room in order. He was nowhere in the house. He was not in the storehouse, nor in that
vicinity. We assembled at the cliff's edge calling, 'Robinson!
Hey there, Robinson!' lest he should be down on the beach,
or have fallen.

We gave Miguel some soup, feeding him by spoonfuls,
for he was sobbing frantically. Jimmie and I, taking with us
some chunky biscuit-sandwiches and the first-aid box, set off
to look for Robinson, for it seemed certain that he had met
with some accident. We took a route over the mountain to
the north-west since this was a part scored with the streams
rich in iron deposits, from which Robinson frequently drew
our mineral water supplies in the early mornings. Tom Wells
remained with Miguel, promising to keep a look-out for
Robinson from the plateau.

We had gone a short way when Miguel climbed up behind us, calling on us to stop. 'Come back now! Come back.'
He had stopped crying. He looked suddenly like an old man

who had started growing downward with age, or again like a child of the very poor, with a face lined with responsibility and want.

'Has Robinson turned up?'

'No. Mr Tom has found the blood.'

'Robinson must be hurt,' I said.

We returned, Jimmie carrying Miguel astride on his shoulders, and Miguel hunched and clinging to him.

Tom Wells came to meet us. He held out towards us a heavy corduroy jacket of a faded tawny colour, which I recognized as one of Robinson's which he would sometimes wear when the weather turned cold, or if he went out of doors at night.

'We found this in the mustard field,' Tom Wells said

'What is with Robinson?' said Jimmie.

'Look at the coat.'

I saw a bright red stain on the coat. I felt it. The stain was damp, it was sticky with blood, and it spread across three separate gashes in the material.

Jimmie exclaimed some words in Dutch.

I said, 'Someone must be hurt.'

'It was lying in the mustard field,' said Wells. 'Miguel lifted it up, and this knife fell out of the pocket.' He reached in the pocket of the coat and produced a clasp-knife. The blade was open. I recognized the knife. It was very sharp, the handle about three inches long, the blade about four inches. Robinson always carried it with him, clasped in its sheath.

I said, 'That's Robinson's knife.'

We went down to the mustard field, and there, even before Miguel ran to point out the spot where the coat had been found, I saw the dark trampled patches among the glaring yellow plants. There was blood on the ground, still slightly sticky. When we came to look closer, there seemed to be the marks of blood all round about. There was also a complete pathway of trodden-down plants spattered with blood, leading out of the field from the spot where the coat had been found. Following this newly-beaten track, towards the mountain path, we found a green silk neck square which was Jimmie's property. This was also soaked in blood, not yet dry.

Jimmie opened our pack and brought out the brandy. This he solemnly handed round. We all had a swig, even Miguel.

Tom Wells said, 'There's something fishy about all this. Someone wounded has been dragged through the field, you realize.'

I lay awake all night, listening to Robinson's elegant eight-day clock chiming the hours. It occurred to me obscurely that I had better wind it in the morning, otherwise we would be without a time-measure on the island. Winding this clock was of course Robinson's concern, and Robinson was gone. But the thought was absurd, muscling its way in among the major disturbances of my mind. For the turmoil and the frightened talk and conjecture, the strangeness and dread of the past day crowded in, almost as if I had a capacity prepared for it; as if, from the time of the crash up to this day I had been a vacuum waiting only for the swift delayed rush of horror to enter in; as if, really, the getting away with a mere concussion and a broken arm, my luck in falling into Robinson's hands, my easy recovery, and the normal life of Robinson's household, were not to have been trusted; and as if the proper consequence of the plane disaster were now upon us. From among the shapes and shadows of the past day I discerned several hard outlines: the trail from the mustard field had led to the mountain. Here, a path linked up with that which crossed the mountain to the Furnace. Now that we were definitely looking for blood, we saw blood smeared everywhere along the trail. There must have been a steady bleeding, a dropping of blood all the way.

Moreover at various stations we came across blood-stained articles either on the actual track or nearby: a shoe belonging to Robinson, a shirt – the one I had been wearing on the previous day while my dress was being washed, and, a little farther up the path, the scarlet cashmere tablecloth which I had worn as a sari. These I had laid aside the previous night, and, putting on my newly washed dress in the morning, had not noticed their absence from my room. The white cotton shirt was streaked with blood which had almost dried and on the red cashmere was a patch of darker red which stained the whole of one side down to the fringe and which, in places, was still sticky. Tom Wells, who had picked it up from the thick plants a few yards off the pathway, pulled his hand away quickly as it touched the sticky patches. I noticed that he did this every time his hand encountered blood not yet dry. I thought this gesture odd, until I noticed that I myself gave the same involuntary jerk of withdrawal when my hand touched wet blood. After stopping to look stupidly at each of these objects, we left them lying on the track and pushed on like somnambulists.

Half-way to the Furnace, at the point where we had sight of the sea on both sides, Tom Wells clutched his ribs and said he could go no farther.

'Go back,' I said, 'and take Miguel with you.'

'No, I'm coming after Robinson,' Miguel said.

'Come with Mr Tom,' said Tom Wells.

'I want Robinson.' He was beside himself, both younger and ages older than his years.

Jimmie and I pressed on while Miguel went fitfully ahead looking from right to left, and behind him to see if we still followed.

At some point I said, 'I wonder, would there be another inhabitant of the island – someone we don't know about?'

'Is possible,' said Jimmie.

He gave me a hand up the steep places, automatically, not with his usual deliberate air.

'It seems that Robinson has been attacked. At least some-one has been attacked,' I said.

'Excuse me,' said Jimmie, 'that I do not converse, as I lose my nerves.'

We found other blood-stained articles on which the blood had dried in the heat of the afternoon. We found a small pocket handkerchief – it was mine, it had been in my pock-et at the time of the crash; we found a blue silk vest which Jimmie had been wearing at the time of the crash; the other of Robinson's shoes; and lastly, at the head of the dip leading to the Furnace, we saw more of Robinson's clothes, another jacket of his, dark tweed, his brown corduroy trousers, his underclothes. These were scattered bloodily down the slope that ran into the gurgling crater, and a clear streak of torn-up vegetation, revealing the raw red earth as if there had been a landslide, completed the run from the rim of the crater to its mouth. The volcano chuckled, and gave out its red vapours, as if that too were a sort of blood. I thought of the crater's scream, and I screamed. Jimmie limply placed the brandy to my lips.

I had all this blood before my eyes as I lay awake, trying to isolate the details of the day. On the journey back we had found other things: a blood-stained scarf which Robinson always wore against the mist; his fountain-pen, his pocket compass.

I did not remember if or how we had eaten that day, nor do I remember this even now, except that we gave Miguel a sedative tablet with warm milk, and that he was asleep before the sun had set.

I recalled, too, there had been some talk between Tom Wells and me. Jimmie had gone out in his stunned silence and was roaming about the beach at the Pomegranate Bay. All I recall of my conversation that evening with Wells was the following:

I said, 'Those blood-stained articles of clothing must have been planted by someone.'

'Oh, must they?'

'They would not be scattered about in quite such an obvious manner if they had been dropped accidentally.'

'Oh, wouldn't they?'

I could not put out of my mind the blood. Even when I closed my eyes it was like a red light penetrating the lids. And when I tried to recall the past day, I had the rare and distressing experience of becoming objectively conscious of my rational mind in action, separate from all others, as one might see the open workings of a clock. This only happens to me when faced with a group of facts which hurt my reasoning powers – as one becomes highly conscious of a limb when it is damaged.

But having set my mind painfully to arrange the facts, I immediately got out of bed and, slipping my coat over my borrowed pyjamas, padded bare-foot along the corridors to Robinson's rooms, aided only by the moon sidling in through the narrow slit windows. There I found Robinson's bunch of house keys hanging in their usual place. At the same time I fumbled among the pigeon-holes in his desk until I found a small electric torch which he usually kept there. I used the torch, since I did not know my way very well, to guide me up a flight of two or three shallow steps, round a stone-flagged bend, and along another corridor to the gun-room. There, without bothering to light the lamp which stood ready with its box of matches, I tried one key after another in the door until I had found the right one. With the help of the torch I extracted this key from the bunch, and locked the door. I re-turned the bunch of keys to its peg in Robinson's room, keep-ing the gun-room key for myself. I went next to the kitchen where string was kept in a drawer. Here in the kitchen my whole body shook as I thought, with a new realization, of Robinson and what could have befallen him. However, I cut myself a length of string, and with this tied the gun-room key round my neck. I snapped out the torch and returned to my room, led by the moonlit window slits. As I passed Jimmie's room I jumped, for instead of the dark shut door there was an open space with Jimmie standing in it, regarding me.

I did not speak to him, but walked on to my room, satisfied that he had only just opened his door having heard the mov-ing about, that he had seen nothing of my performance with the key, and that I had done a reasonable thing, considering that I was on an island with a child and two men, one of them probably a murderer. I had done this, but the small reasonable satisfaction was swallowed up in fear, in the gashes of red on the screen of my mind, and the absurdity of all I had seen, which made me exclaim aloud from time to time throughout the night, 'It can't be so! How *can* it be?' I kept thinking that Robinson was bound to walk in next morning and explain everything, the seriousness of the situation being evident to me then only by my recalling Miguel's distress.

Throughout the next two weeks I lived in a state similar to my first weeks on the island, concussion, stupor. So it appeared. I feared and suspected much. I formed opinions, and wondered sometimes if Robinson's disappearance were a dream or the whole island affair a dream, or life itself, my past life, Brian, Chelsea, were a dream.

We collected the blood-stained clothes from the route. The stains were still sticky, having dried and become moist again from the mists. I piled them up in a heap on the floor of Robinson's bedroom, thinking as I did so that an inquest on Robinson would be held after the boat should come to rescue us with our news.

It took us twelve days to search the island. But already by the third day after Robinson's disappearance we all more or less assented that he was dead.

I thought: either, therefore, he has been killed by Jimmie or Tom Wells, or by both together. Suffering from headaches, I chewed over all other hypotheses – that he had killed himself, had been murdered by Miguel, or by myself in my sleep, or by another, unknown inhabitant of the island; but I rejected these as folly. Again and again I returned to Jimmie, Tom Wells, or both together. I did not think it at all likely that they were accomplices, but I added that possibility to my list for a show of objectivity.

Tom Wells produced a theory of his own, one which I considered brought him under suspicion for having suggested it. A supernatural force, he declared, had done away with Robinson, in revenge for some sacrilege done to the lucky charms which Robinson had confiscated.

'You mean a poltergeist?'

'Something like that.'

There were many difficulties in the way of our searching the island. Tom Wells pleaded his damaged ribs against the exertion required of him for the amount of climbing entailed. And so the task of searching the island fell on Jimmie and me, with Miguel for our guide. Neither Tom Wells nor Jimmie seemed to see it as an imperative task, but I insisted on this course, formality though it might be, so that we should know as far as possible where we stood.

'Is evidence that he lies in the Furnace,' Jimmie said.

'Still, we must eliminate everything else.'

Tom Wells said, 'There's an evil force on this island. I think we should stay put here in the house, I've had a serious time of it with my ribs.'

Now I had resolved, if possible, to avoid being alone with any one of these men, these strangers. Therefore I had to go everywhere, in the course of our examination, with Jimmie and Miguel, rather than stay at the house with Wells. He complained, 'I don't like the idea of your all going off from early morning till late at night. I don't like being alone, quite frankly, after what's happened.'

And then Jimmie's quaintness had altogether lost its charm for me at this time, it exasperated me. And when he declaimed, 'Ah me! Man is born, he suffers, he dies', it sounded to me frivolous, if not false.

Also there was trouble about guns. Jimmie said we must take a gun with us. 'Is only reasonable. We see a stranger, we shoot.'

'Haven't you seen enough blood?' I said. But this was my being afraid, making a diversion while I worked out what could be done.

'The gun-room's locked,' said Tom Wells, 'for some reason which is beyond me.'

I said, 'I have the key.'

'It's time we had a bit of rabbit,' said Wells. 'You'll have to hand over the key. We have to have guns for food.'

I said to Jimmie, 'I'll fetch a gun for you now, if you promise to give it back to me when we return. I want to keep charge of the guns.'

'Is entirely to be understood. Is reasonable,' said Jimmie.

'Look here,' said Wells. 'I don't think a woman should have charge of the guns. I don't agree to that.'

'You will agree,' said Jimmie.

'I hold the key,' I said, or something to that effect, and went to fetch a Winchester rifle for Jimmie, with some cartridges.

For myself I chose a baby Browning automatic. I could not find any cartridges. I have a fear of handling guns, and so it was an effort for me to examine the Browning. I found it loaded. I locked the armoury, went to my room to fetch my coat, gave another neurotic look at the safety-catch of the automatic, and, putting it in my pocket, I then felt safe to take the big gun to Jimmie.

This was Tuesday, the sixth of July. That day we explored the South Arm, descending from our mountain to rich downy grassland. We examined the deserted mill and cottage. We walked round the coast, stopped only by the perpendicular cliffs, which stretched for half a mile on the western seafront of the little peninsula. Here, there was no beach nor access by land, the cliffs dropping sheer into the sea.

Trailing along beside Jimmie, I experienced over again the days of concussion when my actions were mechanical, my senses hazy. But then I had been safe. You must understand that Jimmie and Tom Wells had all at once become strangers to me, far more than when I first fell in with them, for now their familiar characteristics struck me merely as a number of indications that I knew nothing about them.

Five times we were lost in a sudden mist, and once it seemed that we should be wandering all night until, with Miguel huddled on Jimmie's shoulder, we found ourselves to be a few yards from home. Usually, we were home before the big night mists fell.

I remember watching my shadow with the sun behind it, making me tall, very tall, but not so tall as Jimmie in his shadow.

By the end of twelve days we had completed our search, having covered the South Arm, the Headland with its neat pomegranate orchards, the rocky North Arm and North Leg, the ferny meadows of the West Leg. We covered the black and white coast-line, with its cliffs and beaches; we gave two days to the central mountain, climbing, trekking, leaping, and I was glad of our exhaustion and the lack of any energy to speak to one another. Usually I followed after Jimmie, but if ever I found myself in front of him I took firm hold of the automatic concealed in my pocket. Miguel was usually some distance ahead of us. On one of these excursions I had said to him, 'I have a little gun in my pocket. If you should hear me fire it, you must run away.' I said this in case he should be hurt in any tussle between Jimmie and me.

These, I thought, were reasonable precautions. All the time I really suspected Tom Wells. And all the time I smoked cigarettes, Robinson's share as well as my own.

My shoes were worn through. I rummaged among the tidy bundles of salvage, for I had no more squeamishness after the sight of so much blood. At last I found a pair of shoes only slightly too big, and a little charred at the toe.

On the eleventh day we rested. On the twelfth day we set out for the subterranean caves. Miguel was at first reluctant to take us. I suppose he felt their secrets were a sort of possession of Robinson.

'It's important, Miguel. Suppose we should find Robinson?'

'Robinson could not live in the caves. They aren't for living in. They're for going through.'

'Someone else may be hiding there.'

'There's no one on the island.'

Miguel was still frightened. We kept telling him that everything would be all right, that we would look after him, that he was our boy. He did not take in this talk. He did not fail to interpret the strangeness, the suspicion, and the fear between us.

At last I had to say to Miguel, 'If you won't take us to the caves we will have to look for them ourselves. We might get lost and never come back.' And so he set off with us on the twelfth day of our search.

There were three tunnels in all, one leading from the Pomegranate Bay in the south to the region of the deserted mill and homestead at the South Arm. A second passage cut through the mountain from the cliff-top behind our plateau, its entrance being a vertical cleft among some thick shrubbery; this led to a point in the mountain approaching the Furnace. The third tunnel started among the lava boulders of the North Arm. This was the longest, and most difficult to negotiate. It emerged at the beach on the east side of Vasco da Gama's Bay.

The first tunnel was the one through which Miguel had given me the slip when I had taken my first walk down to the beach. The entrance was amazingly obvious once it was pointed out. I had passed it several times without noticing how it stood like a slim shadow in the mountain wall, within a fluted grotto. Miguel led the way, then Jimmie. After the narrow mouth the tunnel was about nine feet in width, the height here being about seven feet, although presently Jimmie had to stoop. I began to cough. I said, 'I shall choke.' This was caused by a combination of sulphurous dust, breathless heat and a powerful lava smell. I felt we were walking into the hot centre of the earth. 'I shall choke, choke,' said my echo.

'Please to return and wait for us,' said Jimmie. He too seemed suffocated by the dust and heat. Miguel coughed, but did not seem to mind.

I could not answer Jimmie for coughing, but I intended to agree to his suggestion, when he added, 'Is not suitable conditions for a lady.'

I do not know why, but his phraseology caused me to remember that Jimmie was heir to Robinson's fortunes. And when I had recovered from my fit of coughing, I said, 'I'm coming with you. I wish to satisfy myself that the caves are empty.'

His flashlamp cast a rusty light: I suppose the place was filled with motes of red dust. By this light Miguel's dark skin and lean figure showed up fiendishly. Jimmie's head was in darkness, and I could only see the dim red glow of the man's long body. Very much later, thinking over the scene, it occurred to me that I too must have looked ghoulish in the caves.

A shallow rivulet led to the entrance of the cave, and was flowing feebly beside us. Jimmie turned and squelched his way down into the tunnel. Miguel and I followed. I stopped every few minutes to recover from my coughing.

We came to a point where even Miguel had to stoop very low, and to squeeze round a narrow bend in the rock. Here the stream was deeper, reaching my knees and Miguel's thighs. This narrow passage gave out on to a vast chamber all over which Jimmie directed his torch. The air here was cleaner. I could not see any further opening from this huge cave-room, but Miguel splashed over to the far wall and there he seemed to climb up the wall and melt into it. We followed him to that spot, and found a small shelf behind which lay a gap. We heaved ourselves up and slid through, emerging at the foot of a steep, slippery, black cliff which Miguel had started to climb very skilfully. Several times I had to take the hand which Jimmie held down to help me. At the top we came to daylight, and the tall grasses of the South Arm. We had been in the tunnel about twenty minutes.

I could see that Jimmie did not want to do any more subterranean crawls. Nor would I have been reluctant to put off our ventures into the two remaining tunnels until the next day. But Jimmie did not make any suggestion to this effect – I think because he was convinced I would disagree. And I said nothing, fearing he would think my vigilance was waning. I was not in a condition which could be called vigilant: I was half-doped, my imagination overwhelmed. I could hardly look at the facts, far less piece them together, but I felt bound to impress on Jimmie and Tom Wells that I was capable of doing so.

We returned to the house to wash, for we were covered with rusty grime. Immediately after our meal we set out for the second tunnel, the entrance to which lay near the back of the house. 'Is pity,' said Jimmie, 'that no policeman resides here who should undertake these searchings.' I thought, Perhaps it is irony, or perhaps it is only one of his silly remarks.

The second tunnel took fifteen minutes to explore. This too was full of volcanic dust and on the floor throughout lay a lot of slimy weed which made our progress dangerous. When Jimmie called back to me, 'Is dangerous,' the words were repeated again and again on the walls of the cave and its recesses and I listened to the 'dangerous, dangerous', encouraging myself with the thought that although I was outmatched in physical strength by Jimmie and Tom Wells, their joint intelligence was probably not superior to mine. I realized that my sense of danger was enhanced by the loss of Robinson's intelligence. It also occurred to me that Tom Wells, should he become troublesome, would not hesitate to use Miguel as an ally. Miguel was well acquainted with the island. On the other hand he was not clever in the sense that Tom Wells would find cleverness useful.

Towards the end of the second tunnel we had to stoop very low, and to crawl for several yards, the smell of the Furnace increasing as we approached the exit. The cave widened gradually, and still stooping we assisted our progress by clutching at various shelves and protrusions in the walls. The last few steps, and I slipped, grazing my knee. Jimmie heaved me up, and it was not until we were standing outside that he handed me the automatic which, unnoticed by me, had fallen out of my pocket when I fell.

'Thanks, Jimmie,' I said, giving him a sort of pleasant smile.

But he was not deceived; he seemed to expect such tactics from me.

It was impossible to be near the Furnace without being drawn to gaze into it. We walked across to the crater's edge and stood staring into the wide bubbling basin. Jimmie unlodged a rock and shoved it down the slide. It entered the turmoil with a scream. I looked up, and caught him watching my face. It came to me with a shock that he might be testing my reaction to the scream. I had never thought that I myself could be under suspicion. Immediately, of course, I felt myself to be looking guilty, and quickly to cover it I said, 'That scream makes me feel ill', which immediately seemed the wrong thing to say. That I should be thought a potential killer was a large new idea. Nervously, I unloosed a rock substantially bigger than that which Jimmie had thrown in, and I sent it screaming into the Furnace. I suppose my intention was to prove that I was not really afraid of the scream. Jimmie looked at the large patch of earth from which I had heaved the boulder, and remarked, 'You are strong.'

Just then, from the depth of the turbulent mud there came a sudden splutter, followed by a loud sigh. Jimmie looked as startled as I was, but instantly I remembered that Robinson had told me, of the Furnace, 'Sometimes it sighs.'

I said to Jimmie, 'Did you get a fright?'

'Ah, no.'

I said, 'I thought you had lost your nerve.'

He said, 'Is not at this moment that I lose my nerves. Is when I have descended from the skies into this island of sorrows.'

Our last excursion under the mountain took forty minutes. This tunnel we approached by a grotto on the narrow beach of Vasco da Gama's Bay, at the North Arm. The light was so refracted from its walls that one did not see, until one had fairly penetrated the cave, that a flight of steps had been hacked out of the rock, leading into a deep dark pit. It smelt of lime and lava, and a fairly deep stream gurgled along the floors at about twenty feet below sea level. The path along the edge of the river was jagged and slippery. Miguel produced a rope from a corner of the cave where it had been left in readiness, and bade us make a chain, walking in single file clutching the rope. He showed off a bit, which was a cheering sight, and I saw that Jimmie, too, smiled. Eventually we came to a precipitous dip, where further steps had been hewn in the path. The stream here splashed over the underground rocks in a waterfall which drenched us with its spray. At the foot of these steps a boat was moored. The tunnel spread wide, and now the stream covered the whole ground. Miguel warned us that it was too deep to wade through. We got into the boat, and splashed along for a few yards until we came to a circular chamber of the tunnel, over which Jimmie flashed his torch. Its walls were fluted fanwise like the surface of a shell. Here the river ended in a large pool which swirled in a constant eddy. We landed on a mooring stage at the far shore and from there climbed steadily to the light and air of the exit at the North Arm. It was a boulder-strewn landscape which, if one half-closed one's eyes, resembled a battle-field newly deserted.

On our return late that afternoon Tom Wells said,

'Been through all the caves?'

Jimmie said, 'Yes, but they lack.'

'Lack what?'

'Robinson,' said Jimmie.

'Naturally,' said Wells.

I X

I WAS ON THE PATIO, pulling faces, when I noticed Tom Wells standing in the shadow of the fountain. I do not know how long he had been standing there, watching me.

The object of my facial contortions was to attempt to discover what it felt like to be Jimmie and Tom Wells respectively. My method was not infallible, but it sometimes served as an aid to perception. I had practised it since childhood. You simply twist your face into the expression of the person whose state of mind and heart you wish to know, and then wait to see what sort of emotions you feel. I had begun with Jimmie. First I considered myself to be standing high and lean, very fair, with a straight wide mouth; and I pulled my mouth straight and wide, I made my eyes close down at the far corners, widening at the inner corners; I raised my eyebrows and furrowed my brow; I put my tongue inside my lower lip, pulled my chin long; my nose, so concentratedly did I imagine it, curving up slightly at the bridge. Then I was self-consciously Jimmie. I said 'Is so', and nodded my head sagely. A sense of helplessness came over me, and I said to myself, though not aloud, 'I lose my nerves.' I placed Robinson in the picture and was filled with awe and exasperation by his standing before me, righteous, austere, a living rebuke. I clasped the fingers of my right hand round an invisible knife, but I did not stab. I was overwhelmed with cousinly love. Widening the inner corner of my eyes, and moving my straight lips soundlessly, I said, 'Is the motor-scooter business', and Robinson replied, 'I have no need of motor-scooters on the island.' But still Jimmie did not stab him, and, as I resumed my normal face, I did not see how he could, in fact, have done so.

I do not know how much of this pantomime was observed by Tom Wells, concealed in the shadow of the fountain, for I had not seen him yet.

Next, I was Tom Wells. I placed my legs solidly apart and sat staring ahead with my bag of lucky charms on my lap, some of them spread out on the patio by my side. I opened my mouth and let the lower lip droop. I turned down the corners of my mouth, and pressed my chin down to make other chins, as flabby as I could think them to be. My skin was mottled and scored with red veins. I rounded my eyes, made them small and light blue, rather watery, and felt beneath them the drag of sallow pouches. My hair was crinkly, partly grey. Moving my lower lip freely I formed the words, 'We're lucky to be alive. A very natural type of woman is my wife.' I had a profound sensation of heat, of sweating about the neck, and my hands were podgy and damp. A longing came over me for the region of Piccadilly Circus and Soho on a summer afternoon; Dean Street, Frith Street, with the dust and paper on the pavement, the smell of garlic and then people scuttling shiftily from door to door, plump men on business, small men popping out of shops in their grey suits and rimless glasses. I longed to be there. But in the middle of this longing I thought, 'No, this isn't Tom Wells. I'm doing Curly Lonsdale.'

And so I started again, the round pouchy eyes, the chin. This time I smiled Tom Wells's smile, which was unlike Curly's, and which showed his upper gums. This made all the difference, and I felt myself raging against the inconvenience of the plane crash, still showing the gums in the smile, and suffering a sensation of furious impatience at the waste of time, the loss of money, and the doubtful fate of my magazine *Your Future*. The more I felt this anger, the more I smiled. When Robinson appeared before me and said 'How are you feeling today?' I clutched my ribs and said, 'Pretty bad. But we're lucky to be alive,' meanwhile closing my fingers round Ethel of the Well, and wishing upon her, 'Bring me luck, Ethel. Don't let Henry marry my wife. Make the airline company pay compensation. Make the insurance pay up. Make Robinson pay up.' Ethel of the Well changed into a knife. Robinson had stolen my lucky charms. He had done away with my luck. I kept on smiling. 'Where's Ethel, what have you done to Ethel?' I mouthed. Robinson replied, 'They are bad for Miguel. They are evil.' I desired to murder Robinson but I couldn't bring Tom Wells to do that to a goose that might yet lay eggs of gold. Instead I said contemptuously, 'Talking of evil, how's your boy-friend?' Robinson looked at me wearily and walked away. I was still smiling after him with the loose moist lower lip curling like a cup and the wet artificial gums glistening above the top teeth, when I noticed Tom Wells himself in the shadow of the fountain, watching me with his smile. When he saw that he had been observed he nodded, as if to say, 'I can see you.' He walked across to me and said, 'Feeling all right?' I had not pulled my face straight immediately, hoping to mislead him into thinking there was some obvious physical cause for my facial contortions. Instead, I screwed up my eyes and wrinkled my nose, finally passing my hand in an exaggerated gesture across my eyes. I said, 'The sun's horribly strong. I have a headache.' I screwed up my face again so that there should be no mistake.

He stopped smiling and looked at me closely.

'Things worrying you, honey?'

'Oh, just the sun. It gives me a headache.'

I was actually sitting in the shadow of the house and the sun was shining on the opposite half of the patio. Still, it gave off a plausible glare.

'Silly to sit out of doors if the sun gives you a headache,' said Wells.

'Oh, I like the fresh air.'

'Where's your boy-friend?' he said.

'Who?'

'Pardon me,' he said, 'I should have said, Robinson's boy-friend.'

I did not reply.

'Maybe,' he said, 'boy-friend isn't the word after all. *Boy's* the word. But hardly *friend*. Do you get me?'

'I did get your meaning,' I said, 'the first time.'

'Oh, you did?' he said.

I said, 'If you have any complaint against Jimmie, you must make it to him.'

He said, 'Faithful for ever. Well, you've no competition now, have you?'

I went indoors. It was a question whether I was under suspicion and by whom, for the murder of Robinson. I kept thinking of Jimmie's remark, 'You are strong.' Could it reasonably be held that I could have stabbed Robinson, and alone dragged him all the way from the mustard field to the Furnace? The question disturbed me profoundly for two main reasons. One, that my physical ability being proved, I might, when our existence on the island was discovered and the murder disclosed, be under equal suspicion as a killer with Tom Wells and Jimmie. Motives would be probed: what were Mrs Marlow's relations with the dead man? Friendly, unfriendly? I thought of other unanswerable questions that might be asked. I reflected, also, that if Jimmie truly thought it possible that I had killed Robinson, he himself was obviously innocent. The same applied to Tom Wells.

I went into Robinson's study and stood by his tidy desk. I lifted a corner of the desk. It was heavy. Still holding the end of the desk, tilted about nine inches above the ground, I looked at Robinson's eight-day clock. I watched four aching minutes pass until my arms and fingers gave out. It was not a bad effort, and my strength was not impaired but for the terrible pain in my arms and hands. I supposed that it was not an improbable idea that I could drag Robinson's body up the mountain. I had heard that some types of murderers have access to superhuman strength in the hour of their kill.

It was the beginning of our eleventh week on the island, two weeks since Robinson's disappearance. I had recovered my senses; the stunned feeling had gone. My moods were like a pendulum. In the mornings I was jumpy with impatience and indignation, longing to be active, to clear up the mystery and know where we stood. Towards evening I would feel desolate and nostalgic, brooding on Robinson.

The blue exercise book which Robinson had given me for my journal was full. I took some loose sheets from the drawer of Robinson's desk, the very drawer in which I had discovered the rosary, and this, too, troubled me. However, I set to write as I had intended.

Journal, Monday 19th July.
Supposing that
1) Robinson was murdered by one man only.
2) And that he was killed by stabbing with the knife, in the mustard field, probably between midnight on the 2nd July and dawn on the 3rd.
3) That the murderer carried him to the Furnace.
4) The evidence of this journey, the track of blood, being impossible to conceal, the murderer decided to confuse the evidence. Various garments

and objects were soaked in Robinson's blood and scattered indiscriminately along the route.

I note that

5) All the blood-soaked garments we found were either the possessions of Jimmie, myself, or Robinson, or had been lent to Jimmie and me by Robinson. Nothing was found belonging to Tom Wells or Miguel.

6) The murderer must be one physically capable of carrying or dragging Robinson's body over the mountain to the Furnace.

7) Therefore Miguel is not questionable, although an official investigator may have to rule out the possibility of his being an accomplice.

8) From my point of view, the suspects are Jimmie Waterford and Tom Wells. One is innocent, the other guilty.

9) *Motives.* Jimmie Waterford inherits Robinson's fortune. The disposition of the fortune was under discussion at the time of Robinson's death. The discussions were proving unfavourable to Jimmie.

10) I may remark that he is Robinson's cousin, was brought up by Robinson's mother, and was emotionally attached to Robinson.

11) Also I observe that my friendship with Jimmie did not please Robinson, and one may suppose some discussion on this subject had taken place.

12) Further, I note that Jimmie himself told me the facts of his inheritance. One may think this was strange, if he meditated murder for gain.

13) Tom Wells had a grievance against Robinson for taking away his lucky charms. He discovered the

loss of his bag on the night of 2nd July, during which Robinson disappeared.

14) Wells was of the belief, or said he was of the belief, that a homosexual relationship existed between Jimmie and Robinson.

15) As he conveyed this sentiment to me, he also expressed personal horror.

16) I observe that Tom Wells, whether sincerely or not, ascribes the cause of Robinson's death to a supernatural agency.

17) And that Tom Wells exaggerates his injury. He runs about playing the fool with Miguel in the hot sun, but when there is any useful exertion demanded of him he clasps his ribs as if in pain.

Other Observations:

18) Jimmie Waterford's relations with Robinson, though they were unsatisfactory, were not acrimonious.

19) Tom Wells's mind is opaque. One cannot tell the extent of his superstitions, whether they could so obsess him as to provoke murder, whether the removal of his samples by Robinson was sufficient cause. Of course, one side of his personality is simply materialistic, the other side extremely problematic. (Can he be mad? Can he have murdered unawares?)

20) *Further considerations.* The innocent man will necessarily speculate on the identity of the murderer. His suspicions may fall on the other man. However, he will not be able to rule out the possibility that I am the murderer.

21) It may be expected that the innocent party will avoid as far as possible the company of the likely suspects, e.g. if Jimmie is innocent he will not wish to associate very closely with Wells and me. He may fear us. Wells, if he is innocent, should also react accordingly.

22) The murderer, on the other hand, may wish to maintain a friendly position with his companions, he will be eager to do so, for security's sake.

23) Is it possible to infer guilt or innocence from such attitudes? If Jimmie does not try to avoid Wells and me as if we were potentially dangerous and murderous, does it follow that he is guilty?

24) There remains the question, whether Robinson was killed single-handed.

25) Jimmie is making a memorial to Robinson, consisting of a plain wooden cross on a stand.

I put down the pencil and wished I were at home in Chelsea where once, in the middle of the night, hearing voices and footsteps in the small paved back garden, simply by lifting the telephone I caused policemen to spring up all over the premises as from the dragon's teeth. The police were instantly at the front door and over the garden wall. They marched through the hall and crowded through the kitchen to the back door. Just when they had got the man, another consignment braked up outside, while round the corner of the street four more came walking two abreast at their steady, doom-like and almost contemplative pace. It is true that a dangerous armed lunatic was at this time at large in the district. My intruder turned out to be only the lover of my upstairs lodger making his getaway before dawn. But I appreciated the attention of the Force, as I told it many times as it streamed out of the house, dark blue and corporate, into its line of cars beneath the lamplight.

Telling Agnes about the incident because there was so little to talk to Agnes about, I yet felt wearily sure Ian Brodie would have something to say about it. He said, next day on the telephone, 'You must give that whore a week's notice. A woman in your position can easily let herself in for – '

'How about minding your own business?'

For in any case, even if I had very much wanted to, I would not have had the courage to make a fuss with the girl on such an issue; a woman in my position can easily let herself in for ridicule, can easily be marked down for a wishful widow, and the awful thing about those sort of insinuations, you never know, they might be true.

'Well, if you *want* to keep a disorderly house. . . . ' Ian said, his voice rising an octave on the word 'want'.

What struck me as I sat at Robinson's desk with my murder dossier in front of me was wonder at how I had ever found any resemblance between squeaky Ian Brodie and solemn Robinson.

On the walls were two engravings by Blake, an El Greco reproduction, and a remarkable picture, by or in the manner of Stubbs, of a splendid chestnut horse surrounded by rather wooden people. The question kept tapping at the door, how to reconcile Robinson's tastes, what had been his *centre*? And yet since people do have inconsistencies of taste, or merely inherit the objects they have around them, this question had only symbolic importance. I was thinking of the mystery of his death; all the time I snooped around his rooms I tried to locate his destiny; what indication had he carried about within him, that he should die by murder, at whose hands?

I wandered round the room, looking at Robinson's books behind their glass, and recalling my first repulsion to the neat sets carefully arranged, at this moment I could not see why they had affected me in this way. The bookcases were graceful and the glass fronts enhanced their dignity. And I could think of numerous respectable people who kept their books behind glass. The books themselves seemed admirable, quite enviable; thirty-eight volumes of Bohn's Antiquarian Library, twelve volumes of Bohn's Historical Library, a run of Johnson's *Lives of the Poets*, a number of Pickering reprints, a complete set of the works of Hegel in German alongside some handsome impressive philosophers – Bosanquet, and some whose names I now learned for the first time, Green, Caird, Wallace. The major English and German poets, nothing minor, but possibly Robinson did not care for poetry. There were also numerous publications of the Bacon Society, and I thought, Why not? Shakespeare isn't a religion. Some bound monographs of the *Aristotelian Society*, the complete *Golden Bough*. All the Greek dramatists and the Greek and Roman philosophers in the Loeb Classics, Lamennais, Von Hügel, Lacordaire, hundreds of others, and in a case by themselves, the uncut first editions.

When I had first seen the books I had felt sickly, had thought: *whole* sets of *everything*. Big names everywhere. But now, after all, it was a reference library, suitable for an island.

I opened a bookcase by the window wall, where the light was poor, and peering close I found the top shelves filled with mystical theology, about a hundred books – writings of the Christian mystics, concordances and commentaries. The lower shelves were occupied by patristic literature in Latin and Greek, and all the English volumes of the Library of the Fathers. Placed to the left of these, a corner bookcase was devoted to the Marian section, all heavily thumbed and annotated. I thought, Well, poor Robinson did at least give thought to the question, Ian Brodie only gives his screeching disapproval supported by misapplied theological quotations.

'Should you desire to possess some of the volumes around us, please to make a choice.' This was Jimmie, standing in the door of Robinson's study. 'Please to retain those which you fancy.'

'Oh, I wouldn't take Robinson's books,' I said.

'Is not now the property of Robinson,' he said mournfully. 'Is mine.'

Jimmie would not avoid me, and so prove his innocence. It was like a game, I played the pipe and he would not dance. I went out of my way to be by his side, watching surreptitiously to see if he flinched from contact with me. He seemed only relieved by this apparent melting on my part. Clearly, I argued with myself, he did not suspect me of murdering Robinson, and his remark, 'You are strong,' had been, most likely, intended to check my intrusive suspicions of himself, as who, whether innocent or not, should say, 'Be careful. If you blame me, I can equally blame you.'

At times I asked myself, What purpose is served by the worry? What was Robinson to you? Why bother? It was, I thought, always desirable that justice should be done, but I had never thought of myself as an avenger, a hunter-down of evil. It was one thing to applaud justice, another to bring it about. My fervour surprised me, of course. One thing I do know: I was just as anxious to prevent injustice as to cause justice. There, I was personally endangered, and I could not help feeling that so, to a greater extent, was Jimmie. In fact, without evidence, I suspected Tom Wells of the murder.

And because Jimmie would not treat me as a candidate for the crime, rather than put this down to his guilt I concluded that he, too, had fixed on Tom Wells as the criminal.

It had come as a new idea to me that the island now belonged to Jimmie. Soon afterwards, when Tom Wells and Miguel were out of the way, I said to him,

'We ought to discuss the murder.'

'Is not to be endured. I lose my nerves.'

'If the island is yours, you are responsible for what happens. You must call a conference.'

'Wherefore a conference? Is enough that I grieve in my heart.'

I had not intended confiding in Jimmie, but his answer annoyed me, it struck me as irresponsible.

I said, 'Tom Wells is a killer.'

Jimmie said, 'As for my part, I do not accuse.'

I stood by the open door, actually ready to run for it in case of trouble, since really I knew very little of Jimmie, and said, 'If it wasn't him it must have been you, Jimmie.'

'Not so,' he said.

'In that case,' I said, 'you believe me to be the murderer.'

'Please not to utter such a declaration.'

'Look here,' I said, 'you don't suppose Miguel – '

'Is not within reason. I do not study to accuse.'

'Then perhaps you share the view,' I said, 'with Wells that Robinson was stabbed by a spook?'

'Is folly,' he said, 'to imagine such an irrational occurrence.'

'What *is* your opinion?'

'Opinion? Alas, is not a time for opinions. I sorrow, I lose my nerves.'

After that I reluctantly and tentatively placed Jimmie again under suspicion.

Less than three weeks remained before the pomegranate boat was due. Miguel was off his food. When we managed, by coaxing, to get him to eat something he frequently vomited half an hour later. Sometimes he lay in a fever which lasted about two hours. We dosed and injected him, but his sickness kept recurring. We put it down to 'the terrible strain', without ever mentioning of what. In between his sick attacks he lolled about the patio with Tom Wells, or followed me about the house. He did not seem to take to Jimmie. Not that he took against him, it was only that he seemed to regard Jimmie as a fool, not worth considering.

I often wondered how he worked out Robinson's death in his mind, and whether the question of its cause and agency had occurred to him at all. He was not apparently afraid of us, but had acquired a general nerviness.

I found it hard to believe that Robinson had made no provision for Miguel in the event of his death. I said to Jimmie, 'Robinson must have left a will. Perhaps it is among his papers. Perhaps the island is not yours, after all.'

'Is mine, as I have knowledge, seeing that I already discover the will of Robinson among his papers.'

'Well, you might have mentioned it before.'

'Is our family business.'

'Ah, well, so is the murder, I suppose.'

'Is so, mayhaps.'

'What is to happen to Miguel?'

'Is our family business. I take him to the aunties.'

On Thursday, the twenty-second of July, a plane flew fairly high over the island. There was a drizzle that day. I was in Robinson's study at the time making a rosary for Miguel out of a string of amber beads that had been amongst the salvage. I had become quite callous about the salvage, and had already made free of the frocks.

Miguel's temperature was normal that day, though he was still sickly and restless. He had been wandering about the house, watching Tom Wells at his writing and me at my rosary-making, and he had drifted silently down to the mustard field where Jimmie had already erected his memorial to Robinson and was now carving some words on the base. About half-past two in the afternoon Miguel came bursting into the house.

'There's an aeroplane coming over from the sky.'

Outside I could see the mist was partially covering the island from the west. The plane approached from the northeast. Jimmie had hurried in from the mustard field and made for the gun-room where the rockets were kept. I fetched the big red signal kite from Robinson's study and brought it out to the patio where I found Tom Wells gazing skyward and clutching his ribs. The plane was over the island and away before Jimmie came back to demand the key of the gun-room which I kept on a string round my neck.

I handed him the kite. 'Unwind it,' I said. 'I'll fetch the rockets.'

'Too late,' said Tom Wells, 'the plane's gone.'

'It may come back.'

There was insufficient breeze to carry the kite but we fired rockets at intervals throughout the afternoon and the following night. There was no further sign of the plane, which must have observed nothing special to report about our island, a minute green rock in the Atlantic. But the excitement of our rockets far into the night had a good effect on Miguel. Although he had a fever next morning, he was in better spirits and by the afternoon he was recovered. As there was a high breeze that day, I gave him Robinson's splendid red kite with its long sequin tail which previously had been forbidden to him. I showed him how to fly it, and as he stood unwinding, holding the heavy apparatus with difficulty, he said,

'Is it mine to keep?'

'See if you can signal the aeroplane to come back,' I said.

'Is it mine to keep?'

'You'll have to ask Jimmie,' I said.

'Does it belong to Jimmie now that Robinson's dead?' he said, quite casually, with his eye on the kite.

'Yes. The island belongs to Jimmie.'

I could see that he was beginning to forget his loss of Robinson, less than three weeks after his death, and I was thankful, because his brooding had been a worry; and I wondered if Brian, though older and different, might by now have accepted my death.

The pomegranate boat was expected between the eighth and tenth of August. I allowed myself to sit gazing out to sea in the hope that it would appear before time, and also in dread, since the boat would find us with a murder on our hands. Meanwhile I made the rosary for Miguel. It was a difficult process, for the tiny holes in the golden beads were too small for the needle; and as I had to make each hole larger with a canvas-bodkin, I worked slowly. I had not quite finished it when Jimmie announced the completion of the memorial. Miguel and I went down to the mustard field. The memorial had been placed at the spot where Robinson's blood-stained jacket and the clasp-knife had been found. It consisted of a wooden cross, very neatly made and joined, although the left arm was longer than the right, and the shaft was set at a slight angle. On the plain block base was inscribed in uneven lettering:

IN MEMORIAM
MILES MARY ROBINSON
1903 – 1954

131

This filled up the whole of the space on the front of the block. 'Is no further room for R.I.P.' said Jimmie. 'Initially I did aim to insert R.I.P. but is not possible. The first letters I create too tall, and then, behold, is no more space.'

Miguel said to Jimmie, pointing at the memorial, 'Is that Robinson?'

'How is that you mean?' said Jimmie.

Miguel looked baffled at this question and though Jimmie pressed him he would not answer. I supposed he thought of the memorial as a sort of statue of Robinson when, later on in the house, he asked me, 'Why is one of Robinson's arms longer than the other?' and after considering his meaning I said, 'Oh, you mean the memorial?' And sometimes, though he referred to it as a memorial, he seemed to hold some sort of pathetic fallacy: 'Won't the memorial be cold out there all night?' He seemed to feel that Robinson's real presence had been transformed into the memorial. It was always impossible to know exactly what was going on in his mind.

The more I pondered the murder the more did I come to think of Robinson as a kind of legendary figure since it was hard to believe that only a few weeks had passed since he had led me on my first visit to the Furnace. Perhaps, even at that time, he had assumed near-mythical dimensions in my eyes. I saw him now as an austere sea-bound hero, a noble heretic, who to follow his mystical destiny, had hidden himself away from the world with only a child-disciple for company. I supposed he had recognized in Miguel a strong unformed religious potentiality. Robinson himself was essentially a religious man. Jimmie had once, in the manner of one who had a relative bitten with an eccentric ambition, referred to Robinson's desire for spiritual advancement. In thinking of Robinson, I had to perform an act of imaginative distortion in that I could not think of him as a part of the present tense, a human creature who had been born into a particular age and at a particular point of developed doctrine – I vaguely thought of him as having no proper station in life like the rest of us. I thought of his rescue work at the time of the crash, his nursing us to health, the burial of the dead, and his patience with our ungrateful intrusion into his elected solitude. That he should have met his end at the hands of one of his beneficiaries seemed to me the essence of his tragedy. And in this interesting light he took on the heroic character of a pagan pre-Christian victim of expiation.

I used to spend a lot of time in Robinson's rooms, recalling his attempts to entertain us with his Rossini recordings, and sometimes imparting information about the history and legends of the island. Robinson's evenings had clearly been an effort to him; I recalled the prevalent feeling of his trying to bring order out of chaos in a schoolmasterly way, never really trusting the evening to go smoothly unless he organized it for us.

I was surprised at the clarity and number of his incidental remarks, which my memory, like a recording instrument, now played back to me. And for the first time I recalled certain pieces of information which I had not really listened to when Robinson had imparted them.

He had told us that if the island was the southernmost part of Atlantis, as the legends suggested, this would extend the current speculations about the size of Atlantis by fifteen hundred miles. The island had been a peninsula, famous for its pomegranate orchards which had been planted by King Arthur. Another legend told of a beautiful northern princess who had been carried there by a half-human demon and imprisoned in the mountain beneath the Furnace. From there her screams attracted a shepherd who gallantly threw himself in the Furnace to be imprisoned with her. The scream could still be heard whenever the crater was disturbed by an object entering it. The lovers can only be released if a priest is prepared to bless them and die immediately afterwards. Another group of legends claimed the island to be the home of the Greek Hesperus, and assigned an oracular function to the Furnace.

Chance fragments of Robinson's conversation recurred to me at this time, although when he told these stories I had usually been thinking of something else, had been occupied with Jimmie's intriguing qualities, or burned-up with irritation at Tom Wells, or day-dreaming about Chelsea. In fact, it was not until some months after I had left the island, when I was questioned about its history, that I remembered points in Robinson's conversations that I had previously forgotten. And even now I keep remembering new facts which Robinson gave us then, night after night, as if compelled to do so lest we should run amok.

When I sat in Robinson's rooms summoning up his presence, it was not only the substance of his conversation that returned to me, but also the tone of his voice, even, rhythmical, almost a chant, which had a slightly mesmeric effect:

'The history is obscure. . . .

'Traditional hermits' home. Five of them . . . one on each Arm, one on each Leg, and one . . .

'A few Arabs, Danes . . .

'A line of Portuguese have successively owned the island.

'Yes, eccentrics, I dare say . . .

'The history is obscure. . . .

'The island has always been privately owned.

'Bought and sold. . . .

'Smugglers' hide-out, of course. . . .

'Too small to need more than nominal protection. . . .

'Ruling powers not really interested. . . .

'The history is obscure. . . .

'Most of the craters active six hundred years ago. . . .

'Vasco da Gama's fleet nosed in. . . . '

In the late afternoon of the day when Jimmie finished the memorial I mooned round Robinson's rooms, flicking a duster, touching books, and almost hearing his voice intone on the subject of the island. On a side table lay his reading glasses face-down with the shafts upright, in the position in which he had left them. From curiosity, and because I had been considering the peculiar essence of Robinson, I tried on the glasses. Usually when, for some idle reason, I have tried on other people's glasses everything has looked out of focus, has appeared to swim, as if I were unwell. I expected some mild sensation of this kind when I tried on Robinson's glasses, but I did not expect what happened. The room swung over and round in a swivel movement. The books leaped from the shelves and piled over the carpet. Everything on the tables and the desk whirled on to the floor, and even then did not stay still. I myself staggered and reeled with the room, and as I clung to the back of a heavy leather chair the El Greco *Agony* flew off the wall, to which it had been very tightly clamped, just missing me. As for Robinson's glasses, they had not been on my nose for the space of a blink, but I did not need their absence to tell me that the room was rocking in any case, without their aid. The pitch and toss grew gradually milder. I fixed my eye on one of the books spread open on the floor. It steadied up, so that I could see the bookplate on the inside of the cover, and it remained quite still, '*Nunquam minus solus quam cum solus*'. I caught sight of Miguel running past the window with a grin on his face. He came inside and opened the study door, smiling excitedly.

'Mr Tom is under his bed,' he said.

'Do you often have earthquakes here?'

'I think so. Jimmie has cut his hand on a piece of glass.'

'Are they all as severe as this?' I said.

'All what?'

'Severe. Bad. Are they all bad, like this?'

'They aren't bad. Robinson said so.'

'I call it bad,' I said.

'Mr Tom is under his bed.'

Tom Wells must have emerged from his shelter, for he was now crossing the patio looking pale, flabby and troubled in the half-light.

'Where's your boy-friend?' he said sharply to me.

Jimmie emerged from the kitchen door with his hand bound in a towel like a huge stump.

'I have received a shock,' he said.

'Look here, Waterford,' said Tom Wells, 'you own this island, don't you?'

'Is mine,' said Jimmie, unwinding the towel slightly, then quickly, at the sight of his blood, replacing the fold.

'Take it from me,' said Wells, 'you're going to have to pay me damages.'

'Alas, where have you been damaged?' said Jimmie, nursing the towel.

'I'm covered with knocks. I'm going to claim damages.'

'Tell him it's an Act of God,' I said to Jimmie.

'Is an act from God,' said Jimmie.

'Like the murder,' said Wells.

'How do you mean?' said Jimmie. But Tom Wells walked tremulously into the house.

Miguel had started clearing up the mess, as if by routine. I joined him in the kitchen, separating the broken crockery and glass from that which was left intact, or merely cracked. Very soon, however, the delayed effects of the earthquake overtook me, and the lamplit kitchen went out of focus, swimming before my eyes as if I had tried on someone else's glasses. I went to my room and lay down, not sure if, on entering the room, I had encountered Tom Wells again, startled and guilty, outside the door of my room, or if I had imagined it.

Next day Jimmie had to set up the memorial again. It had toppled over during the earthquake. Miguel, however, did not accompany him, but instead hung round me to see the completion of the rosary which was now quite presentable. I fixed to the chaplet a cross which I had made, with difficulty, from the smallest of the amber beads threaded with thin wire. Miguel was magnetized by this new trinket, and when I showed him how to use it he was not content until he had mastered the technique, holding between his frail brown fingers and thumb glittering bead by bead, nodding his head in time to the repetitive prayers, completely under the spell. It crossed my mind how easily he was influenced. '*Santa Maria*,' he said suddenly. '*Mãe de Deus*,' and I realized he had heard the rosary recited in his infancy.

By way of conversation, and because he liked to know the ins and outs of anything, once it had captured his interest, I said, 'It ought to be blessed by a priest, but as there isn't a priest on the island I dare say you can gain all the indulgences without a blessing.' These words, which he but dimly understood, dazzled him considerably. I suppose the unknown element, 'indulgences', to be gained from a 'priest's blessing', gave extra glamour to his rosary. He questioned me all afternoon.

'What is indulgences?' 'Can you pray on Ethel of the Well?' 'Is Mr Tom a Catholic?' 'Is Jimmie . . . ?'

He displayed the rosary to Tom Wells at the first opportunity.

Wells said: 'That's an R.C. item. Robinson wouldn't have approved.'

Miguel sensed danger and hurried off with his treasure.

'You should respect Robinson's wishes,' said Wells. 'He always said how easily anyone could corrupt the boy.'

'You speak too late,' I said, 'since I've already started to corrupt him.'

'It isn't a laughing matter.'

'Very true.'

Something else about his words sounded odd to me: I could hardly believe that Robinson's murderer would say, 'You should respect Robinson's wishes.'

X

IT IS NOT THAT I JUDGE PEOPLE by their appearance, but it is true that I am fascinated by their faces. I do not stare in their presence. I like to take the impression of a face home with me, there to stare at and chew over it in privacy, as a wild beast prefers to devour its prey in concealment.

As a means of judging character it is a misleading practice and as for physiognomy the science, I know nothing of that. The misleading element, in fact, provides the essence of my satisfaction. In the course of deciphering a face, its shape, tones, lines and droops as if these were words and sentences of a message from the interior, I fix upon it a character which, though I know it to be distorted, never quite untrue, never entirely true, interests me. I am as near the mark as myth is to history, the apocrypha to the canon. I seek no justification for this habit, it is one of the things I do. Most of all, I love to compare faces. I have seen a bus conductor who resembles a woman don of my acquaintance, I have seen the face of Agnes throwing itself from side to side in the pulpit; I make a meal of these.

All the time I was on the island I set considerable store by faces; and in the absence of normal criteria of judgement, I fell back on intuitions of faces whenever I was frightened.

The facial resemblance between Tom Wells and Curly Lonsdale lay more in the expression than the actual features.

Curly's mouth was not so loose. But both had the habit of keeping their mouths open all the time, and you would sometimes think they were smiling when they were not.

Curly Lonsdale once remarked, 'Life is based on blackmail', but I have since come to think he had himself in mind, not as the blackmailer but the blackmailed. I think he had in mind the fact that he had always operated within an inch of the law; and 'life' for Curly consisted of those standards of behaviour which he had set up for himself.

The pomegranate boat was expected in nine or ten days. I was more and more impatient, and at the same time apprehensive. It gave rise to a feeling not unlike guilt to imagine in advance the men spilling ashore on the white beach. 'Where's Robinson?' Or perhaps they spoke only Portuguese, and would question Jimmie or Miguel. Tom Wells and I would look on, as if we were both of a piece. And they would, in turn, look at us, would of course put us under arrest. Probably weeks and months of detention and inquiries would transpire before I could go home.

Tom Wells found me alone in Robinson's study and said, 'There's something I want to say to you privately.'

I said, 'If it's blackmail, sorry I'm not rich.'

He said, 'I don't understand.'

'True enough,' I said. 'No one will believe you if you try to pin the murder on me.'

'Honey, I wouldn't dream of framing you. What I wanted to say was – '

'Why are you blackmailing Jimmie?' I thought for a moment that he was still smiling, but I was wrong, it was his loose mouth. He said, 'If you know what's good for you, you'll keep your mouth shut.'

'I do not, as a rule, go about with it hanging open.'

'That's the bitch,' he said. 'You were always a bitch to Robinson.'

'You are trying to blackmail Jimmie.'

'I'm negotiating for a settlement. I've sustained damages on his island. If he doesn't want a reckon-up with me, he'll get it elsewhere.'

'You'll never get away with that,' I said.

'Listen,' he said, 'be reasonable. Do you want to put your boy-friend in the way of difficulties?'

I said, 'What difficulties?' and looked out of the window to see if Jimmie or Miguel were about.

'What I want to say to you,' he said, 'is this. We'd better have an understanding about the murder.'

'In my opinion,' I said, 'it was occasioned by a supernatural force.'

He looked at me to see what I meant, and was not sure. He said, 'That's a good enough yarn for ourselves, dear – or rather, was until your boy-friend settled down a bit. He must have been worried, naturally, after what he did. But you mustn't talk about the supernatural to the dicks, dear, it makes them cross as hell.'

'No,' I said, 'I shall not say things like that.' I looked out of the window.

'Now you're talking sense, sweetie, you're talking good sense. Now, we'd better have an understanding. I did think of suicide. What do you think of suicide?'

'If you care to commit suicide,' I said, 'that's your affair. But I'm bound to point out it is a mortal sin.'

'You playing dumb, dear?'

I said, 'I don't agree to put out the tale that Robinson committed suicide,' and took another look out of the window to see if anyone was nearby.

'Then it'll have to be an accident. Robinson had an accident. He slipped and fell on the mountain and he broke his neck. His face was badly bashed in, d'you see, not recognizable. We buried him among the victims of the crash, poor chap.'

'Anything else?' I said. 'Because I'm busy at the moment.'

'We'll burn the evidence tonight,' he said, 'and we shall sign the statement tomorrow.'

'What statement?'

'The one I'm going to prepare. I just wanted to know whether you preferred suicide or an accident. Mind you, suicide would be sound, because he was a bit touched in the head, Robinson.'

I said, 'Have you consulted Jimmie?'

'About the damages? That's another matter, you don't come into that. We sign the statement about Robinson's misfortune *after* Jimmie has signed his agreement with me about the damages.'

'Has Jimmie agreed to swear that Robinson was killed in an accident?'

'Oh yes, and he'll come across with it. What d'you take him for?'

'I don't believe you.' There was no sign of anyone from the window. I did not know if Jimmie or Miguel were near the house.

'D'you suppose he's going to give himself up?' said Wells.

'No; why should he?'

Tom Wells said, 'Yes, *why* should he?' He looked at me in a frightening way and said, 'You're not such an unnatural bitch that you'd shop your man, are you?' He laid his large hand on my shoulder, gripping painfully.

I said, 'Take your hand off my shoulder.'

He said, 'You'll sign the statement.'

I said, 'Take your hand off my shoulder or I shall scream.'

He dropped his hand, and said, 'You'll sign the statement.'

I said, 'I don't see why I should put Jimmie's money your way.'

'What you say, honey,' he said, 'is natural enough. I'd give you a slice, but you won't need it, that's honest, if you know how to handle your boy-friend. You're on to a good thing there, and some of it's in motor-scooters – you can't go wrong with motor-scooters.'

'You have forgotten Miguel,' I said.

He said, 'Tom Wells never forgets.'

'He saw the blood,' I said, 'and the bloodstains and the knife.'

'Naturally,' said Wells, 'he saw the blood and the knife. Anyone can see the youngster's backward. And he has a lot of imagination, and he has a touch of fever besides being a bit peculiar in the head – not surprising when you think of the unnatural life. No one's going to listen to Miguel about the blood and the knife.'

'Anything else? Because I'm busy.'

He said, 'You'll sign the agreement.' Out of the window I saw Jimmie and Miguel walking across the patio. I said to Tom Wells, 'Go to hell,' and left him.

Ten minutes later I saw Miguel sidle up to Tom Wells on the patio. I had long been disabused of the idea that a child is an instinctive judge of character, but I never ceased to wonder at the attraction Miguel felt towards Tom Wells, who more-over treated him quite roughly.

'Sign his paper,' said Jimmie. 'Is best.'

'You must be mad,' I said.

'Is so,' said Jimmie, 'that I want my head examined. But I see is best to sign.'

'You must be guilty,' I said, 'of killing Robinson.'

'Is not so. Never do I think to take care of Robinson.'

'Then I'd see Tom Wells in hell before I would sign his statement. And mind you don't sign any agreement to pay him money.'

'Is a dangerous man,' said Jimmie. 'You do not conceive what story he has prepared, in the event we do not sign.'

'He will accuse you of the murder. Don't worry, the motive of Robinson's inheritance doesn't count for everything. The police usually find the guilty man; and if you're innocent, simply say so.'

'Is not the story which he has prepared,' said Jimmie. 'He has prepared to accuse you, that you have stabbed with the knife.'

'I really don't think that would be believed,' I said. 'I don't think I look strong enough to drag a body up the mountain.'

'Tom Wells has prepared to accuse that you did knife Robinson at the dawn in the mustard field, and he accuses that he has heard you return to the house and confide these doings to me, which this Wells declares he has heard. Whereafter together we depart to the place where is the body of Robinson, and we transport this body to the Furnace.'

I said, 'Why should *I* kill Robinson?'

'Is the declaration of Tom Wells that you have done the crime on purpose to gain for me the fortune. Whereafter you marry me.'

I said, 'You must see now, Jimmie, that Tom Wells is the criminal.'

'I do not accuse. Is dangerous to accuse. Mayhaps in consequence he should request a duel. He is entitled to make such demand. Then is mayhaps blood shed. Is serious to say to a man, "Behold, you have killed." Is better to sign the statement.'

This speech gave me no pleasure.

'Do you really think,' I said, 'anyone would believe his story?'

'Is better to sign,' he said.

I wrote my island journal that night, Saturday, the thirty-first July. I did not know at the time that it was to be the last entry, but I realized for the first time that my journal might be a fateful sort of document, might come in useful, and so I wrote with special thought.

1) I begin by stating that I have reached the conclusion that T. Wells murdered Robinson.

2) I may remark that the motive of gain which might lay suspicion on Jimmie Waterford or on myself is not likely to be thought unquestionably conclusive. The question would arise, might not the transparency of this motive deter a potential murderer? Further, would not the criminal take the utmost care to conceal his guilt? It must be remembered that the bloodstained articles which were found between the mustard field and the Furnace had been in use by Jimmie, Robinson and myself. Nothing belonging to Tom Wells was found. Far from contributing to the case against Jimmie and me, this casts suspicion, I believe, on Tom Wells.

3) Also, I observe that from the type and position of the bloodstained articles they had been deliberately planted there.

4) Tom Wells is a blackmailer. He has put it to me that we all three sign a statement to the effect that Robinson died of an accident. I say 'put it to me' but in fact he seemed to think it certain I would agree. I gained the impression from Wells that he was counting on my affection for Jimmie, and my desire to cover up for him.

The price of this hushing up of the murder is a sum of money to be extorted from Jimmie.

But I have further information from Jimmie about Wells's intentions. Failing our agreement to sign his statement, he proposes to inform the Portuguese authorities that I murdered Robinson by stabbing with a knife, subsequently persuading Jimmie to assist me in disposing of the body; motive being to acquire for Jimmie Robinson's fortune, and later to marry Jimmie.

5) Jimmie tells me he is prepared to sign the statement. This may mean one of four things:
   i) That he is guilty.
   ii) That he is innocent but afraid of being implicated, or desires to avoid trouble in general.
   iii) That he desires to save me from being implicated.
   iv) That he is in league with Tom Wells.

6) I favour the proposition that Jimmie is innocent but wants to avoid trouble and so is prepared to acquiesce in Tom Wells's demands.

7) I leave the possibility of Jimmie's guilt to consider the question of Tom Wells.

8) I know him to be a blackmailer in one instance. I think he may be a professional blackmailer.

If that is so, and Robinson had evidence of it, that would provide a motive for murder.

I am thinking of the papers which were missing from Tom Wells's bag when it was restored to him by Robinson, and about which Wells made a fuss (see Journal 1st July), and I think it possible that his luck-and-occult racket is a cover for trade in blackmail, and a means to it. I am thinking

of all the people who write and tell him their
secrets.

9) It is possible that the body may be retrieved from
the Furnace.

10) I do not think of signing Tom Wells's statement.

I had been using loose sheets of paper for my journal since
I had filled the blue exercise book which Robinson had
given to me. I slipped the sheets inside the back cover of
the exercise book and put it in a drawer in my room where
I kept it.

The question of signing the statement was giving me more
trouble than I had allowed to appear in the journal. The morals of the question apart, I felt strongly that it would be the
greatest folly to falsify evidence in a way that might easily be
detected by expert criminologists, and I also had a horror of
placing myself in Tom Wells's power.

I felt that in opposing Jimmie and Wells I was up against
two different types of the melodramatic mind; one coloured
by romance, the other by crime. We were on the same island
but in different worlds.

Although these things were clear to me, I was afraid of
pressure. I feared the united pressure of Jimmie and Tom
Wells, and, more, the pressure of the scheme's expedient at-
tractions. If successful, it would facilitate my homegoing – no
interrogations, no unpleasantness in the newspapers. I was
beginning to think up an idea that really there was no reason
why the scheme should not be successful, when I decided to
put the temptation out of my reach. I went to find Miguel. He
was fishing in the lake. 'Miguel,' I said, 'do you know what
a lie is?'

He said, 'Yes.'

'What is a lie?'

He screwed up his face to search his memory, then he said, 'When you say something is different from what you think it is.' It sounded like a set piece of Robinson's teaching. Although Miguel was truthful, I was not sure that he understood the formula.

'Do you remember,' I said, 'the day that Robinson disappeared?'

He screwed up his face as if to recall something and I understood that he was trying to remember the date.

'I mean, do you remember what happened on that day, and what we did?'

'Yes, Mr Tom found the knife and Robinson's jacket. We went to look for Robinson.'

I said, 'What do you think happened to Robinson?'

'Someone killed him,' he said.

'Who do you think killed him?'

'The Parroveevil,' he said.

'Say it again.'

He repeated it twice, and presently I discerned the influence of Tom Wells and his Power of Evil.

'Suppose someone said that Robinson fell down, alone by himself on the mountain, and was killed?'

'Who said it?'

'*Suppose* someone said it, what would that be?'

He said, 'A mistake.'

I said, 'Do you remember the things we found when we were looking for Robinson?'

He said, 'All the clothes.'

'That's right. What did they look like?'

'They were all over blood,' he said.

'Suppose,' I continued, 'that one of us said we didn't find any clothes at all, and that there wasn't any blood?'

'That would be silly,' he said.

'Would it be true?'

'No, they must be making a mistake.'

I thought, What odds if he doesn't know what a lie is, so long as he speaks the truth? And by his puzzled look I was satisfied that the present conversation would stick in his mind. It would be difficult, now, to persuade him that he had dreamt the evidence of Robinson's death.

The swimming suit was slightly too big for me, but it was the best I could find among the salvage. I regretted not availing myself of it earlier, when I had been obliged to sit enviously on the shore of the lake and watch Jimmie and Robinson splashing about in bathing trunks and Miguel swimming naked, diving like a rocket. There had been no garment for me to bathe in. 'Bathe in nothing at all,' Jimmie had advised, 'and we avert our gaze.'

'There's a woman's swimming suit amongst the salvage,' Robinson had said.

I had come to the lake to cool off after a violent encounter with Tom Wells and Jimmie. I had told them both at breakfast that I would not sign the statement, and I deliberately spoke in front of Miguel, hoping that he would take in something of the meaning rather than the mere vibrations.

'Better to sign,' said Jimmie.

'Look, let's all get together and discuss it in private,' said Wells, looking at Miguel.

'There's nothing to discuss.'

'We meet at two p.m.,' said Wells. 'That's final.'

'Better to sign,' said Jimmie.

I said to Jimmie, 'You make me sick.'

He sprang up and banged the table. 'Is on your behalf that I make you sick.'

I had not seen Jimmie lose his temper before. I was taken aback and must have shown it, for Tom Wells was quick to follow this advantage with a loud-voiced, 'You'll sign, if it's the last thing you do. Robinson died of an accident – get it?'

Jimmie turned on him and said, 'Get it – is not nice to address a lady like the thunder, get it.'

'Come away, Miguel,' I said loftily. 'Come with me.'

He came hesitantly. Tom Wells called after me. 'Two p.m.'

At two o'clock I was cooling myself in the lake. I had avoided the house all day and had brought food to eat by the lake. I was regretting that I had not availed myself of the salvaged bathing dress in our early days on the island. I would have preferred the sea, but Robinson had warned us of the sharks. Apart from the streams which scored the island, and which were often only ankle-deep, the lake was the only bathing place.

It was wonderfully soothing and the blue-green effect was only slightly diminished when one was actually in the water. I think the colour was caused by some mineral in the lake water rather than reflection from the sky; when I sent a splash into the air, it looked like a shower of transparent blue gems. Making big splashes to some extent alleviated the apprehensive pain about my stomach, a physical pain which I had been going about with for the last two weeks, and which I realized had been nibbling inside me since Robinson's disappearance.

It had been a favourite game of Bluebell, when Robinson was swimming in the lake, to race along the bank trying to catch the glittering blue beads of water which he threw in her direction. I caught sight of the cat on the bank as I dabbled around, saw it was trying to egg me on to play. It did this by planting its forepaws together on the very verge of the lake and waggling its hindquarters ready to spring. The technique of the game, on the swimmer's part, was to send a shower of spray a little above and in front of the cat, and then she would leap, almost fly in the air after the elusive drops. Bluebell did not seem to mind when it occasionally drenched her, but would shake the blue water off her head and crouch for the next spring. I swam in to the edge and obliged her with a high-thrown handful of lake water. She gave a beautiful leap, her slate-blue coat looking far more blue beside the lake. I swam farther round, churning out Bluebell's shower with the back of my hand. 'Come on, Bluebell,' I called to her, 'water's good for the nerves.' I wondered how soon the cat would tire, and decided to see if she would follow me all round the lake, trotting, crouching, leaping, in her wonderful rhythm. We were more than half-way round when she got bored, and browsed off among the ferns towards the cliff edge. I drifted for a small while, then decided to set off again towards the bank where I had left my clothes. I did not intend to return to the house just yet; I had it in mind to walk down the cliff-path and through the copse of blue-gum trees to the Pomegranate beach, there to let the white sand trickle through my toes and fingers. I started cutting across the lake, and when I had almost reached the middle I caught sight of Tom Wells disappearing behind some shrubbery near the spot where I had left my clothes. At first I thought he was lying in wait for me behind the shrubbery, but as I came up to the bank I saw him retreating farther off, shuffling up to the house.

The key of the gun-room, which I usually kept on a string round my neck, was missing from among my clothes, where I had left it. The pain above my stomach returned.

I dressed quickly and went in search of Jimmie. He was drinking brandy in Robinson's study. When he saw me he said:

'Alas, I am abased to the servile floor.'

I shivered, for in my haste I had not dried myself properly. I said, 'I'd like a drink.'

He poured some brandy for me. 'I lose my nerves.'

I said, 'Wells has stolen the key of the gun-room from me.'

He jumped up. 'He has assaulted you to obtain this key?'

'No, I left it lying about.'

Jimmie filled his glass and said, 'Is my key – lo, all is mine.'

I said, 'Take care what you do. He has probably armed himself.'

'He is angered in the extreme, that you do not sign the statement today,' Jimmie said. 'Thus mayhaps he shall insist by pointing the pistol. Is not humorous.'

'Have you signed his statement?'

'No, no. Is fruitless if all do not agree.'

'Have you signed any agreement to pay him the money?'

'No, is fruitless if all do not agree to Robinson's accident.'

I said, 'I have a sort of weapon against Tom Wells.'

'Yes, yes,' said Jimmie. 'I do recall the pistol.'

'I don't mean the pistol,' I said. 'I mean my journal. It is a sort of evidence, a dossier. People would find it difficult to reconcile Tom Wells's story with the journal.'

Jimmie was only half-listening. 'If you please,' he said, 'is best to place the little gun into my charge. Is necessary, in the event that I am obliged to protect you.'

I kept the baby Browning in the pocket of my coat. I am always rather afraid of firearms; and without actually believing they can go off by themselves, I have one of those shadowy fears that they will. Every morning I had checked the Browning to see if the safety-catch was still on, and sometimes in the night I would get up to have another look; that was the relationship between myself and the automatic.

I said to Jimmie, 'I may need the automatic myself. In fact, I think I need it now more than you do.'

'Is like this,' Jimmie said. 'Is not nice to have a gun except in the event that you understand it. Many ladies do not understand what is a gun. In the event that words should occur, pouff – the lady will shoot and the gentleman is killed.'

'I ought to keep it for security. I don't like the thought of Tom Wells having the key of the gun-room.'

'Is my intention to arrange that he should render up that key.'

'My God!' I said. 'If I give you the pistol there will be another murder.'

'No, no,' said Jimmie. 'Is to go too far. Never in my life do I shoot to kill. I understand what is a gun. Is best for you to give to me my gun, then is no killing in the event that you make mistakes.'

I did not miss the words 'my gun'. The automatic was undoubtedly Jimmie's property, and I felt, if it came to that, he could easily force his gun from me. But I was more impressed by the idea that I might kill Tom Wells, should I be provoked to wield the automatic against him. In fact, I thought, this would be very likely, since I was on edge with fear of him, and the possibility of what he might do in the days ahead. Seven or eight days, I thought, is a long time when you can kill a man in less than a second, and so complicate your life. Self-defence is all very well, but two murders on the island . . .

'Is best,' said Jimmie, 'not to have a gun if you are not experienced with shooting. In the course of the hostilities I have had the occasion . . . '

Like a fool, I went and fetched the Browning. Even as I handed it over I regretted it; I was insecure, and overcome with a feeling of distrust for Jimmie.

I left him immediately, resolved to make a record in my journal of my having given him the gun, and the reasons why I had done so.

The journal was gone from its drawer. It was nowhere in my room. I had been altogether counting on it to counteract Tom Wells's accusation against me. Of course, it contained no direct proof, but it had struck me, on reading it through, that it was not at all the sort of journal that anyone would write who was gradually meditating murder. And also it contained the 'dossier' of the murder itself, the notes of my suspicions and reflections which I had intended to hand over to the Portuguese. I set particular store by my theory that Robinson had discovered some blackmailing activity of Wells, and so been silenced.

For some reason, when I was satisfied that the blue exercise book was not in my room, I felt light-headed. I felt carefree and reckless. I went to Robinson's apartments and put a recording of Mozart on the gramophone, poured myself a drink, lit a cigarette, sat back, and closed my eyes. Bluebell, who had sidled into the room with me, leapt on to my lap and, purring loudly, started to pummel me with her paws, prior to nestling down. When the record came to an end I turned it over and had some more Mozart. I had another drink. When I felt I was bored with music, I cast round for a novel and found that Robinson's few novels had apparently been chosen for their bibliographical charms. I pulled out of the case a leather-bound volume of a novel, and opened it in the middle of a chapter. The eighteenth-century typography, with its s's like f's, irritated me. I threw it on to a nearby sofa. I put on another record, poured myself another drink. I took up the book again:

> Now the agonies which affected the mind of Sophia rather augmented than impaired her beauty; for her tears added brightnefs to her eyes, and her breafts rofe higher with her fighs. Indeed, no one hath feen beauty in its highest luftre, who hath never feen it in diftrefs. . . .

I put it by, and settled down to the interesting thought of how like I was at this moment to my sister Julia. There is something about too much worry that brings out Julia in me, a temporary reaction which is typical of her constant behaviour. Julia spends her life putting discs on and off her electric gramophone, switching on the television, switching it off, pouring herself a drink, taking up a book, throwing it on a near-by sofa, lifting the telephone, then changing her mind. And I mused on other occasions of special stress when on the other hand, I was Agnes to the life. That was when I had been over-excited by some event, such as a play, or a letter with a surprise cheque, or a party where I had chattered all night very successfully and been much talked to. My hangover, perhaps a kind of protection against excitability, took the form of a fat-headed domestic triviality, and I would make it a big issue to consider how long, to the very month, the curtains had been in use, resolving to clean out cupboards that had not been touched for fifteen years, writing out timetables to follow, writing out my expenditure in one column, my income in another, adding up and glumly comparing them. This would last but a few hours, but Agnes did it all her life.

While I pondered the genetic question involved in these self-observations, the irrelevant idea flashed upon me that Tom Wells was the sort of person likely to hide my journal under his mattress.

I was almost right. The blue exercise book was under the counterpane at the foot of his bed. I examined it and found it intact, loose pages and all. I had ascertained his presence on the patio before entering his room. He had been sitting out there, looking suddenly quite horrible with a hand on each knee, and the key of the gun-room hanging conspicuously round his neck. Now, from his window, I saw the back of his head above the chair where he was seated, and I thought how stupid he was.

It was about five o'clock. I had just time to reach my destination and return before the mists should fall. I quickly cut a square piece out of Robinson's waterproof – the handiest thing I could find for the purpose – and, wrapping my notebook in this to protect it from dampness, I set off for the secret tunnel which led from the cliffs at the Pomegranate Bay to the South Arm. It was my plan to conceal my journal near the South Arm end of the tunnel, so that there should be no chance of Wells coming upon it by accident. He had never been to the caves, and seldom walked far beyond the vicinity of the house. A visit to the scene of the accident had been his longest venture, and he had gone there only to assure himself that his missing papers were not among the debris at the spot where he had been found. He had returned from this visit, complaining of exhaustion and clutching his ribs.

I chose the Pomegranate Bay tunnel because it was sufficiently near at hand to enable me to reach it and return before the fall of the mist, and yet not too near. The tunnel whose entrance led from the cliff just behind the house to the Furnace was, I felt, too near-by to be safe from anyone really on the hunt. And, of course, the cave on the North Arm was too far away, although I would gladly have hidden my book that distance from Tom Wells.

I had only got as far as the beach when I realized I had forgotten to bring a light, without which it was impossible to penetrate the tunnel. I returned as quickly as possible up the mountain path. I stopped only to stuff my package out of sight for the time being in a hollow at the bole of a tree, covering it up with whin, and placing some small black pebbles on the path in the form of a cross, to mark the place. I saw that a light mist had begun to curl round the mountain.

There was a powerful flashlamp about nine inches long in Robinson's study; all the others were weak, the batteries running out. It usually lay on the wide window ledge.

In Robinson's study I found Tom Wells sitting at the desk.

'Good evening,' he said. 'So I murdered Robinson to keep him quiet?'

'You know best,' I said.

'I'm a blackmailer, you say?'

'Yes, that's what I say.'

'Well,' he said, 'naturally you'll be disappointed to hear that I've destroyed your little notebook.'

'You haven't stolen my journal?' I said, making frightened eyes.

'I've burnt it.'

'Burnt it? When? I've always thought blackmailers never destroy papers.'

'I burnt it a few hours ago. It made interesting reading. Do you know what?'

'What?'

'You're going to sign my statement.' He opened a drawer of the desk and taking out a fair-sized revolver placed it before him.

I said, 'You won't get away with two murders.'

He said, 'There's ways of going about a job like that, and there's ways of putting the remains out of sight.'

'A gun makes a lot of noise on this island,' I said. 'It echoes all over the place.'

'O.K., it makes a lot of noise. Who's going to hear it?'

'Jimmie is not deaf.'

'No, but he's dumb. I'll see to it that he's dumb for the rest of his life. No one squeals once Tom Wells says they're dumb. And as for the boy – well, I'll settle with anyone that tries to make evidence of what that half-wit says.'

I started to retreat. He stood up. 'Listen, honey. I don't want to do you any harm. There's no need to get alarmed. You'll sign my statement, it's for your own good. And I just want to warn you, if there's any retraction when you get home, I've got my boys in London. They can pay you a visit. I just want you to know, honey, that you'd better see my way of things.'

'I must find Jimmie,' I said, backing slowly out of the door.

'Naturally,' he said, 'of course. By all means talk it over with the boy-friend. He's got the right slant, he'll tell you the same as I've done.'

I was half-way out of the doorway when he said, 'You'll find him in the cellar. I've put him to crating the wines and liquor ready to take away. No use leaving that good stuff on the island.'

'Then I'll need the torch,' I said.

'That's right,' he said. He lifted the flashlamp off the window ledge and handed it to me. 'Don't break your neck down the steps, we don't want two corpses. Go and talk to Jimmie, dear.'

I slipped out by way of the storehouse, and made my way through the film of blue rising vapour down the mountain path again and, retrieving my parcel, continued my way along the beach to the aperture in the cliff which concealed the mouth of the tunnel.

I coughed my way through the sulphurous dust, my cough echoing on the walls of the cave, as if there were three or four people ahead of me, three or four behind. Twice I slipped on the slimy weeds, once scraping my elbow badly, but hardly noticing it in my efforts to make progress. My flashlamp cast a red glare in the volcanic dust. I came to that part of the tunnel where it dwindled to a hole, and I was obliged to crawl along the muddy floor with the parcel between my teeth. At last the cave widened, but it was low; I was forced to stoop and clutch the jutting shelves to assist my advance. It was here I looked for a suitable hiding-place for the journal, feeling with my hand the top surfaces of the protruding shelves, hoping to come across a flat rest. None of them had sufficient surface to retain my flat parcel, but running my hand over the upper face of a ledge I found that it fell back into a hole in the rock. I had to bend the parcel to squeeze it in.

My next plan was to return to the house, avoiding Wells if possible, and find Jimmie. If this could be done before Wells discovered the disappearance of the journal it might be possible for us, supported by the Browning, to take Wells by surprise and place him under arrest.

It seemed the wisest course to turn and retrace my journey through the tunnel to the beach, since by this route there would be less chance of my being overcome by the mist than if I emerged higher up on the South Arm. I still hesitated to return through the tunnel, for I was quite near to the South Arm door and I felt a suffocating desire for open air. However, I crouched under the shelf where my journal lay concealed, and gathered up my strength for the return journey through the caves. What I hated most in anticipation was the few yards of crawling. After a few minutes I set off, stooping and clutching at the rocky protuberances; and when the tunnel closed in to the dimensions of a tube, I crawled through as quickly as possible. The moment I emerged into the wider walls I had a fit of coughing. My cough echoed around me and, as it seemed, a short distance ahead. My cough subsided a little but the echoes from the interior seemed stronger and more frequent than my cough itself. I held my breath for a few seconds; and hearing a choking cough approach me, I knew it was not an echo. At that moment I saw the light of a flashlamp casting a weak pink glow. I flashed my stronger torch in that direction, and saw Tom Wells stumbling and slithering towards me. I turned to make my escape the way I had come. His voice, spluttered with coughs, followed me: 'Don't move or I'll shoot. Don't move there.' The cave coughed and echoed his words: 'Don't move there. There, there, there.' I put out my torch and, crouching low, I pressed sideways against the wall. His flashlamp found me as he approached. He held it in his left hand, while his right hand was poised, as I thought, with the pistol.

'Where's that book?'

'What book?'

'Your diary.'

'You burnt it. You told me so.'

My eye was on his right hand. By the dim light of his weak torch I saw that he was holding a knife, not a revolver.

'I took your tip,' he said. 'Guns make too much noise.'

I flashed on my light. He blinked, and while he did so I bashed the flashlamp hard into the pit of his stomach. He cried, slipped and fell backwards.

I crawled back through the terrible hole, emerging to stumble along towards the air, clutching carelessly at rock ledges, so that my hands and arms were torn. When at last I came out of the cave the mist had fallen. I took refuge in a shallow crater, and lay there for about twenty minutes, not caring that the mist was pouring over me. Presently I pulled myself stiffly out of the crater and made my way to the deserted mill. There I spent the night, for the fog was too thick to permit my finding my way to the house. I spent most of the night listening fitfully for a sound and watching the dense air fearfully from the broken windows. Eventually I fell asleep on the soaking floor.

It must have been about six in the morning when I heard a sound. The mist was unfurling and the sun had risen. Light footsteps came round from the back of the house. I was getting ready to run for it when Miguel appeared.

He said, 'Mr Tom has got a bad cold. He got lost in the mist. He fell and hurt his head.'

'Is he in the house?'

'Yes. He came home this morning early. He fell and hurt himself.'

'What are you doing here?'

'I came to look for you. Jimmie has been to the Furnace to look for you.'

'Is Jimmie at home now?'

'Yes. He's looking after Mr Tom. Mr Tom is sitting out in the sun with his feet up.'

'You are sure Jimmie is in the house?'

'Naturally,' said Miguel in the accents of his idol.

'All right, I'll come with you.'

He made to set off in the direction of the tunnel.

'No,' I said, 'I'd rather not go home that way.'

'It's quicker,' said Miguel.

'This way's nice,' I said.

'I like that way,' said Miguel.

'You go that way,' I said, 'and I'll go this.'

But he decided to accompany me, and on the way he chatted about how Mr Tom's ribs were better, because last night he had taken a walk. 'And I showed him,' said Miguel, 'the secret tunnel at the beach, and he went in all by himself. But afterwards he got lost in the mist.'

Jimmie was in the kitchen, mixing rum with hot water and sugar.

'Ah,' said Jimmie, 'I lose my nerves that you have been lost. Where have you lodged?'

I said, 'At the mill.'

'You lose your way?' said Jimmie. 'We are in great desolation that you are endangered last night from the mist.'

'Wells came after me with a knife,' I said.

'Is not so!' said Jimmie.

'It's true,' I said. 'I believe he would have killed me if I hadn't pushed him over and got away.'

I sat down and started to cry.

Jimmie said, 'Is to go too far. I am a man of patience but is to go too far. I attend to this Wells for you.'

He tasted the rum posset and seemed to approve of it. Then he carried it out to the patio where Tom Wells was sitting in the sun, nursing himself among a lot of garments. I stood by the door and watched him take the drinks over to Wells. He threw the drink in Wells's face. Then he took from his pocket the baby Browning and pointed it at Wells's head.

'Jimmie!' I shouted. 'Don't shoot at his head!'

He pressed the trigger. Nothing happened, not even a click. He pressed the trigger again and again, looking angrily at the gun, giving no attention to its aim.

Wells so far overcame his surprise as to throw off the coats in which he was swaddled. The rum was still running down his face when he saw that Jimmie's pistol was not working. He swiped at Jimmie and got him above the eye. Jimmie threw down the pistol and hit him back; it was a dreadful thud on the mouth, and blood began to run down Wells's shirt. I wish I knew the technical terms for fights; for, thinking it over afterwards, this between Wells and Jimmie seemed to me rather professional. Jimmie hit fast, one hand after the other. Wells was slow, but more powerful. I retrieved the automatic from the ground. I think I had the feeling that the violence might set it off. I glanced at it, and saw that the safety-catch was still on.

Wells had been knocked over. He rose, shook his head violently, and faced Jimmie again, in readiness. Jimmie was beginning to look glaze-eyed and exhausted when Miguel came running on to the patio with a very strange look. He seemed not to notice the fight, and ran up to the two breathless heaving men.

'Out of the way, boy,' said Wells.

But Miguel was already tugging his arm, and Wells seemed glad of the pause.

'What's the matter, child?' he said.

Miguel's eyes were round and startled.

'Robinson is looking at the memorial,' he said.

'What's that you say?' said Wells.

'What is?' said Jimmie.

Miguel pointed towards the mustard field. Even from my place by the door I could see a man's figure stooping, with his hands on his knees, to read the words on Robinson's memorial. He straightened up and started walking slowly up to the house. Thinner and more weary than before, he was none the less unmistakably Robinson.

XI

JIMMIE HAD TO TAKE THE BOTTLES out of the crates where they were stacked in the storehouse for shipment. All the bottles went back into the cellar. Slowly, and by request, Tom Wells rendered up the key of the armoury, three boxes of cigars, two shirts, a camera, the *Shorter Oxford English Dictionary*, a pair of ormulu vases, a Bible, and other surprising objects which lay in the packing case he had prepared to take away with him. All that week Robinson went about inquiring after his goods: where was this and that? And he sat in his study like a potentate receiving tribute as his possessions came flowing back to him. Jimmie gave back the will. I had Robinson's fat fountain-pen. He asked for that, of course.

He did not appear at all to see why he should explain his disappearance. As soon as I realized that he had gone by his own choice, my fury rose.

'You might have thought of Miguel. It was a mean trick to play on Miguel. It made him ill,' I said, three or perhaps four times during our last week on the island.

Robinson would sigh, 'One can only act according to one's capacity,' or 'Miguel is to go to school in any case. He has to leave me. It will be less difficult now.'

Once he said, 'Yours is, of course, the obvious view. Well, my actions are beyond the obvious range. It surely needs only that you should realize this, not that you should understand my actions.'

I replied, 'I chucked the antinomian pose when I was twenty. There's no such thing as a private morality.'

'Not for you. But for me, living on an island – I have a system.'

On another occasion he said, 'Normally, my life is regulated, it is a system. It was disrupted by your arrival.'

'Any system,' I said, 'which doesn't allow for the unexpected and the unwelcome is a rotten one.'

At last he said, 'Things mount up inside one, and then one has to perpetrate an outrage.'

Owing to the strangeness of our predicament, the touchiness of our minds, the qualities of the island, and perhaps the shock of our plane accident, we did not for a moment suspect what had really happened. The blood was lying about everywhere. Our minds were on the blood.

When I think of Robinson now, I think of him as a selfish but well-meaning eccentric, but during our last week on the island I felt violently against him: one, because he went about with a lofty air; two, as a reaction against my romantic conception of him when I had thought him dead; and, three, because I had caught a heavy cold on the night I had spent in the old mill. I thought, noble heretic indeed. But really, after all, it was his island, and he probably, at the start, had saved our lives.

Tom Wells, with his face and eyes bruised from the fight, took to bed the day Robinson returned, and stayed there all week. Robinson attempted to commission me to look after him. I refused. 'He might catch my cold.'

'Is humorous,' Jimmie pointed out.

Robinson showed little interest when Jimmie and I gave him a graphic account of our ordeals. Our story was illustrated by Jimmie's black eye and my hands which had been cut and scratched in the tunnel.

Robinson said, 'It was only to be expected.'

Once he said to me, 'Wells is complaining of stomach trouble through living on tinned food. That's your fault for depriving him of wildfowl and rabbit. You ought not to have locked up the guns.'

I said, 'We caught some fish.'

He said, 'That's insufficient diet for a man like Wells.'

'He would never have stirred himself to go shooting game.'

'Jimmie might have done so.'

'Jimmie knows nothing about guns.'

Then I noticed that Robinson was laughing silently to himself.

'Tom Wells nearly killed me,' I said.

'That would not have been serious for you,' he said. 'You've got to die sometime.'

I felt there was a flaw in this argument, but because of my cold in the head I simply could not think how to refute it with dignity on the spot. Instead, I took another line: 'It would have been serious for Wells.'

'Yes, it would have been serious for Wells,' he said.

'And for me too,' I said then, 'for I'm not ready to die yet.'

Robinson would not be drawn into telling where he had concealed himself. When Jimmie told him of our long search he assumed the air of a triumphant schoolmistress.

Bit by bit we got the story out of Miguel, whose manner with Robinson was now rather restrained, and to whom Robinson, in the hope of regaining his confidence, had given an account of his late whereabouts.

A few weeks before his disappearance he had planned to leave us; he began to lay up stores for himself in the old smugglers' storehouse, of which he had told us, the cave called The Market. The last of these stores were conveyed from the house at the time when, some of our food having gone bad, he and Jimmie had made up packages for the Furnace. He managed to bamboozle Jimmie, which did not surprise me, and got some good stores away without suspicion.

The Market, lying among the sheer cliffs on the west coast of the South Arm, was quite inaccessible from the island.

'Have you ever seen The Market?' I asked Miguel.

'No, naturally.'

'How did Robinson get there with all his stores?'

'He took the little boat.'

A few days before Robinson's disappearance, he had been mending this boat with the aid of Jimmie.

'Did Robinson often go to The Market in the boat?'

'No, naturally. It's dangerous among the rocks, with a little boat.'

'I think I want my head examined,' Jimmie said, 'as I have assisted Robinson to mend this boat.'

'Yes,' I said, 'why didn't we think of the boat?'

'We were taking thought for the blood,' Jimmie said.

It was the blood which gave me to think of the well of darkness in Robinson's character. Of course, it was amusing in a sense, his having led the goat to the mountain, fired the shot for all to hear, without shooting the goat. He cut its throat a few days later in the mustard field, during the night of the second of July, had soaked in its blood everything he could lay hands on, and, dragging the carcass to the Furnace, had scattered the bloody evidence all along the path. I pictured how he had plastered goat's blood over our clothes, carefully omitting those of Tom Wells and Miguel. I could not deny the comic element, at the same time as I could not help thinking, There is something vicious in him. What urged him to make such a display of blood? Why? What bloody delight was satisfied?

Once, in my presence, Ian Brodie telephoned to Curly Lonsdale to tell him, confidentially, that Julia had cancer of the womb. I knew that Julia had been rather unwell, but this was the first I had heard of cancer. I gasped, and looked at Agnes. She was sitting fatly in the chair, giggling quietly to herself. Agnes always abetted her husband in his practical jokes, as unconscious of her motives in this as she was in her habit of giving Ian for birthdays and Christmas photographic books of 'art studies' – that is, representations of nude girls, and making no secret of it, for wasn't it art?

'Nothing much,' Ian Brodie said into the telephone, 'to worry about, only cancer of the womb.' I thought, 'What's Julia to him? What cancer of the soul is venting itself?'

All through that week Jimmie continued to press garrulously upon Robinson the details of what had occurred during his absence. Robinson would usually reply, 'It was only to be expected.' I found this phrase unendurable with its implication that he had foreseen all the consequences of his action to the last detail, and that he more or less held the wires that made us move.

Towards the end of the week I said to Robinson, 'I believe Tom Wells is a professional blackmailer.'

'You are full of suspicions,' he said.

'What about his trying to blackmail Jimmie and me?' I said.

'That does not prove him a professional.'

'I think those documents he missed from his bag were to do with blackmail.'

'In fact,' said Robinson, 'they were obscene photographs. I burnt them.'

'He's a criminal type,' I said.

'You are full of suspicions. You thought he had murdered me, and you were wrong.'

'Not far wrong. He tried to kill me.'

'It was only to be expected.'

I turned on him. I said, 'What do you mean, it was only to be expected.'

He sighed, and I could have thrown something at him for it.

'Generally,' he said, 'people act in this way. Human nature does not vary much. It was to be expected that a man like Wells would turn a situation to his own interests. It was to be expected that a woman like you would, in the circumstances, withdraw very rapidly from a man like Jimmie.'

'That was the reason!' I said.

He looked troubled. 'What reason for what?'

'Your reason for arranging this farce – it was to separate Jimmie and me. You need not have bothered, I'm quite capable of judging for myself – '

'I don't want you to think – I mean, you never know where these things may lead.'

'It would never do,' I said, 'to keep a disorderly island.'

He said, 'I don't want you to think that I had nothing else in mind but your relationship with Jimmie when I decided to leave. Motives are seldom simple. I find no call upon me to go into my motives. Of course, you are annoyed. It is only to be expected.'

I said, 'I have taught the child the rosary.'

He said, 'I didn't think you would do that.'

I said, 'It was only to be expected. I made a very nice rosary for him from the amber beads among the salvage.'

'The salvage is not your property,' he said helplessly.

'There was no one to guard the salvage and so I helped myself. It was only to be – '

'Miguel's religion was not your business,' he said.

'True,' I said, 'it was yours. But I charge no fee.'

'Did you do this to revenge yourself in some way? What exactly was your reason? That you wanted to gain influence over the boy? Was it to feed your possessive instincts? Some unconscious urge? Was it – '

'I see no call to tear myself to bits over motives,' I said. 'They are never simple. I am happy to say I have taught the child the rosary.'

'What else have you taught him? Have you put something against me into his mind? He has been strange with me since my return.'

'You are full of suspicions,' I said.

'Miguel is not the same,' he said.

'If you choose to depart in a sudden shower of blood, leaving him with strangers, he will of course have reservations on your return. It is only to be expected.'

'He will forget the rosary,' said Robinson, 'in time.'

I said, 'He wants to go to a Catholic school.'

'You have been really hostile to my intentions,' Robinson said.

'In fact,' I said, 'it was Jimmie who put the idea into his head.' This was true. Often, in the course of entertaining Miguel with stories about his schooldays in a priory, Jimmie had advised, 'Is best to go to a Catholic school. Is more strict and terrible than any other, and in consequence is more delight and joy to infringe the rules.'

'I shall be glad,' said Robinson, 'to see the pomegranate boat.'

On the late afternoon of Sunday, the eighth of August, the pomegranate men spilt ashore. It was strange to see so many people, to hear so many voices, and all talking at once. They were highly intrigued and puzzled by the memorial, which Robinson had refused to let Jimmie dismantle.

I had vaguely imagined that the pomegranate boat would take us aboard and set off with us. Instead, they sent wireless messages, and early next morning three planes circled the island, dipped low and disappeared. Another plane arrived. Robinson sent up his kite from the flat pastureland of the West Leg, and there, as the plane made to land, Robinson drew it in again, like a fluttering red bird coming wearily to roost.

Robinson handed to Tom Wells a cardboard box which, it transpired, contained his lucky charms. 'Thanks a lot,' said Wells. He was grinning to right and left. He grimaced at me, 'I hope we're going to let bygones be bygones.' I stooped to stroke the cat.

My journal, which Miguel had retrieved from the tunnel and which was still wrapped in the piece of Robinson's waterproof, was my only luggage.

Before we left, Robinson asked me if I would like to take the cat home with me. I half-thought this was an ironic question, since Bluebell now took hardly any notice of Robinson. But he went on to explain that he would be leaving the island for a few weeks with the pomegranate boat, in order to take Miguel to school. He could not leave the cat on the island, and the pomegranate boat was already equipped with a cat. He would be obliged if I would accept the gift of Bluebell if I didn't mind waiting for the period of quarantine.

He also gave me a print of the photograph of the stream gushing from the cactus, which he had taken on the mountain.

XII

I STARED AT WHAT JULIA was carrying. She became aware of my attention; then, embarrassed by a sudden recollection, tucked it away under her arm. It was my real crocodile leather handbag, left to me by my grandmother.

'Of course, you understand, your house is up for sale,' said Agnes.

Curly's car splashed through the downpour, carrying us from the airport. 'Take it from me, she doesn't want to talk business now,' said Curly.

I sat between Brian and Julia at the back. Julia whispered, 'We would have had a lot of business trouble with your affairs. I've had a lot of trouble with Agnes. It was foolish of you to die intestate. You'd better make a will in case it happens again.'

Brian fairly rocked.

'What's the joke back there?' said Curly.

I said, 'Julia wants me to make a will.'

'So you should,' said Agnes.

'In the name of God,' said Curly, 'can't you talk about something more cheerful? This is an occasion, it's an occasion.'

Tom Wells gave the exclusive story to a Sunday paper the following week, whether in his own words or not makes little difference.

172

What's it like to be an island castaway? To come face to face with the Alone? ... To endure the agony of loneliness, knowing that the folks at home have given up hope? ...

A Family Man

Mind you, it was hard work to keep alive. *It was a constant contest with Nature and Death.* ... My one thought was for my wife. ... Jan was the only woman among us three men, and naturally there might have been some awkward situations. I'm a family man myself. But I saw to it from the start that *the strictest proprieties were observed.* Nights, it was oh so lonely ...

True Comradeship

Those three months were stark, grim, challenging, but I wouldn't have missed them for worlds. *I never knew what true comradeship was till I lived on that island.* Everyone pulled his or her weight. ...

That Lucky Charm. ...

I happened to have on me a lucky charm, just a tiny metal object of ancient Druid design. It's my firm conviction that *I owe it to that lucky charm.* ...

We never had a moment's disagreement. ...

Of course, it was a strain on Jan's nerves, but she was a brick. ...

Would that I were, I thought, and I would hurl myself at his fat head.

I was staying with Julia and Curly until my house should be put to rights again. I wondered how ever I could have thought of Tom Wells bearing any likeness to Curly. And the facial resemblance now seemed to me superficial – Curly had a way of opening out his face expectantly to the world, which might be difficult to live with all the time, but differed from Tom Wells's open-mouthed regard, so like that of a dew-lapped dog forever wanting a drink.

'I suppose you'll want to sleep late in the mornings?' Julia had inquired dolefully.

'Naturally, naturally,' said Curly. 'After what she's been through she's got to take it easy.'

And when he paddled upstairs with my breakfast tray every morning, and when I heard his voice at the street door discouraging the reporters with terse unprintable phrases, I thought him the kindest of all my relatives.

'Alas, is never that I have luck with the English ladies,' Jimmie had said while we waited for our separate planes in the hotel at Lisbon. 'In the time of the end of the hostilities I have fallen in love with an English lady who is driving the car of a colonel in France. This lady is of noble blood, and she has declared to me, "I am not yet old enough to marry without the permission of my pa, but I go on leave to my home and I tell of you to Pa. Mayhaps he should desire to meet you, and lo! he shall permit the marriage." Now I say to this lady, "What is about the ma?" and she has replied, "Ma has married to another; is necessary only to fix Pa." Alas, then this lady departs to England, and she is writing to me most woeful because the faulty old pa has the plan for his daughter to marry a great lord or mayhaps an American. Then lo! I have a visitor. Is the brother of my lady love, a captain of the English Army. He has declared to me, "Behold, is five hundred pounds, and you bloody well lay off the girl."'

Jimmie sat back in his chair and despondently sipped his brandy and soda. 'Is never any luck with English girls. Is my destiny,' he concluded.

'What happened about this girl? Did you see her again?'

'Never. From that day I cease to write letters to that lady.'

'Did you refuse the five hundred?'

'No, no; on the contrary, I settle for six hundred and fifty. This cash is necessary for my expenses along about that time.'

'Many a man,' I said admiringly, 'would have taken the money *and* the girl.'

'Is to go too far. I am a man of honour,' said Jimmie, 'wherefore is mayhaps the reason that I do not have luck with English ladies.'

'I should think,' said Ian Brodie, 'you were in your element with three men dancing round you, and no other woman around.'

'It was delightful,' I said.

'Nice chaps, were they?'

'Charming.'

'This Robinson seems a peculiar sort, living like that on an island. I don't like the sound of *him*.'

'He was delightful,' I said.

'Oh, was he?'

'Yes, charming.'

'There was a young boy. Supposed to be adopted.'

'Yes, charming.'

'It must have been awkward, all living together like that.'

'It was delightful,' I said, 'it was charming.'

'Well,' he said, 'it's rather embarrassing for me, you know, when people ask what happened.'

'Don't they read the papers?'

'There's always a lot more behind these things – people want to know what really happened.'

'Oh, it was really, tell them, all delightful and charming.'

'What I can't understand is why Brian preferred to stay with the Lonsdales. . . . '

Gradually most of my possessions were returned to me. Sometimes I wondered what happened to my six pairs of nylons. Agnes returned two pairs of gloves. Ian Brodie had already sold some of my books.

Green-eyed Bluebell came out of quarantine within six months. After the first two lessons her memory of ping-pong returned. By this time I was once more settled in Chelsea.

One day, when Brian was telling me how news of the plane crash had arrived, and how, after a week, we were despaired of, he remarked, with his slightly alarming sophistication, 'It's difficult for the young, those without experience of life, to realize death.'

In the autumn of 1955 I read, under the title 'Island Man in Dock,' the case of Tom Wells which was heard at the Old Bailey. He was described as the director of Luck Unlimited Ltd, a firm of wholesalers dealing in lucky charms and medals, and as proprietor of the monthly magazine *Your Future*. Charged with uttering letters of blackmail against an unnamed couple, he pleaded guilty, and asked for twenty-three other charges to be taken into consideration. Plus two more, I thought.

The defending counsel recalled that Mr Wells had undergone a severe nervous strain after a plane crash in which he had sustained serious injuries, and was subsequently exiled on a desert island, where, for three months, he endured pain, hunger and thirst. Mr Wells's business affairs had suffered a severe set-back during his absence and since his return he had also had domestic troubles. Throughout the past twenty years, and in the course of his editorship of *Your Future*, involving a large correspondence of an intimate nature, Mr Wells had given valuable advice and brought comfort to many thousands. Bearing these factors in mind, it was hoped that a lenient view would be taken of Mr Wells's having yielded to the more than usual temptations with which his work presented him.

The prosecution said it was one of the nastiest cases ever to come before those courts. 'In any sense – *nasty*.' Over a period of ten years – stretching back, that was, to a period long preceding his escape from the plane disaster – the accused had been extorting money from men and women who had, in their innocence, confided their most cherished secrets, the deepest anguish of their souls, to Wells. Operating under the name of Dr Benignus, Wells had solicited such confidences through the columns of his paper. The court would agree that *benign* was the very last word one could apply . . .

He got seven years. Two of his associates, a woman secretary charged with aiding and abetting, and a man, said to be in the pay of Wells, charged with trespassing with intent to intimidate, got three and five years respectively.

I supposed that only Miguel would be sorry.

Next spring I learned from a news paragraph in an evening paper that the island was sinking.

'Robinson', the tiny man-shaped Atlantic island owned by the recluse Mr M. M. Robinson, is sinking, say experts.

Within three years, it is estimated, the topmost point of the 3,000-ft. mountain will disappear under the sea. Already the sea level has risen over twenty feet, and a strip of white beach on the south coast, which was the pride of the island, is now under water. The event is explained by volcanic action.

Mr Robinson is already making plans for evacuation.

It will be recalled that a plane bound for the Azores crashed on 'Robinson' in May 1954, the survivors of which . . .

In a sense I had already come to think of the island as a place of the mind. I opened up once more the blue exercise book wrapped in the square from Robinson's waterproof, still smelling so of sulphur that for a moment I was crawling again in the cave with the parcel between my teeth.

It is now, indeed, an apocryphal island. It may be a trick of the mind to sink one's past fear and exasperation in the waters of memory; it may be a truth of the mind.

From time to time since I read this news I have pictured Robinson wearily moving his possessions on to some boat bound for some other isolation. I have thought greedily of the books. And of Miguel, wondering if they think him backward at his school in Lisbon.

And now, perhaps it is because the island is passing out of sight that it rises so high in my thoughts. Even while the journal brings before me the events of which I have written, they are transformed, there is undoubtedly a sea-change, so that the island resembles a locality of childhood, both dangerous and lyrical. I have impressions of the island of which I have not told you, and could not entirely if I had a hundred tongues – the mustard field staring at me with its yellow eye, the blue and green lake seeing in me a hard turquoise stone, the goat's blood observing me red, guilty, all red. And sometimes when I am walking down the King's Road or sipping my espresso in the morning – feeling, not old exactly, but fussy and adult – and chance to remember the island, immediately all things are possible.

The
Abbess
of
Crewe

Come let us mock at the great
That had such burdens on the mind
And toiled so hard and late
To leave some monument behind,
Nor thought of the levelling wind . . .
Mock mockers after that
That would not lift a hand maybe
To help good, wise or great
To bar that foul storm out, for we
Traffic in mockery.

From W. B. Yeats,
'Nineteen Hundred and Nineteen'

I

'WHAT IS WRONG, SISTER WINIFREDE,' says the Abbess, clear and loud to the receptive air, 'with the traditional keyhole method?'

Sister Winifrede says, in her whine of bewilderment, that voice of the very stupid, the mind where no dawn breaks, 'But, Lady Abbess, we discussed right from the start – '

'Silence!' says the Abbess. 'We observe silence, now, and meditate.' She looks at the tall poplars of the avenue where they walk, as if the trees are listening. The poplars cast their shadows in the autumn afternoon's end, and the shadows lie in regular still file across the pathway like a congregation of prostrate nuns of the Old Order. The Abbess of Crewe, soaring in her slender height, a very Lombardy poplar herself, moving by Sister Winifrede's side, turns her pale eyes to the gravel walk where their four black shoes tread, tread and tread, two at a time, till they come to the end of this corridor of meditation lined by the secret police of poplars.

Out in the clear, on the open lawn, two men in dark police uniform pass them, with two Alsatian dogs pulling at their short leads. The men look straight ahead as the nuns go by with equal disregard.

After a while, out there on the open lawn, the Abbess speaks again. Her face is a white-skinned English skull, beautiful in the frame of her white nun's coif. She is forty-two in her own age with fourteen generations of pale and ruling ancestors of England, and ten before them of France, carved also into the bones of her wonderful head. 'Sister Winifrede,' she now says, 'whatever is spoken in the avenue of meditation goes on the record. You've been told several times. Won't you ever learn?'

Sister Winifrede stops walking and tries to think. She strokes her black habit and clutches the rosary beads that hang from her girdle. Strangely, she is as tall as the Abbess, but never will she be a steeple or a tower, but a British matron in spite of her coif and her vows, and that great carnal chastity which fills her passing days. She stops walking, there on the lawn; Winifrede, land of the midnight sun, looks at the Abbess, and presently that little sun, the disc of light and its aurora, appears in her brain like a miracle. 'You mean, Lady Abbess,' she says, 'that you've even bugged the poplars?'

'The trees of course are bugged,' says the Abbess. 'How else can we operate now that the scandal rages outside the walls? And now that you know this you do not know it so to speak. We have our security to consider, and I'm the only arbiter of what it consists of, witness the Rule of St Benedict. I'm your conscience and your authority. You perform my will and finish.'

'But we're something rather more than merely Benedictines, though, aren't we?' says Sister Winifrede in dark naïvety. 'The Jesuits – '

'Sister Winifrede,' says the Abbess in her tone of lofty calm, 'there's a scandal going on, and you're in it up to the neck whether you like it or not. The Ancient Rule obtains when I say it does. The Jesuits are for Jesuitry when I say it is so.'

A bell rings from the chapel ahead. It is six o'clock of the sweet autumnal evening. 'In we go to Vespers whether you like it or whether you don't.'

'But I love the Office of Vespers. I love all the Hours of the Divine Office,' Winifrede says in her blurting voice, indignant as any common Christian's, a singsong lament of total misunderstanding.

The ladies walk, stately and tall, but the Abbess like a tower of ivory, Winifrede like a handsome hostess or businessman's wife and a fair weekend tennis player, given the chance.

'The chapel has not been bugged,' remarks the Lady Abbess as they walk. 'And the confessionals, never. Strange as it may seem, I thought well to omit any arrangement for the confessionals, at least, so far.'

The Lady Abbess is robed in white, Winifrede in black. The other black-habited sisters file into the chapel behind them, and the Office of Vespers begins.

The Abbess stands in her high place in the choir, white among the black. Twice a day she changes her habit. What a piece of work is her convent, how distant its newness from all the orthodoxies of the past, how far removed in its antiquities from those of the present! 'It's the only way,' she once said, this Alexandra, the noble Lady Abbess, 'to find an answer always ready to hand for any adverse criticism whatsoever.'

As for the Jesuits, there is no Order of women Jesuits. There is nothing at all on paper to reveal the mighty pact between the Abbey of Crewe and the Jesuit hierarchy, the overriding and most profitable pact. What Jesuits know of it but the few?

As for the Benedictines, so closely does the Abbess follow and insist upon the ancient and rigid Rule that the Benedictines proper have watched with amazement, too ladylike, both monks and nuns, to protest how the Lady Abbess ignores the latest reforms, rules her house as if the Vatican Council had never been; and yet have marvelled that such a great and so Benedictine a lady should have brought her strictly enclosed establishment to the point of an international newspaper scandal. How did it start off without so much as a hint of that old cause, sexual impropriety, but merely from the little misplacement, or at most the theft, of Sister Felicity's silver thimble? How will it all end?

'In these days,' the Abbess had said to her closest nuns, 'we must form new monastic combines. The ages of the Father and of the Son are past. We have entered the age of the Holy Ghost. The wind bloweth where it listeth and it listeth most certainly on the Abbey of Crewe. I am a Benedictine with the Benedictines, a Jesuit with the Jesuits. I was elected Abbess and I stay the Abbess and I move as the Spirit moves me.'

Stretching out like the sea, the voices chant the Gregorian rhythm of the Vespers. Behind the Abbess, the stained-glass window darkens with a shadow, and the outline of a man climbing up to the window from the outside forms against the blue and the yellow of the glass. What does it matter, another reporter trying to find his way into the convent or another photographer as it might be? By now the scandal occupies the whole of the outside world, and the people of the press, after all, have to make a living. Anyway, he will not get into the chapel. The nuns continue their solemn chant while a faint grumble of voices outside the window faintly penetrates the chapel for a few moments. The police dogs start to bark, one picking up from the other in a loud litany of their own. Presently their noises stop and evidently the guards have appeared to investigate the intruder. The shadow behind the window disappears hastily.

These nuns sing loudly their versicles and responses, their antiphons:

Tremble, O earth, at the presence of the Lord; at the presence of the God of Jacob

Who turned the rock into pools of water: and the strong
hills into fountains of water.
Not to us, O Lord, not to us, but to thy name, give glory:
because of thy mercy and thy faithfulness.

But the Abbess is known to prefer the Latin. It is said that she
sometimes sings the Latin version at the same time as the congregation chants the new reformed English. Her high place is
too far from the choir for the nuns to hear her voice except
when she sings a solo part. This evening at Vespers her lips
move with the others but discernibly at variance. The Lady
Abbess, it is assumed, prays her canticles in Latin tonight.

She sits apart, facing the nuns, white before the altar.
Stretching before her footstool are the green marble slabs, the
grey slabs of the sisters buried there. Hildegarde lies there;
Ignatia lies there; who will be next?

The Abbess moves her lips in song. In reality she is chanting English, not Latin; she is singing her own canticle, not
the vespers for Sunday. She looks at the file of tombs and,
thinking of who knows which occupant, past or to come, she
softly chants:

Thy beauty shall no more be found,
Nor, in thy marble vault, shall sound
My echoing song; then worms shall try
That long-preserved virginity . . .

The cloud of nuns lift their white faces to record before the
angels the final antiphon:

But our God is in heaven:
he has done all that he wished.

'Amen,' responds the Abbess, clear as light.

Outside in the grounds the dogs prowl and the guards patrol silently. The Abbess leads the way from the chapel to the house in the blue dusk. The nuns, high nuns, low nuns, choir nuns, novices and nobodies, fifty in all, follow two by two in hierarchical order, the Prioress and the Novice Mistress at the heels of the Abbess and at the end of the faceless line the meek novices.

'Walburga,' says the Abbess, half-turning towards the Prioress who walks behind her right arm; 'Mildred,' she says, turning to the Novice Mistress on her left, 'go and rest now because I have to see you both together between the Offices of Matins and Lauds.'

Matins is sung at midnight. The Office of Lauds, which few convents now continue to celebrate at three in the morning, is none the less observed at the Abbey of Crewe at that old traditional time. Between Matins and Lauds falls the favourite time for the Abbess to confer with her nearest nuns. Walburga and Mildred murmur their assent to the late-night appointment, bowing low to the lofty Abbess, tall spire that she is.

The congregation is at supper. Again the dogs are howling outside. The seven o'clock news is on throughout the kingdom and if only the ordinary nuns had a wireless or a television set they would be hearing the latest developments in the Crewe Abbey scandal. As it is, these nuns who have never left the Abbey of Crewe since the day they entered it are silent with their fish pie at the refectory table while a senior nun stands at the corner lectern reading aloud to them. Her voice is nasal, with a haughty twang of the hunting country stock from which she and her high-coloured complexion have at one time disengaged themselves. She stands stockily, remote from the words as she half-intones them. She is reading from the great and ancient Rule of St Benedict, enumerating the instruments of good works:

To fear the day of judgement.

To be in dread of hell.

To yearn for eternal life with all the longing of our soul.

To keep the possibility of death every day before our eyes.

To keep a continual watch on what we are doing with our life.

In every place to know for certain that God is looking at us.

When evil thoughts come into our head, to dash them at once on Christ, and open them up to our spiritual father.

To keep our mouth from bad and low talk.

Not to be fond of talking.

Not to say what is idle or causes laughter.

Not to be fond of frequent or boisterous laughter.

To listen willingly to holy reading.

The forks make tiny clinks on the plates moving bits of fish pie into the mouths of the community at the table. The reader toils on . . .

Not to gratify the desires of the flesh.

To hate our own will.

To obey the commands of the Abbess in everything, even though she herself should unfortunately act otherwise, remembering the Lord's command: 'Practise and observe what they tell you, but not what they do.' – Gospel of St Matthew, 23.

At the table the low nuns, high nuns and novices alike raise water to their lips and so does the reader. She replaces her glass . . .

Where there has been a quarrel, to make peace before
    sunset.

Quietly, the reader closes the book on the lectern and
opens another that is set by its side. She continues her
incantations:

A frequency is the number of times a periodic phenome-
    non repeats itself in unit time.
For electromagnetic waves the frequency is expressed in
    cycles per second or, for the higher frequencies, in kilo-
    cycles per second or megacycles per second.
A frequency deviation is the difference between the maxi-
    mum instantaneous frequency and the constant carrier
    frequency of a frequency-modulated radio transmis-
    sion.
Systems of recording sound come in the form of variations
    of magnetization along a continuous tape of, or coated
    with, or impregnated with, ferro-magnetic material.
In recording, the tape is drawn at constant speed through
    the airgap of an electromagnet energized by the audio-
    frequency current derived from a microphone.
Here endeth the reading. *Deo gratias.*

'Amen,' responds the refectory of nuns.
    'Sisters, be sober, be vigilant, for the Devil goes about as a
raging lion, seeking whom he may devour.'
    'Amen.'

The Abbess of Crewe's parlour glows with bright ornaments
and brightest of all is a two-foot statue of the Infant of Prague.
The Infant is adorned with its traditional robes, the episcopal
crown and vestments embedded with such large and so many

rich and gleaming jewels it would seem they could not possibly be real. However, they are real.

The Sisters, Mildred the Novice Mistress and Walburga the Prioress, sit with the Abbess. It is one o'clock in the morning. Lauds will be sung at three, when the congregation arises from sleep, as in the very old days, to observe the three-hourly ritual.

'Of course it's out of date,' the Abbess had said to her two senior nuns when she began to reform the Abbey with the winsome approval of the late Abbess Hildegarde. 'It is absurd in modern times that the nuns should have to get up twice in the middle of the night to sing the Matins and the Lauds. But modern times come into a historical context, and as far as I'm concerned history doesn't work. Here, in the Abbey of Crewe, we have discarded history. We have entered the sphere, dear Sisters, of mythology. My nuns love it. Who doesn't yearn to be part of a myth at whatever the price in comfort? The monastic system is in revolt throughout the rest of the world, thanks to historical development. Here, within the ambience of mythology, we have consummate satisfaction, we have peace.'

More than two years have passed since this state of peace was proclaimed. The Abbess sits in her silk-covered chair, now, between Matins and Lauds, having freshly changed her white robes. Before her sit the two black senior sisters while she speaks of what she has just seen on the television, tonight's news, and of that Sister Felicity we have all heard about, who has lately fled the Abbey of Crewe to join her Jesuit lover and to tell her familiar story to the entranced world.

'Felicity,' says the Abbess to her two faithful nuns, 'has now publicly announced her conviction that we have eavesdropping devices planted throughout our property. She's demanding a commission of inquiry by Scotland Yard.'

'She was on the television again tonight?' says Mildred.

'Yes, with her insufferable charisma. She said she forgives us all, every one, but still she considers as a matter of principle that there should be a police inquiry.'

'But she has no proof,' says Walburga the Prioress.

'Someone leaked the story to the evening papers,' says the Abbess, 'and they immediately got Felicity on the television.'

'Who could have leaked it?' says Walburga, her hands folded on her lap, immovable.

'Her lax and leaky Jesuit, I dare say,' the Abbess says, the skin of her face gleaming like a pearl, and her fresh, white robes falling about her to the floor. 'That Thomas,' says the Abbess, 'who tumbles Felicity.'

'Well, someone leaked it to Thomas,' says Mildred, 'and that could only be one of the three of us here, or Sister Winifrede. I suggest it must be Winifrede, the benighted clot, who's been talking.'

'Undoubtedly,' says Walburga, 'but why?'

' "Why?" is a fastidious question at any time,' says the Abbess. 'When applied to any action of Winifrede's the word "why" is the inscrutable ingredient of a brown stew. I have plans for Winifrede.'

'She was certainly instructed in the doctrine and official version that our electronic arrangements are merely laboratorial equipment for the training of our novices and nuns to meet the challenge of modern times,' Sister Mildred says.

'The late Abbess Hildegarde, may she rest in peace,' says Walburga, 'was out of her mind to admit Winifrede as a postulant, far less admit her to the veil.'

But the living Abbess of Crewe is saying, 'Be that as it may, Winifrede is in it up to the neck, and the scandal stops at Winifrede.'

'Amen,' say the two black nuns. The Abbess reaches out to the Infant of Prague and touches with the tip of her finger a ruby embedded in its vestments. After a space she speaks: 'The motorway from London to Crewe is jammed with reporters, according to the news. The A51 is a solid mass of vehicles. In the midst of the strikes and the oil crises.'

'I hope the police are in force at the gates,' Mildred says.

'The police are in force,' the Abbess says. 'I was firm with the Home Office.'

'There are long articles in this week's *Time* and *Newsweek*,' Walburga says. 'They give four pages apiece to Britain's national scandal of the nuns. They print Felicity's picture.'

'What are they saying?' says the Abbess.

'*Time* compares our public to Nero who fiddled while Rome burned. *Newsweek* recalls that it was a similar attitude of British frivolity and neglect of her national interests that led to the American Declaration of Independence. They make much of the affair of Sister Felicity's thimble at the time of your election, Lady Abbess.'

'I would have been elected Abbess in any case,' says the Abbess. 'Felicity had no chance.'

'The Americans have quite gathered that point,' Walburga says. 'They appear to be amused and rather shocked, of course, by the all-pervading bitchiness in this country.'

'I dare say,' says the Abbess. 'This is a sad hour for England in these, the days of her decline. All this public uproar over a silver thimble, mounting as it has over the months. Such a scandal could never arise in the United States of America. They have a sense of proportion and they understand Human Nature over there; it's the secret of their success. A realistic race, even if they do eat asparagus the wrong way. However, I have a letter from Rome, dear Sister Walburga, dear Sister Mildred. It's from the Congregation of Religious. We have to take it seriously.'

'We do,' says Walburga.

'We have to do something about it,' says the Abbess, 'because the Cardinal himself has written, not the Cardinal's secretary. They're putting out feelers. There are questions, and they are leading questions.'

'Are they worried about the press and publicity?' says Walburga, her fingers moving in her lap.

'Yes, they want an explanation. But I,' says the Abbess of Crewe, 'am not worried about the publicity. It has come to the point where the more we get the better.'

Mildred's mind seems to have wandered. She says with a sudden breakage in her calm, 'Oh, we could be excommunicated! I know we'll be excommunicated!'

The Abbess continues evenly, 'The more scandal there is from this point on the better. We are truly moving in a mythological context. We are the actors; the press and the public are the chorus. Every columnist has his own version of the same old story, as it were Aeschylus, Sophocles or Euripides, only of course, let me tell you, of a far inferior dramatic style. I read classics for a year at Lady Margaret Hall before switching to Eng. Lit. However that may be – Walburga, Mildred, my Sisters – the facts of the matter are with us no longer, but we have returned to God who gave them. We can't be excommunicated without the facts. As for the legal aspect, no judge in the kingdom would admit the case, let Felicity tell it like it was as she may. You cannot bring a charge against Agamemnon or subpoena Clytemnestra, can you?'

Walburga stares at the Abbess, as if at a new person. 'You can,' she says, 'if you are an actor in the drama yourself.' She shivers. 'I feel a cold draught,' she says. 'Is there a window open?'

'No,' says the Abbess.

'How shall you reply to Rome?' Mildred says, her voice soft with fear.

'On the question of the news reports I shall suggest we are the victims of popular demonology,' says the Abbess. 'Which we are. But they raise a second question on which I'm uncertain.'

'Sister Felicity and her Jesuit!' says Walburga.

'No, of course not. Why should they trouble themselves about a salacious nun and a Jesuit? I must say a Jesuit, or any priest for that matter, would be the last man I would myself elect to be laid by. A man who undresses, maybe; but one who unfrocks, no.'

'That type of priest usually prefers young students,' Walburga observes. 'I don't know what Thomas sees in Felicity.'

'Thomas wears civilian clothes, so he wouldn't unfrock for Felicity,' observes Mildred.

'What I have to decide,' says the Abbess, 'is how to answer the second question in the letter from Rome. It is put very cautiously. They seem quite suspicious. They want to know how we reconcile our adherence to the strict enclosed Rule with the course in electronics which we have introduced into our daily curriculum in place of book-binding and hand-weaving. They want to know why we cannot relax the ancient Rule in conformity with the new reforms current in the other convents, since we have adopted such a very modern course of instruction as electronics. Or, conversely, they want to know why we teach electronics when we have been so adamant in adhering to the old observances. They seem to be suggesting, if you read between the lines, that the convent is bugged. They use the word "scandals" a great deal.'

'It's a snare,' says Walburga. 'That letter is a snare. They want you to fall into a snare. May we see the letter, Lady Abbess?'

'No,' says the Abbess. 'So that, when questioned, you will not make any blunder and will be able to testify that you haven't seen it. I'll show you my answer, so that you can say you have seen it. The more truths and confusions the better.'

'Are we to be questioned?' says Mildred, folding her arms at her throat, across the white coif.

'Who knows?' says the Abbess. 'In the meantime, Sisters, do you have any suggestions to offer as to how I can convincingly reconcile our activities in my reply?'

The nuns sit in silence for a moment. Walburga looks at Mildred, but Mildred is staring at the carpet.

'What is wrong with the carpet, Mildred?' says the Abbess. Mildred looks up. 'Nothing, Lady Abbess,' she says.

'It's a beautiful carpet, Lady Abbess,' says Walburga, looking down at the rich green expanse beneath her feet.

The Abbess puts her white head to the side to admire her carpet, too. She intones with an evident secret happiness:

No white nor red was ever seen
So amorous as this lovely green.

Walburga shivers a little. Mildred watches the Abbess's lips as if waiting for another little quotation.

'How shall I reply to Rome?' says the Abbess.

'I would like to sleep on it,' says Walburga.

'I, too,' says Mildred.

The Abbess looks at the carpet:

Annihilating all that's made
To a green thought in a green shade.

'I,' says the Abbess, then, 'would prefer not to sleep on it. Where is Sister Gertrude at this hour?'

'In the Congo,' Walburga says.

'Then get her on the green line.'

'We have no green line to the Congo,' Walburga says. 'She travels day and night by rail and river. She should have arrived at a capital some hours ago. It's difficult to keep track of her whereabouts.'

'If she has arrived at a capital we should hear from her tonight,' the Abbess says. 'That was the arrangement. The sooner we perfect the green line system the better. We should have in our laboratory a green line to everywhere; it would be convenient to consult Gertrude. I don't know why she goes rushing around, spending her time on ecumenical ephemera. It has all been done before. The Arians, the Albigensians, the Jansenists of Port Royal, the English recusants, the Covenanters. So many schisms, annihilations and reconciliations. Finally the lion lies down with the lamb and Gertrude sees that they remain lying down. Meantime Sister Gertrude, believe me, is a philosopher at heart. There is a touch of Hegel, her compatriot, there. Philosophers, when they cease philosophizing and take up action, are dangerous.'

'Then why ask her advice?' says Walburga.

'Because we are in danger. Dangerous people understand well how to avoid it.'

'She's in a very wild area just now, reconciling the witch doctors' rituals with a specially adapted rite of the Mass,' Mildred says, 'and moving the old missionaries out of that zone into another zone where they are sure to be opposed, probably massacred. However, this will be an appropriate reason for reinstating the orthodox Mass in the first zone, thus modifying the witch doctors' bone-throwing practices. At least, that's how I see it.'

'I can't keep up with Gertrude,' says the Abbess. 'How she is so popular I really don't know. But even by her build one can foresee her stone statue in every village square: Blessed Mother Gertrude.'

'Gertrude should have been a man,' says Walburga. 'With her moustache, you can see that.'

'Bursting with male hormones,' the Abbess says as she rises from her silk seat the better to adjust the gleaming robes of the Infant of Prague. 'And now,' says the Abbess, 'we wait here for Gertrude to call us. Why can't she be where we can call her?'

The telephone in the adjoining room rings so suddenly that surely, if it is Gertrude, she must have sensed her sisters' want from the other field of the earth. Mildred treads softly over the green carpet to the adjoining room and answers the phone. It is Gertrude.

'Amazing,' says Walburga. 'Dear Gertrude has an uncanny knowledge of what is needed where and when.'

The Abbess moves in her fresh white robes to the next room, followed by Walburga. Electronics control-room as it is, here, too, everything gleams. The Abbess sits at a long steel desk and takes the telephone.

'Gertrude,' says the Abbess, 'the Abbess of Crewe has been discussing you with her Sisters Walburga and Mildred. We don't know what to make of you. How should we think?'

'I'm not a philosopher,' says Gertrude's deep voice, philosophically.

'Dear Gertrude, are you well?'

'Yes,' says Gertrude.

'You sound like bronchitis,' says the Abbess.

'Well, I'm not bronchitis.'

'Gertrude,' says the Abbess, 'Sister Gertrude has charmed all the kingdom with her dangerous exploits, while the Abbess of Crewe continues to perform her part in the drama of *The Abbess of Crewe*. The world is having fun and waiting for the catharsis. Is this my destiny?'

'It's your calling,' says Gertrude, philosophically.

'Gertrude, my excellent nun, my learned Hun, we have a problem and we don't know what to do with it.'

'A problem you solve,' says Gertrude.

'Gertrude,' wheedles the Abbess, 'we're in trouble with Rome. The Congregation of Religious has started to probe. They have written delicately to inquire how we reconcile our adherence to the Ancient Rule, which as you know they find suspect, with the laboratory and the courses we are giving the nuns in modern electronics, which, as you know, they find suspect.'

'That isn't a problem,' says Gertrude. 'It's a paradox.'

'Have you time for a very short seminar, Gertrude, on how one treats of a paradox?'

'A paradox you live with,' says Gertrude, and hangs up.

The Abbess leads the way from this room of many shining square boxes, many lights and levers, many activating knobs, press-buttons and slide-buttons and devices fearfully and wonderfully beyond the reach of a humane vocabulary. She leads the way back to the Infant of Prague, decked as it is with the glistening fruits of the nuns' dowries. The Abbess sits at her little desk with the Sisters Walburga and Mildred silently composed beside her. She takes the grand writing-paper of the Abbey of Crewe and places it before her. She takes her pen from its gleaming holder and writes:

'Your Very Reverend Eminence,

Your Eminence does me the honour to address me, and I humbly thank Your Eminence.

I have the honour to reply to Your Eminence, to submit that his sources of information are poisoned, his wells are impure. From there arise the rumours concerning my House, and I beg to write no more on that subject.

Your Eminence does me the honour to inquire of our activities, how we confront what Your Eminence does us the honour to call the problem of reconciling our activities in the field of technological surveillance with the principles of the traditional life and devotions to which we adhere.

I have the honour to reply to Your Eminence. I will humbly divide Your Eminence's question into two parts. That we practise the activities described by Your Eminence I agree; that they present a problem I deny, and I will take the liberty to explain my distinction, and I hold:

That Religion is founded on principles of Paradox.

That Paradox is to be accepted and presents no Problem.

That electronic surveillance (even if a convent were one day to practise it) does not differ from any other type of watchfulness, the which is a necessity of a Religious Community; we are told in the Scriptures "to watch and to pray", which is itself a paradox since the two activities cannot effectively be practised together except in the paradoxical sense.'

'You may see what I have written so far,' says the Abbess to her nuns. 'How does it strike you? Will it succeed in getting them muddled up for a while?'

The black bodies lean over her, the white coifs meet above the pages of the letter.

'I see a difficulty,' says Walburga. 'They could object that telephone-tapping and bugging are not simply an extension of listening to hearsay and inviting confidences, the steaming open of letters and the regulation search of the novices' closets. They might well say that we have entered a state where a difference of degree implies a difference in kind.'

'I thought of that,' says the Abbess. 'But the fact that we have thought of it rather tends to exclude than presume that they in Rome will think of it. Their minds are set to liquidate the convent, not to maintain a courtly correspondence with us.' The Abbess lifts her pen and continues:

'Finally, Your Eminence, I take upon myself the honour to indicate to Your Eminence the fine flower and consummation of our holy and paradoxical establishment, our beloved and renowned Sister Gertrude whom we have sent out from our midst to labour for the ecumenical Faith. By river, by helicopter, by jet and by camel, Sister Gertrude covers the crust of the earth, followed as she is by photographers and reporters. Paradoxically it was our enclosed community who sent her out.'

'Gertrude,' says Mildred, 'would be furious at that. She went off by herself.'

'Gertrude must put up with it. She fits the rhetoric of the occasion,' says the Abbess. She bends once more over her work. But the bell for Lauds chimes from the chapel. It is three in the morning. Faithful to the Rule, the Abbess immediately puts down her pen. One white swan, two black, they file from the room and down to the waiting hall. The whole congregation is assembled in steady composure. One by one they take their cloaks and follow the Abbess to the chapel, so softly ill-lit for Lauds. The nuns in their choirs chant and reply, with wakeful voices at three in the morning:

> O Lord, our Lord, how wonderful is thy name in all the
>   earth:
> Thou who hast proclaimed thy glory upon the heavens.
> Out of the mouths of babes and sucklings thou hast pre-
>   pared praise to confuse thy adversaries:
> to silence the enemy and the revengeful.

The Abbess from her high seat looks with a kind of wonder at her shadowy chapel of nuns, she listens with a fine joy to the keen plainchant, as if upon a certain newly created world.

She contemplates and sees it is good. Her lips move with the Latin of the psalm. She stands before her high chair as one exalted by what she sees and thinks, as it might be she is contemplating the full existence of the Abbess of Crewe.

Et fecisti eum paulo minorem Angelis:
Gloria et honore coronasti eum.

Soon she is whispering the melodious responses in other words of her great liking:

Every farthing of the cost,
All the dreaded cards foretell,
Shall be paid, but from this night
Not a whisper, not a thought,
Not a kiss nor look be lost.

II

IN THE SUMMER BEFORE the autumn, as God is in his heaven, Sister Felicity's thimble is lying in its place in her sewing-box.

The Abbess Hildegarde is newly dead, and laid under her slab in the chapel.

The Abbey of Crewe is left without a head, but the election of the new Abbess is to take place in twenty-three days' time. After Matins, at twenty minutes past midnight, the nuns go to their cells to sleep briefly and deeply until their awakening for Lauds at three. But Felicity jumps from her window on to the haycart pulled up below and runs to meet her Jesuit.

Tall Alexandra, at this time Sub-Prioress and soon to be elected Abbess of Crewe, remains in the chapel, kneeling to pray at Hildegarde's tomb. She whispers:

> Sleep on, my love, in thy cold bed
> Never to be disquieted.
> My last good night! Thou wilt not wake
> Till I thy fate shall overtake:
> Till age, or grief, or sickness must
> Marry my body to that dust
> It so much loves, and fill the room
> My heart keeps empty in thy tomb.

She wears the same black habit as the two sisters who wait for her at the door of the chapel.

She joins them, and with their cloaks flying in the night air they return to the great sleeping house. Up and down the dark cloisters they pace, Alexandra, Walburga and Mildred.

'What are we here for?' says Alexandra. 'What are we doing here?'

'It's our destiny,' Mildred says.

'You will be elected Abbess, Alexandra,' says Walburga.

'And Felicity?'

'Her destiny is the Jesuit,' says Mildred.

'She has a following among the younger nuns,' Walburga says.

'It's a result of her nauseating propaganda,' says lofty Alexandra. 'She's always talking about love and freedom as if these were attributes peculiar to herself. Whereas, in reality, Felicity cannot love. How can she truly love? She's too timid to hate well, let alone love. It takes courage to practise love. And what does she know of freedom? Felicity has never been in bondage, bustling in, as she does, late for Mass, bleary-eyed for Prime, straggling vaguely through the Divine Office. One who has never observed a strict ordering of the heart can never exercise freedom.'

'She keeps her work-box tidy,' Mildred says. 'She's very particular about her work-box.'

'Felicity's sewing-box is the precise measure of her love and her freedom,' says Alexandra, so soon to be Abbess of Crewe. 'Her sewing-box is her alpha and her omega, not to mention her tiny epsilon, her iota and her omicron. For all her talk, and her mooney Jesuit and her pious eyelashes, it all adds up to Felicity's little sewing-box, the norm she departs from, the north of her compass. She would ruin the Abbey if she were elected. How strong is her following?'

'About as strong as she is weak. When it comes to the vote she'll lose,' Mildred says.

Walburga says sharply, 'This morning the polls put her at forty-two per cent according to my intelligence reports.'

'It's quite alarming,' says Alexandra, 'seeing that to be the Abbess of Crewe is my destiny.' She has stopped walking and the two nuns have stopped with her. She stands facing them, drawing their careful attention to herself, lighthouse that she is. 'Unless I fulfil my destiny my mother's labour pains were pointless and what am I doing here?'

'This morning the novices were talking about Felicity,' Mildred says. 'She was seen from their window wandering in the park between Lauds and Prime. They think she had a rendezvous.'

'Oh, well, the novices have no vote.'

'They reflect the opinions of the younger nuns.'

'Have you got a record of all this talk?'

'It's on tape,' says Mildred.

Walburga says, 'We must do something about it.' Walburga's face has a grey-green tinge; it is long and smooth. An Abbess needs must be over forty years, but Walburga, who has just turned forty, has no ambition but that Alexandra shall be elected and she remain the Prioress.

Walburga is strong; on taking her final vows she brought to the community an endowment of a piece of London, this being a section of Park Lane with its view of Rotten Row, besides an adjoining mews of great value. Her strength resides in her virginity of heart combined with the long education of her youth that took her across many an English quad by night, across many a campus of Europe and so to bed. A wealthy woman, more than most, she has always maintained, is likely to remain virgin at heart. Her past lovers had been the most learned available; however ungainly, it was invariably

205

the professors, the more profound scholars, who attracted her. And she always felt learned herself, thereafter, by a kind of osmosis.

Mildred, too, has brought a fortune to the Abbey. Her portion includes a sizeable block of Chicago slums in addition to the four big flats in the Boulevard St Germain. Mildred is thirty-six and would be too young to be a candidate for election, even if she were disposed to be Abbess. But her hopes, like Walburga's, rest on Alexandra. This Mildred has been in the convent since her late schooldays; it may be she is a nourisher of dreams so unrealizable in their magnitude that she prefers to keep them in mind and remain physically an inferior rather than take on any real fact of ambition that would defeat her. She has meekly served and risen to be Novice Mistress, so exemplary a nun with her blue eyes, her pretty face and nervous flutter of timidity that Thomas the Jesuit would at first have preferred to take her rather than Felicity. He had tried, following her from confession, waiting for her under the poplars.

'What did you confess?' he asked Mildred. 'What did you say to that young priest? What are your sins?'

'It's between myself and God. It is a secret.'

'And the priest? What did you tell that young confessor of your secrets?'

'All my heart. It's necessary.'

He was jealous but he lost. Whatever Mildred's deeply concealed dreams might be, they ran far ahead of the Jesuit, far beyond him. He began at last to hate Mildred and took up with Felicity.

Alexandra, who brought to the community no dowry but her noble birth and shrewd spirit, is to be Abbess now that Hildegarde lies buried in the chapel. And the wonder is that she bothers, or even her favourite nuns are concerned, now, a few weeks before the election, that Felicity causes a slight stir amongst the forty nuns who are eligible to vote. Felicity has new and wild ideas and is becoming popular.

Under the late Abbess Hildegarde this quaint convent, quasi-Benedictine, quasi-Jesuit, has already discarded its quasi-natures. It is a mutation and an established fact. The Lady Abbess Hildegarde, enamoured of Alexandra as she was, came close to expelling Felicity from the Abbey in the days before she died. Alexandra alone possesses the authority and the means to rule. When it comes to the vote it needs must be Alexandra.

They pace the dark cloisters in such an evident happiness of shared anxiety that they seem not to recognize the pleasure at all.

Walburga says, 'We must do something. Felicity could create a crisis of leadership in the Abbey.'

'A crisis of leadership,' Mildred says, as one who enjoys both the phrase and the anguish of the idea. 'The community must be kept under the Rule, which is to say, Alexandra.'

Alexandra says, 'Keep watch on the popularity chart. Sisters, I am consumed by the Divine Discontent. We are made a little lower than the angels. This weighs upon me, because I am a true believer.'

'I, too,' says Walburga. 'My faith remains firm.'

'And mine,' Mildred says. 'There was a time I greatly desired not to believe, but I found myself at last unable not to believe.'

Walburga says, 'And Felicity, your enemy, Ma'am? How is Felicity's faith. Does she really believe one damn thing about the Catholic faith?'

'She claims a special enlightenment,' says Alexandra the Abbess-to-be. 'Felicity wants everyone to be liberated by her vision and to acknowledge it. She wants a stamped receipt from Almighty God for every word she spends, every action, as if she can later deduct it from her income-tax returns. Felicity will never see the point of faith unless it visibly benefits mankind.'

'She is so bent on helping lame dogs over stiles,' Walburga says. 'Then they can't get back over again to limp home.'

'So it is with the Jesuit. Felicity is helping Thomas, she would say. I'm sure of it,' Mildred says. 'That was clear from the way he offered to help me.'

The Sisters walk hand in hand and they laugh, now, together in the dark night of the Abbey cloisters. Alexandra, between the two, skips as she walks and laughs at the idea that one of them might need help of the Jesuit.

The night-watch nun crosses the courtyard to ring the bell for Lauds. The three nuns enter the house. In the great hall a pillar seems to stir. It is Winifrede come to join them, with her round face in the moonlight, herself a zone of near-darkness knowing only that she has a serviceable place in the Abbey's hierarchy.

'Winifrede, *Benedicite*,' Alexandra says.

'*Deo Gratias*, Alexandra.'

'After Lauds we meet in the parlour,' Alexandra says.

'I've got news,' says Winifrede.

'Later, in the parlour,' says Walburga. And Mildred says, 'Not here, Winifrede!'

But Winifrede proceeds like beer from an unstoppered barrel. 'Felicity is lurking somewhere in the avenue. She was with Thomas the Jesuit. I have them on tape and on video-tape from the closed-circuit.'

Alexandra says, loud and clear, 'I don't know what rubbish you are talking.' And motions with her eyes to the four walls. Mildred whispers low to Winifrede, 'Nothing must be said in the hall. How many times have we told you?'

'Ah,' breathes Winifrede, aghast at her mistake. 'I forgot you've just bugged the hall.'

So swiftly to her forehead in despair goes the hand of Mildred, so swivelled to heaven are Walburga's eyes in the exasperation of the swifter mind with the slow. But Alexandra is calm. 'Order will come out of chaos,' she says, 'as it always has done. Sisters, be still, be sober.'

Walburga the Prioress turns to her: 'Alexandra, you are calm, so calm . . . '

'There is a proverb: Beware the ire of the calm,' says Alexandra.

Quietly the congregation of nuns descends the great staircase and is assembled. Walburga the Prioress now leads, Alexandra follows, and all the community after them, to sing the Hour.

It is the Hour of None, three in the afternoon, when Sister Felicity slips sleepily into the chapel. She is a tiny nun, small as a schoolgirl, not at all like what one would have imagined from all the talk about her. Her complexion looks as if her hair, sprouting under her veil, would be reddish. Nobody knows where Felicity has been all day and half the night, for she was not present at Matins at midnight nor Lauds at three in the morning, nor at breakfast at five, Prime at six, Terce at nine; nor was she present in the refectory at eleven for lunch, which comprised barley broth and a perfectly nourishing and tasty, although uncommon, dish of something unnamed on toast, that something being in fact a cat-food by the name of Mew, bought cheaply and in bulk. Felicity was not there to partake of it, nor was she in the chapel singing the Hour of Sext at noon. Nor between these occasions was she anywhere in the convent, not in her cell nor in the sewing-room embroidering the purses, the vestments and the altar-cloths;

nor was she in the electronics laboratory which was set up by the great nuns Alexandra, Walburga and Mildred under the late Abbess Hildegarde's very nose and carefully unregarding eyes. Felicity has been absent since after Vespers the previous day, and now she slips into her stall in the chapel at None, yawning at three in the afternoon.

Walburga, the Prioress, temporarily head of the convent, turns her head very slightly as Felicity takes her place, and turns away again. The community vibrates like an evanescent shadow that quickly fades out of sight, and continues fervently to sing. Puny Felicity, who knows the psalter by heart, takes up the chant but not her Office book:

> They have spoken to me with a lying tongue and have
>   compassed me about with words of hatred:
> And have fought against me without cause.
> Instead of making me a return of love, they slandered me:
> but I gave myself to prayer.
> And they repaid evil for good:
> and hatred for my love.

The high throne of the Abbess is empty. Felicity's eyes, pink-rimmed with sleeplessness, turn towards it as she chants, thinking, maybe, of the dead, aloof Abbess Hildegarde who lately sat propped in that place, or maybe how well she could occupy it herself, little as she is, a life-force of new ideas, a quivering streak of light set in that gloomy chair. The late Hildegarde tolerated Felicity only because she considered her to be a common little thing, and it befitted a Christian to tolerate.

'She constitutes a reliable something for us to practise benevolence upon,' the late Hildegarde formerly said of Felicity, confiding this to Alexandra, Walburga and Mildred one summer afternoon between the Hours of Sext and None.

Felicity now looks away from the vacant throne and, intoning her responses, peers at Alexandra where she stands mightily in her stall. Alexandra's lips move with the incantation:

As I went down the water side,
None but my foe to be my guide,
None but my foe . . .

Felicity, putting the finishing touches on an altar-cloth, is sewing a phrase into the inside corner. She is doing it in the tiniest and neatest possible satin-stitch, white upon white, having traced the words with her fine pencil: '*Opus Anglicanum*'. Her little frail fingers move securely and her silver thimble flashes.

The other sewing nuns are grouped around her, each busy with embroidery but none so clever at her work as Felicity.

'You know, Sisters,' Felicity says, 'our embroidery room is becoming known as a hotbed of sedition.'

The other nuns, eighteen in all, murmur solemnly. Felicity does not permit laughter. It is written in the Rule that laughter is unseemly. 'What are the tools of Good Works?' says the Rule, and the answers include, 'Not to say what is idle or causes laughter.' Of all the clauses of the Rule this is the one that Felicity decrees to be the least outmoded, the most adapted to the urgency of our times.

'Love,' says Felicity softly, plying her little fingers to her satin-stitch, 'is lacking in our Community. We are full of prosperity. We prosper. We are materialistic. May God have mercy on our late Lady Abbess Hildegarde.'

'Amen,' say the other eighteen, and the sun of high summer dances on their thimbles through the window panes.

'Sometimes,' Felicity says, 'I think we should tend more towards the teachings of St Francis of Assisi, who understood total dispossession and love.'

One of her nuns, a certain Sister Bathildis, answers, her eyes still bent on her beautiful embroidery, 'But Sister Alexandra doesn't care for St Francis of Assisi.'

'Alexandra,' says Felicity 'has actually said, "To hell with St Francis of Assisi. I prefer Sextus Propertius who belongs also to Assisi, a contemporary of Jesus and a spiritual fore-runner of Hamlet, Werther, Rousseau and Kierkegaard." According to Alexandra these fellows are far more interesting neurotics than St Francis. Have you ever heard of such names or such a doctrine?'

'Never,' murmur the nuns in unison, laying their work on their laps the easier to cross themselves.

'Love,' says Felicity as they all take up their work again, 'and love-making are very liberating experiences, very. If I were the Abbess of Crewe, we should have a love-Abbey. I would destroy that ungodly electronics laboratory and install a love-nest right in the heart of this Abbey, right in the heart of England.' Her busy little fingers fly with the tiny needle in and out of the stuff she is sewing.

'What do you make of that?' says Alexandra, switching off the closed-circuit television where she and her two trusted nuns have just witnessed the scene in the sewing-room, re-corded on video and sound tape.

'It's the same old song,' Walburga says. 'It goes on all the time. More and more nuns are taking up embroidery of their own free will, and fewer and fewer remain with us. Since the Abbess died there is no more authority in the convent.'

'All that will be changed now,' Alexandra says, 'after the election.'

212

'It could be changed now,' Mildred says. 'Walburga is Prioress and has the authority.'

Walburga says, 'I thought better than to confront Felicity with her escapade last night and half of the day. I thought better of it, and I think better of preventing the nuns from joining the sewing-room faction. It might provoke Felicity to lead a rebellion.'

'Oh, do you think the deserters can have discovered that the convent is bugged?' says Mildred.

'Not on your life,' says Alexandra. 'The laboratory nuns are far too stupid to do anything but wire wires and screw screws. They have no idea at all what their work adds up to.'

They are sitting at the bare metal table in the private control room which was set up in the room adjoining the late Abbess's parlour shortly before her death. The parlour itself remains as it was when Hildegarde died although within a few weeks it will be changed to suit Alexandra's taste. For certainly Alexandra is to be Abbess of Crewe. And as surely, at this moment, the matter has been thrown into doubt by Sister Felicity's glamorous campaign.

'She is bored,' says the destined Abbess. 'That is the trouble. She provides an unwholesome distraction for the nuns for a while, and after a while they will find her as boring as she actually is.'

'Gertrude,' says Alexandra into the green telephone. 'Gertrude, my dear, are you not returning to your convent for the election?'

'Impossible,' says Gertrude, who has been called on the new green line at the capital city nearest to that uncharted spot in the Andes where she has lately posted herself. 'I'm at a very delicate point in my negotiations between the cannibal

213

tribe and that vegetarian sect on the other side of the mountain.'

'But, Gertrude, we're having a lot of trouble with Felicity. The life of the Abbey of Crewe is at stake, Gertrude.'

'The salvation of souls comes first,' says Gertrude's husky voice. 'The cannibals are to be converted to the faith with dietary concessions and the excessive zeal of the vegetarian heretics suppressed.'

'What puzzles me so much, Gertrude, my love, is how the cannibals will fare on the Day of Judgement,' Alexandra says cosily. 'Remember, Gertrude, that friendly little verse of our childhood:

It's a very odd thing –
As odd as can be –
That whatever Miss T. eats
Turns into Miss T. . . .

And it seems to me, Gertrude, that you are going to have a problem with those cannibals on the Latter Day when the trumpet shall sound. It's a question of which man shall rise in the Resurrection, for certainly those that are eaten have long since become the consumers from generation to generation. It is a problem, Gertrude, my most clever angel, that vexes my noon's repose and I do urge you to leave well alone in that field. You should come back at once to Crewe and help us in our time of need.'

Something crackles on the line. 'Gertrude, are you there?' says Alexandra.

Something crackles, then Gertrude's voice responds, 'Sorry, I missed all that. I was tying my shoelace.'

'You should be here, Gertrude. The nuns are beginning to murmur that you're avoiding us. Felicity is saying that if she's elected Abbess of Crewe she wants an open audit of all the dowries and she advocates indiscreet sex. Above all, she has proclaimed a rebellion in the house and it's immoral.'

'What is her rebellion against?' Gertrude inquires.

'My tyranny,' says Alexandra. 'What do you think?'

'Is the rebellion likely to succeed?' says Gertrude.

'Not if we can help it. But she has a chance. Her following increases every hour.'

'If she has a chance of success then the rebellion isn't immoral. A rebellion against a tyrant is only immoral when it hasn't got a chance.'

'That sounds very cynical, Gertrude. Positively Machiavellian. Don't you think it a little daring to commit yourself so far?'

'It is the doctrine of St Thomas Aquinas.'

'Can you be here for the election, Gertrude? We need to consult you.'

'Consult Machiavelli,' says Gertrude. 'A great master, but don't quote me as saying so; the name is inexpedient.'

'Gertrude,' says Alexandra. 'Do bear in mind that

Tiny and cheerful,
And neat as can be,
Whatever Miss T. eats
Turns into Miss T.'

But Gertrude has hung up.

'Will she come home?' says Walburga when Alexandra turns from the telephone.

'I doubt it,' says Alexandra. 'She is having a great success with the cannibals and has administered the Kiss of Peace according to the photograph in today's *Daily Mirror*. Meanwhile the vegetarian tribes have guaranteed to annihilate the cannibals, should they display any desire to roast her.'

'She will be in trouble with Rome,' says Mildred, 'if she absents herself from the Abbey much longer. A mission takes so long and no longer according to the vows of this Abbey.'

'Gertrude fears neither Pope nor man,' says Alexandra. 'Call Sister Winifrede on the walkie-talkie. Tell Winifrede to come to the Abbess's parlour.' She leads the way into the parlour which is still furnished in the style of the late Hildegarde, who had a passion for autumn tints. The carpet is figured with fallen leaves and the wallpaper is a faded glow of browns and golds. The three nuns recline in the greenish-brown plush chairs while Winifrede is summoned and presently appears before them, newly startled out of a snooze.

Alexandra, so soon to be clothed in white, fetches from her black pocket a bunch of keys. 'Winifrede,' she says, indicating one of the keys, 'this is the key to the private library. Open it up and bring me Machiavelli's *Art of War*.' Alexandra then selects another key. 'And while you are about it go to my cell and open my locked cupboard. In it you will find my jar of *pâté*, some fine little biscuits and a bottle of my Le Corton, 1959. Prepare a tray for four and bring it here with the book.'

'Alexandra,' whines Winifrede, 'why not get one of the kitchen nuns to prepare the tray?'

'On no account,' says Alexandra. 'Do it yourself. You'll get your share.'

'The kitchen nuns are so ugly,' says Mildred.

'And such common little beasts,' says Walburga.

'Very true,' says Winifrede agreeably and departs on her errands.

'Winifrede is useful,' says Alexandra.

'We can always make use of Winifrede,' says Mildred.

'Highly dependable,' says Walburga. 'She'll come in useful when we really come to grips with Felicity.'

'That, of course, is for you two nuns to decide,' Alexandra says. 'As a highly obvious candidate for the Abbey of Crewe, plainly I can take no personal part in whatever you have in mind.'

'Really, I have nothing in mind,' Mildred says.

'Nor I,' says Walburga. 'Not as yet.'

'It will come to you,' says Alexandra. 'I see no reason why I shouldn't start now arranging for this room to be newly done over. A green theme, I think. I'm attached to green. An idea of how to proceed against Felicity will occur to you quite soon, I imagine, tomorrow or the day after, between the hours of Matins and Lauds, or Lauds and Prime, or Prime and Terce, or, maybe, between Terce and Sext, Sext and None, None and Vespers, or between Vespers and Compline.' Winifrede returns, tall and handsome as a transvested butler, bearing a tray laden with their private snack for four. She sets it on a table and, fishing into her pocket, produces a book and Alexandra's keys which she hands over.

They are seated at the table, and the wine is poured. 'Shall I say grace?' says fair-faced, round-eyed Winifrede, although the others have already started to scoop daintily at the *pâté* with their pearl-handled knives. 'Oh, it isn't necessary,' says Alexandra, spreading the *pâté* on her fine wafer, 'there's nothing wrong with *my* food.'

Winifrede, with her eyes like two capital Os, leans forward and confides, 'I've seen the print of that telephoto of Felicity with Thomas this morning.'

'I, too,' says Walburga. 'I don't understand these fresh-air fiends when the traditional linen cupboard is so much better heated and equipped.'

Alexandra says, 'I glanced at the negative. Since when my spirit is impure. It does not become them. Only the beautiful should make love when they are likely to be photographed.'

'The double monasteries of the olden days were so discreet and so well ordered,' Mildred says, wistfully.

'I intend to reinstate the system,' says Alexandra. 'If I am the Abbess of Crewe for a few years I shall see to it hat each nun has her own private chaplain, as in the days of my ancestor St Gilbert, Rector of Sempringham. The nuns will have each her Jesuit. The lay brothers, who will take the place of domestic nuns as in the eleventh century, will be Cistercians, which is to say, bound to silence. Now, if you please, Walburga, let's consult *The Art of War* because time is passing and the sands are running out.'

Alexandra gracefully pushes back her plate and leans in her chair, one elbow resting on the back of it and her long body arranged the better to finger through the pages of the book placed on the table before her. The white coifs meet in a tent of concentration above the book where Alexandra's fingers trace the passages to be well noted.

'It is written,' says Alexandra with her lovely index finger on the margin as she reads:

After you have consulted many about what you ought to do, confer with very few concerning what you are actually resolved to do.

The bell rings for Matins, and Alexandra closes the book. Walburga leads the way while Alexandra counsels them, 'Sisters, be vigilant, be sober. This is a monastery under threat, and we must pray to Almighty God for our strength.'

'We can't do more,' says Mildred.

'To do less would be cheap,' Walburga says.

'We are corrupt by our nature in the Fall of Man,' Alexandra says. 'It was well exclaimed by St Augustine, "O happy fault to merit such a Redeemer! O *felix culpa!*" '

'Amen,' respond the three companions.

They start to descend the stairs. 'O happy flaw!' says Alexandra.

Felicity is already waiting with her assembled supporters and the anonymous files of dark-shaped nuns when the three descend, graceful with Walburga in the lead, each one of them so nobly made and well put together. One by one they take their capes and file across the midnight path to their chapel.

Felicity slips aside, waiting with her cloak folded in the dark air until the community has entered the chapel. Then, while the voices start to sound in the ebb and flow of the plainchant, she makes her way back across the grass to the house quickly as a water bird skimming a pond. Felicity is up the great staircase, she is in the Abbess's parlour and switches on the light. Her little face looks at the remains of the little feast; she spits at it like an exasperated beggar-gypsy, and she breathes a cat's hiss to see such luxury spent. But soon she is about her business, through the door, and is occupied with the apparatus of the green telephone.

At the end of a long ring someone answers.

'Gertrude!' she says. 'Can that really be you?'

'I was just about to leave,' Gertrude says. 'The helicopter is waiting.'

'Gertrude, you're doing such marvellous work. We hear –'

'Is that all you want to say?' Gertrude says.

'Gertrude, this convent is a hotbed of corruption and hypocrisy. I want to change everything and a lot of the nuns agree with me. We want to break free. We want justice.'

'Sister, be still, be sober,' Gertrude says. 'Justice may be done but on no account should it be seen to be done. It's always a fatal undertaking. You'll bring down the whole community in ruins.'

'Oh, Gertrude, we believe in love in freedom and freedom in love.'

'That can be arranged,' Gertrude says.

'But I have a man in my life now, Gertrude. What can a poor nun do with a man?'

'Invariably, a man you feed both ends,' Gertrude says. 'You have to learn to cook and to do the other.'

The telephone then roars like a wild beast.

'What's going on, Gertrude?'

'The helicopter,' Gertrude says, and hangs up.

'Read it aloud to them,' Alexandra says. Once more it is lunch time. 'Let it never be said that we concealed our intentions. Our nuns are too bemused to take it in and those who are for Felicity have gone morbid with their sentimental Jesusism. Let it be read aloud. If they have ears to hear, let them hear.' The kitchen nuns float with their trays along the aisles between the refectory tables, dispensing sieved nettles and mashed potatoes.

Winifrede stands at the lectern. She starts to read, announcing Ecclesiasticus, chapter 34, verse 1:

Fools are cheated by vain hopes, buoyed up with the fancies of a dream. Wouldst thou heed such lying visions? Better clutch at shadows, or chase the wind. Nought thou seest in a dream but symbols; man is but face to face with his own image. As well may foul thing cleanse, as false thing give thee a true warning. Out upon the folly of them, pretended divination, and cheating omen, and wizard's dream! Heart of woman in her pangs is not more fanciful. Unless it be some manifestation the most High has sent

thee, pay no heed to any such; trust in dreams has crazed
the wits of many, and brought them to their ruin. Believe
rather the law's promises, that cannot miss their fulfilment,
the wisdom that trusty counsellors shall make clear to thee.

Winifrede stops to turn the pages to the next place marked
with a book-marker elaborately embroidered from the sewing-
room. Her eyes remotely sweep the length of the room, where
the kitchen nuns are bearing jugs up the aisles, pouring water which has been heated for encouragement into the nuns'
beakers. The forks move to the faces and the mouths open to
receive the food. These are all the nuns in the convent, with
the exception of kitchen nuns and the novices who do not
count and the senior nuns who do. A less edifying crowd of
human life it would be difficult to find; either they have become so or they always were so; at any rate, they are in fact
a very poor lot, all the more since they do not think so for a
moment. Up pop the forks, open go the mouths, in slide the
nettles and the potato mash. They raise to their frightful little
lips the steaming beakers of water and they sip as if fancying
they are partaking of the warm sap of human experience, ripe
for Felicity's liberation. Anyway, the good Winifrede reads
on, announcing Ecclesiastes, chapter 9, verse 11. 'Sisters, hear
again,' she says, 'the wise confessions of Solomon':

Then my thought took a fresh turn; man's art does not
avail, here beneath the sun, to win the race for the swift,
or the battle for the strong, a livelihood for wisdom, riches
for great learning, or for the craftsman thanks; chance and
the moment rule all.

The kitchen staff is gliding alongside the tables now, re-
moving the empty plates and replacing them with saucers

of wholesome and filling sponge pudding which many more deserving cases than the nuns would be glad of. Winifrede sips from her own glass of water, which is cold, puts it down and bends her eyes to the next book marked with its elaborate markers, passage by passage, which she exchanges with the good book on her lectern. She dutifully removes a slip of paper from the inside cover and almost intelligent-looking in this company reads it aloud in her ever-keening voice: 'Further words of wisdom from one of our Faith':

> If you suspect any person in your army of giving the enemy intelligence of your designs, you cannot do better than avail yourself of his treachery, by seeming to trust him with some secret resolution which you intend to execute, whilst you carefully conceal your real design; by which, perhaps, you may discover the traitor, and lead the enemy into an error that may possibly end in their destruction . . .
>
> In order to penetrate into the secret designs, and discover the condition of an enemy, some have sent ambassadors to them with skilful and experienced officers in their train, dressed like the rest of their attendants . . .
>
> As to private discords amongst your soldiers, the only remedy is to expose them to some danger, for in such cases fear generally unites them . . .

'Here endeth the reading,' Winifrede says, looking stupidly round the still more stupid assembly into whose ears the words have come and from which they have gone. The meal over, the nuns' hands are folded.

'Amen,' they say.

'Sisters, be vigilant, be sober.'

'Amen.'

Alexandra sits in the downstairs parlour where visitors are generally received. She has laid aside the copy of *The Discourses of Machiavelli* which she has been reading while awaiting the arrival of her two clergymen friends; these are now ushered in, accompanied by Mildred and Walburga.

Splendid Alexandra rises and stands, quiet and still, while they approach. It is Walburga, on account of being the Prioress, who asks the company to be seated.

'Father Jesuits,' says Walburga, 'our Sister Alexandra will speak.'

It is summer outside, and some of the old-fashioned petticoat roses that climb the walls of the Abbey look into the window at the scene, where Alexandra sits, one arm resting on the table, her head pensively inclining towards it. The self-controlled English sun makes leafy shadows fall on this polished table and across the floor. A bee importunes at the window-pane. The parlour is cool and fresh. A working nun can be seen outside labouring along with two pails, one of them probably unnecessary; and all things keep time with the season.

Walburga sits apart, smiling a little for sociability, with her eye on the door wherein soon enters the tray of afternoon tea, so premeditated in every delicious particular as to make the nun who bears it, leaves it, and goes away less noteworthy than ever.

The two men accept the cups of tea, the plates and the little lace-edged napkins from the sewing-room which Mildred takes over to them. They choose from among the cress sandwiches, the golden shortbread and the pastel-coloured *petit fours*. Both men are grey-haired, of about the same middle age as the three nuns. Alexandra refuses tea with a mannerly inclination of her body from the waist. These Jesuits are her friends. Father Baudouin is big and over-heavy with a face full of high blood-pressure; his companion, Father Maximilian, is more handsome, classic-featured and grave. They watch Alexandra attentively as her words fall in with the silvery acoustics of the tea-spoons.

'Fathers, there are vast populations in the world which are dying or doomed to die through famine, under-nourishment and disease; people continue to make war, and will not stop, but rather prefer to send their young children into battle to be maimed or to die; political fanatics terrorize indiscriminately; tyrannous states are overthrown and replaced by worse tyrannies; the human race is possessed of a universal dementia; and it is at such a moment as this, Fathers, that your brother-Jesuit Thomas has taken to screwing our Sister Felicity by night under the poplars, so that her mind is given over to nothing else but to induce our nuns to follow her example in the name of freedom. They thought they had liberty till Felicity told them they had not. And now she aspires to bear the crozier of the Abbess of Crewe. Fathers, I suggest you discuss this scandal and what you propose to do about it with my two Sisters, because it is beyond me and beneath me.'

Alexandra rises and goes to the door, moving like a Maharajah aloft on his elephant. The Jesuits seem distressed.

'Sister Alexandra,' says the larger Jesuit, Baudouin, as he opens the door for her, 'you know there's very little we can do about Thomas. Alexandra – '

'Then do that very little,' she says in the voice of one whose longanimity foreshortens like shadows cast by the poplars amid the blaze of noon.

Fathers Baudouin and Maximilian will sit late into the night conferring with Mildred and Walburga.

'Mildred,' says handsome Maximilian, 'I know you can be counted on to be tough with the nuns.'

That Mildred the Novice Mistress is reliably tough with the lesser nuns is her only reason for being so closely in Alexandra's confidence. Her mind sometimes wavers with little gusts of timidity when she is in the small environment of her equals. She shivers now as Maximilian addresses her with a smile of confidence.

Baudouin looks from Mildred's heart-shaped white face to Walburga's strong dark face, two portraits in matching white frames. 'Sisters,' Baudouin says, 'Felicity ought not to be the Abbess of Crewe.'

'It must be Alexandra,' Walburga says.

'It shall be Alexandra,' says Mildred.

'Then we have to discuss an assault strategy in dealing with Felicity,' says Baudouin.

'We could deal with Felicity very well,' Walburga says, 'if you would deal with Thomas.'

'The two factors are one,' Maximilian says, smiling wistfully at Mildred.

The bell rings for Vespers. Walburga, looking straight ahead, says, 'We shall have to miss Vespers.'

'We'll miss all the Hours until we've got a plan,' Mildred says decisively.

'And Alexandra?' says Baudouin. 'Won't Alexandra return to join us? We should consult Alexandra.'

'Certainly not, Fathers,' Walburga says. 'She will not join us and we may not consult her. It would be dishonourable – '

'Seeing she is likely to be Abbess,' says Mildred.

'Seeing she will be Abbess,' Walburga says.

'Well, it seems to me that you girls are doing plenty of campaigning,' Baudouin says, looking round the room uncomfortably, as if some fresh air were missing.

Maximilian says, 'Baudouin!' and the nuns look down, offended, at their empty hands in their lap.

After a space, Mildred says, 'We may not canvass for votes. It is against the Rule.'

'I see, I see,' says large Baudouin, patiently.

They talk until Vespers are over and the black shape comes in to remove the tea tray. Still they talk on, and Mildred calls for supper. The priests are shown to the visitors' cloakroom and Mildred retires with Walburga to the upstairs lavatories where they exchange a few words of happiness. The plans are going well and are going forward.

The four gather again, conspiring over a good supper with wine. The bell rings for Compline, and they talk on.

Upstairs and far away in the control-room the recorders, activated by their voices, continue to whirl. So very much elsewhere in the establishment do the walls have ears that neither Mildred nor Walburga are now conscious of them as they were when the mechanisms were first installed. It is like being told, and all the time knowing, that the Eyes of God are upon us; it means everything and therefore nothing. The two nuns speak as freely as the Jesuits who suspect no eavesdropping device more innocuous than God to be making a chronicle of their present privacy.

The plainchant of Compline floats sweetly over from the chapel where Alexandra stands in her stall nearly opposite Felicity. Walburga's place is empty, Mildred's place is empty. In the Abbess's chair, not quite an emptiness as yet, but the absence of Hildegarde.

The voices ripple like a brook:
Hear, O God, my supplication:
be attentive to my prayers.
From the ends of the earth I cry to thee:
when my heart fails me.
Thou wilt set me high upon a rock, thou wilt
give me rest:

thou art my fortress, a tower of strength against the face
of the enemy.

And Alexandra's eyes grieve, her lips recite:

For I am homesick after mine own kind
And ordinary people touch me not.
And I am homesick
After my own kind . . .

Winifrede, taking over Mildred's duty, is chanting in true
tones the short lesson to Felicity's clear responses:

Sisters: Be sober and vigilant:
for thy enemy the devil, as a raging lion, goeth about seeking whom he may devour. Him do thou resist . . .

'Aye, I am wistful for my kin of the spirit'; softly flows the
English verse beloved of Alexandra:

Well then, so call they, the swirlers out of the mist of my
soul,
They that come mewards, bearing old magic.
But for all that, I am homesick after mine own kind . . .

III

FELICITY'S WORK-BOX IS KNOWN as Felicity's only because she brought it to the convent as part of her dowry. It is no mean box, being set on fine tapered legs with castors, standing two and a half feet high. The box is inlaid with mother-of-pearl and inside it has three tiers neatly set out with needles, scissors, cottons and silks in perfect compartments. Beneath all these is a false bottom lined with red watered silk, for love-letters. Many a time has Alexandra stood gazing at this box with that certain wonder of the aristocrat at the treasured toys of the bourgeoisie. 'I fail to see what mitigation soever can be offered for that box,' she remarked one day, in Felicity's hearing, to the late Abbess Hildegarde who happened to be inspecting the sewing-room. Hildegarde made no immediate reply, but once outside the room she said, 'It is in poison-bad taste, but we are obliged by our vows to accept mortifications. And, after all, everything is hidden here. Nobody but ourselves can see what is beautiful and what is not.'

Hildegarde's dark eyes, now closed in death, gazed at Alexandra. 'Even our beauty,' she said, 'may not be thought of.'

'What should we care,' said Alexandra, 'about our beauty, since we are beautiful, you and I, whether we care or not?'

Meanwhile Felicity, aggrieved, regarded her work-box and opened it to see that all was in order. So she does every morning and by custom, now, she once more strokes the elaborate shining top after the Hour of Prime while the ordinary nuns, grown despicable by profession, file in to the sewing-room and take their places.

Felicity opens the box. She surveys the neat compartments, the reels and the skeins, the needles and the little hooks. Suddenly she gives a short scream and with her tiny bad-tempered face looking round the room at everybody she says, 'Who has touched my work-box?'

There is no answer. The nuns have come all unprepared for a burst of anger. The day of the election is not far off. The nuns have come in full expectance of Felicity's revelations about the meaningful life of love as it should be lived on the verge of the long walk lined with poplars.

Felicity now speaks with a low and strained voice. 'My box is disarranged. My thimble is missing.' Slowly she lifts the top layer and surveys the second. 'It has been touched,' she says. She raises the lowest recess and looks inside. She decides, then, to empty the work-box the better to examine the contents of its secret compartment.

'Sisters,' she says, 'I think my letters have been discovered.'

It is like a wind rushing over a lake with a shudder of birds and reeds. Felicity counts the letters. 'They are all here,' she says, 'but they have been looked at. My thimble is lost. I can't find it.'

Everyone looks for Felicity's thimble. Nobody finds it. The bell goes for the Hour of Terce. The first part of the morning has been a sheer waste of sensation and the nuns file out to their prayers, displaying, in their discontent, a trace of individualism at long last.

How gentle is Alexandra when she hears of Felicity's distress! 'Be gentle with her,' she tells the senior nuns. 'Plainly she is undergoing a nervous crisis. A thimble after all – a thimble. I wouldn't be surprised if she has not herself, in a moment of unconscious desire to pitch all her obsessive needlework to hell and run away with her lover, mislaid the ridiculous thimble. Be gentle. It is beautiful to be gentle with those who suffer. There is no beauty in the world so great as beauty of action. It stands, contained in its own moment, from everlasting to everlasting.'

Winifrede, cloudily recognizing the very truth of Alexandra's words, is yet uncertain what reason Alexandra might have for uttering them at this moment. Walburga and Mildred stand silently in the contemplative hush while Alexandra leaves them to continue their contemplations. For certainly Alexandra means what she says, not wishing her spirit to lose serenity before God nor her destiny to be the Abbess of Crewe. Very soon the whole community has been informed of these thoughts of the noble Alexandra and marvel a little that, with the election so close at hand, she exhorts gentleness towards her militant rival.

Felicity's rage all the next day shakes her little body to shrieking point. There is a plot, there is a plot, against me, is the main theme of all she says to her sewing companions between the Hours of Lauds and Prime, Prime and Terce, Terce and Sext. In the afternoon, she takes to her bed, while her bewildered friends hunt the thimble and are well overheard in the control room in all their various exchanges and conjectures.

Towards evening Walburga reports to Alexandra, 'Her supporters are wavering. The nasty little bitch can't stand our gentleness.'

'You know, Walburga,' Alexandra muses, 'from this moment on, you may not report such things to me. Everything now is in your hands and those of Sister Mildred; you are together with Fathers Baudouin and Maximilian, and you are with the aid of Winifrede. I must remain in the region of unknowing. Proceed but don't tell me. I refuse to be told, such knowledge would not become me; I am to be the Abbess of Crewe, not a programmed computer.'

Felicity lies on her hard bed and at the midnight bell she rises for Matins. My God, there is a moving light in the sewing-room window! Felicity slips out of the file of black-cloaked nuns who make their hushed progress to the chapel. Alexandra leads. Walburga and Mildred are absent. There is a light in the sewing-room, moving as if someone is holding an electric torch.

The nuns are assembled in the chapel but Felicity stands on the lawn, gazing upward, and eventually she creeps back to the house and up the stairs.

So it is that she comes upon the two young men rifling her work-box. They have found the secret compartment. One of the young men holds in his hand Felicity's love-letters. Screaming, Felicity retreats, locks the door with the intruders inside, runs to the telephone and calls the police.

In the control-room, Mildred and Walburga are tuned in to the dim-lit closed-circuit television. 'Come quickly,' says Walburga to Mildred, 'follow me to the chapel. We must be seen at Matins.' Mildred trembles. Walburga walks firmly.

The bell clangs at the gate, but the nuns chant steadily. The police sirens sound in the drive, their car having been admitted by Felicity, but the Sisters continue the night's devotions:

He turned rivers into a desert:
and springs of water into parched ground,
A fruitful land into a salt waste:
because of the wickedness of those who dwelt therein.
He turned a desert into a pool of water:

and an arid land into springs of water.
And there he settled the hungry:
and they founded a city to dwell in.

Alexandra hears the clamour outside.

Sisters, be sober, be vigilant, for the devil as a raging
lion . . .

The nuns file up to bed, anxiously whispering. Their heads bend meekly but their eyes have slid to right and to left where in the great hall the policemen stand with the two young men, dressed roughly, who have been caught in the convent. Felicity's voice comes in spasmodic gasps. She is recounting her story while her closest friend Bathildis holds her shaking body. Down upon them bear Walburga and Alexandra, swishing their habits with authority. Mildred motions the nuns upward and upward to their cells out of sight, far out of sight. Alexandra can be heard: 'Come into the parlour, sirs. Sister Felicity, be still, be sober.'

'Pull yourself together, Felicity,' Walburga says.

As the last nun reaches the last flight of stairs Winifrede in her handsome stupor comes out of the dark cupboard in the sewing-room and descends.

And, as it comes to pass, these men are discovered to be young Jesuit novices. In the parlour, they admit as much, and the police take notes.

'Officer,' says Walburga. 'I think this is merely a case of high spirits.'

'Some kind of a lark,' Alexandra says with an exalted and careless air. 'We have no charge to bring against them. We don't want a scandal.'

'Leave it to us,' says Walburga. 'We shall speak to their Jesuit superiors. No doubt they will be expelled from their Order.'

Sister Felicity screams, 'I bring a charge. They were here last night and they stole my thimble.'

'Well, Sister . . . ' says the officer in charge, and gives a little grunt.

'It was a theft,' says Felicity.

The officer says, 'A thimble, ma'am, isn't much of a crime. Maybe you just mislaid it.' And he looks wistfully into the mother-of-pearl face of Alexandra, hoping for her support. These policemen, three of them, are very uneasy.

Young Bathildis says, 'It isn't only her thimble. They wanted some documents belonging to Sister Felicity.'

'In this convent we have no private property,' Walburga says. 'I am the Prioress, officer. So far as I'm concerned the incident is closed, and we're sorry you've been troubled.'

Felicity weeps loudly and is led from the room by Bathildis, who says vulgarly, 'It was a put-up job.'

In this way the incident is closed, and the two Jesuit novices cautioned, and the police implored by lovely Alexandra to respect the holiness of the nuns' cloistered lives by refraining from making a scandal. Respectfully the policemen withdraw, standing by with due reverence while Walburga, Alexandra and Mildred lead the way from the parlour.

Outside the door stands Winifrede. 'What a bungle!' she says.

'Nonsense,' says Walburga quickly. 'Our good friends, these officers here, have bungled nothing. They understand perfectly.'

'Young people these days, Sisters . . . ' says the elder policeman.

They put the two young Jesuits in a police car to take them back to their seminary. As quietly as they can possibly go, they go.

Only a small piece appears in one of the daily papers, and then only in the first edition. Even so, Alexandra's cousins, Walburga's sisters and Mildred's considerable family connections, without the slightest prompting, and not even troubling to question the fact, weigh in with quiet ferocity to protect their injured family nuns. First on the telephone and then, softly, mildly, in the seclusion of a men's club and the demure drawing-room of a great house these staunch families privately and potently object to the little newspaper story which is entitled 'Jesuit Novices on the Spree'. A Catholic spokesman is fabricated from the clouds of nowhere to be quoted by all to the effect that the story is a gross exaggeration, that it is ungallant, that it bears the heavy mark of religious prejudice and that really these sweet nuns should not be maligned. These nuns, it is pointed out, after all do not have the right of reply, and this claim, never demonstrated, is the most effective of all arguments. Anyway, the story fades into almost nothing; it is only a newspaper clipping lying on Alexandra's little desk. 'Jesuit Novices on the Spree', and a few merry paragraphs of how two student Jesuits gatecrashed the enclosed Abbey of Crewe and stole a nun's thimble. 'They did it for a bet,' explained Father Baudouin, assistant head of the Jesuit College. Denying that the police were involved, Father Baudouin stated that the incident was closed.

'Why in hell,' demands Alexandra, in the presence of Winifrede, Walburga and Mildred, 'did they take her thimble?'

'They broke in twice,' Winifrede says in her monotone of lament. 'The night before they were caught and the night they were caught. They came first to survey the scene and test the facility of entry, and they took the thimble as a proof they'd done so. Fathers Baudouin and Maximilian were satisfied and therefore they came next night for the love-letters. It was – '

'Winifrede, let's hear no more,' Walburga says. 'Alexandra is to be innocent of the details. No specific items, please.'

'Well,' says obstinate Winifrede, 'she was just asking why the hell – '

'Alexandra has said no such thing,' Walburga menaces. 'She said nothing of the kind,' Mildred agrees.

Alexandra sits at her little desk and smiles.

'Alexandra, I heard it with my own ears. You were inquiring as to the thimble.'

'If you believe your own ears more than you believe us, Winifrede,' says Alexandra, 'then perhaps it is time for us to part. It may be you have lost your religious vocation, and we shall all quite understand if you decide to return to the world quietly, before the election.'

Dawn breaks for a moment through the terribly bad weather of Winifrede's understanding. She says, 'Sister Alexandra, you asked me for no explanation whatsoever, and I have furnished none.'

'Excellent,' says Alexandra. 'I love you so dearly, Winifrede, that I could eat you were it not for the fact that I can't bear suet pudding. Would you mind going away now and start giving all the nuns a piece of your mind. They are whispering and carrying on about the episode. Put Felicity under a three days' silence. Give her a new thimble and ten yards of poplin to hem.'

'Felicity is in the orchard with Thomas,' states Winifrede.

'Alexandra has a bad cold and her hearing is affected,' Walburga observes, looking at her pretty fingernails.

'Clear off,' says Mildred, which Winifrede does, and faithfully, meanwhile, the little cylindrical ears in the walls transmit the encounter; the tape-recorder receives it in the control-room where spools, spools and spools twirl obediently for hours and many hours.

When Winifrede has gone, the three Sisters sit for a moment in silence, Alexandra regarding the press cutting, Walburga and Mildred regarding Alexandra.

'Felicity is in the orchard with Thomas,' Alexandra says, 'and she hopes to be Abbess of Crewe.'

'We have no video connection with the orchard,' says Mildred, 'not as yet.'

'Gertrude,' says Alexandra on the green telephone, 'we have news that you've crossed the Himalayas and are preaching birth-control. The Bishops are demanding an explanation. We'll be in trouble with Rome, Gertrude, my dear, and it's very embarrassing with the election so near.'

'I was only preaching to the birds like St Francis,' Gertrude says.

'Gertrude, where are you speaking from?'

'It's unpronounceable and they're changing the name of the town tomorrow to something equally unpronounceable.'

'We've had our difficulties here at Crewe,' says Alexandra. 'You had better come home, Gertrude, and assist with the election.'

'One may not canvass the election of an Abbess,' Gertrude says in her deepest voice. 'Each vote is a matter of conscience. Winifrede is to vote for me by proxy.'

'A couple of Jesuit novices broke into the convent during Compline and Felicity is going round the house saying they were looking for evidence against her. They took her thimble. She's behaving in a most menopausal way, and she claims there's a plot against her to prevent her being elected Abbess. Of course, it's a lot of nonsense. Why don't you come home, Gertrude, and make a speech about it?'

'I wasn't there at the time,' Gertrude says. 'I was here.'

'Have you got bronchitis, Gertrude?'

'No,' says Gertrude, 'you'd better make a speech yourself. Be careful not to canvass for votes.'

'Gertrude, my love, how do I go about appealing to these nuns' higher instincts? Felicity has disrupted their minds.'

'Appeal to their lower instincts,' Gertrude says, 'within the walls of the convent. It's only when exhorting the strangers outside that one appeals to the higher. I hear a bell at your end, Alexandra. I hear a lovable bell.'

'It's the bell for Terce,' Alexandra says. 'Are you not homesick, Gertrude, after your own kind?'

But Gertrude has rung off.

The nuns are assembled in the great chapter hall and the Prioress Walburga addresses them. The nuns are arranged in semicircles according to their degree, with the older nuns at the back, the lesser and more despised in the middle rows and the novices in the front. Walburga stands on a dais at a table facing them, with the most senior nuns on either side of her. These comprise Felicity, Winifrede, Mildred and Alexandra.

'Sisters, be still, be sober,' says Walburga.

The nuns are fidgeting, however, in a way that has never happened before. The faces glance and the eyes dart as if they were at the theatre waiting for the curtain to go up, having paid for their tickets. Outside the rain pelts down on the green, on the gravel, on the spreading leaves; and inside the nuns rustle as if a small tempest were swelling up amongst them.

'Be sober, be vigilant,' says Walburga the Prioress, 'for I have asked Sister Alexandra to speak to you on the subject of our recent disturbances.'

Alexandra rises and bows to Walburga. She stands like a lightning-conductor, elegant in her black robes, so soon to be more radiant in white. 'Sisters, be still. I have first a message from our esteemed Sister Gertrude. Sister Gertrude is at present settling a dispute between two sects who reside beyond the Himalayas. The dispute is on a point of doctrine which apparently has arisen from a mere spelling mistake in English. True to her bold custom, Sister Gertrude has refused to furnish Rome with the tiresome details of the squabble and bloodshed in that area and she is settling it herself out of court. In the midst of these pressing affairs Sister Gertrude has found time to think of our recent trifling upset here at cosy Crewe, and she begs us to appeal to your higher instincts and wider vision, which is what I am about to do.'

The nuns are already sobered and made vigilant by the invocation of famous Gertrude, but Felicity on the dais causes a nervous distraction by bringing out from some big pocket under her black scapular a little embroidery frame. Felicity's fingers busy themselves with some extra flourish while Alexandra, having swept her eyes upon this frail exhibition, proceeds.

'Sisters,' she says, 'let me do as Sister Gertrude wishes; let me appeal to your higher instincts. We had the extraordinary experience, last week, of an intrusion into our midst, at midnight, of two young ruffians. It's natural that you should be distressed, and we know that you have been induced to gossip amongst yourselves about the incident, stories of which have been circulated outside the convent walls.'

Felicity's fingers fly to and fro; her eyes are downcast with pale, devout lashes, and she holds her sewing well up to meet them.

'Now,' says Alexandra, 'I am not here before you to speak of the ephemera of every day or of things that are of no account, material things that will pass and will become, as the poet says,

The love-tales wrought with silken thread
By dreaming ladies upon cloth
That has made fat the murderous moth . . .

I call rather to the attention of your higher instincts the en-
during tradition of one belonging to my own ancestral lineage, Marguerite Marie Alacoque of the seventeenth century,
my illustrious aunt, founder of the great Abbeys of the Sacré
Cœur. Let me remind you now of your good fortune, for in
those days, you must know, the nuns were rigidly divided in
two parts, the *sœurs nobles* and the *sœurs bourgeoises*. Apart
from this distinction between the nobility and the bourgeoisie, there was of course a third section of the convent comprising the lay sisters who hardly count. Indeed, well into this
century the Abbey schools of the Continent were divided; the
filles nobles were taught by nuns of noble lineage while *sœurs
bourgeoises* taught the daughters of the *vils métiers*, which is
to say the tradesmen.'

Winifrede's eyes, like the wheels of a toy motor car, have
been staring eagerly from her healthy fair face; her father is
the rich and capable proprietor and president of a porcelain
factory, and has a knighthood.

Walburga's pretty hands are folded on the table before
her and she looks down at them as Alexandra's voice comes
sounding its articulate sweet numbers. Walburga's long face
is dark grey against the white frame of her coif; she brought
that great property to the convent from her devout Brazilian
mother; her father, now dead, was of a military family.

Mildred's blue eyes move to survey the novices, how they
are comporting themselves, but the heart-shape of her face is
a motionless outline as if painted on to her coif.

Alexandra stands like the masthead of an ancient ship.
Felicity's violent fingers attack the piece of stuff with her

accurate and ever-piercing needle; she had sometimes amused the late Abbess Hildegarde with her timid venom for although her descent was actually as noble as Alexandra's she demonstrated no trace at all of it. 'Some interesting sort of genetic mutation,' Hildegarde had said, 'seeing that with so fine a lineage she is, you know, a common little thing. But Felicity, after all, is something for us to practise benevolence upon.' The rain pelts harder, pattering at the window against Alexandra's clear voice as Felicity stabs and stabs again, as it might be to draw blood. Alexandra is saying:

'You must consider, Sisters, that very soon we shall have an election to appoint our new Abbess of Crewe, each one of us who is sufficiently senior and qualified to vote will do so according to her own conscience, nor may she conspire or exchange opinions upon the subject. Sisters, be vigilant, be sober. You will recall your good fortune, daughters as the majority of you are of dentists, doctors, lawyers, stockbrokers, businessmen and all the Toms, Dicks and Harrys of the realm; you will recognize your good fortune that with the advance of the century this Congregation no longer requires you to present as postulants the *épreuves*, that is to say, the proofs of your nobility for four generations of armigerious forebears on both sides, or else of ten generations of arms-bearers in the male line only. Today the bourgeois mix indifferently with the noble. No longer do we have in our Abbey the separate entrances, the separate dormitories, the separate refectories and staircases for the *sœurs nobles* and the *sœurs bourgeoises*; no longer is the chapel divided by the screens which separated the ladies from the bourgeoisie, the bourgeoisie from the baser orders. We are left now only with our higher instincts to guide us in the matter of how our Order and our Abbey proceeds. Are we to decline into a community of the total bourgeois or are we to retain the characteristics of a society of ladies? Let me recall at this point that in 1873 the Sisters of the Sacred Heart made a pilgrimage to Paray le Monial to the shrine of my ancestral aunt, headed by the Duke of Norfolk in his socks. Sisters, be vigilant. In the message conveyed to me by our celebrated Sister Gertrude, and under obedience to our Prioress Walburga, I am exhorted to appeal to your higher instincts, so that I put before you the following distinctions upon which to ponder well:

'In this Abbey a Lady places her love-letters in the casket provided for them in the main hall, to provide light entertainment for the community during the hour of recreation; but a Bourgeoise keeps her love-letters in a sewing-box.

A Lady has style; but a Bourgeoise does things under the poplars and in the orchard.

A Lady is cheerful and accommodating when dealing with the perpetrators of a third-rate burglary; but a Bourgeoise calls the police.

A Lady recognizes in the scientific methods of surveillance, such as electronics, a valuable and discreet auxiliary to her natural capacity for inquisitiveness; but a Bourgeoise regards such innovations in the light of demonology and considers it more refined to sit and sew.

A Lady may or may not commit the Cardinal Sins; but a Bourgeoise dabbles in low crimes and safe demeanours.

A Lady bears with fortitude that *Agenbite of Inwit*, celebrated in the treatise of that name in Anglo-Saxon by my ancestor Michel of Northgate in the year 1340; but a Bourgeoise suffers from the miserable common guilty conscience.

A Lady may secretly believe in nothing; but a Bourgeoise invariably proclaims her belief, and believes in the wrong things.

A Lady does not recognize the existence of a scandal which touches upon her own House; but a Bourgeoise broadcasts it *urbi et orbi*, which is to say, all over the place.

A Lady is free; but a Bourgeoise is never free from the desire for freedom.'

Alexandra pauses to smile like an angel of some unearthly intelligent substance upon the community. Felicity has put down her sewing and is looking out of the window as if angry that the rain has stopped. The other Sisters on the dais are looking at Alexandra who now says, 'Sisters, be sober, be vigilant. I don't speak of morals, but of ethics. Our topics are not those of sanctity and holiness, which rest with God; it is a question of whether you are ladies or not, and that is something *we* decide. It was well said in my youth that the question "Is she a lady?" needs no answer, since, with a lady, the question need not arise. Indeed, it is a sad thought that necessity should force us to speak the word in the Abbey of Crewe.'

Felicity leaves the table and walks firmly to the door where, as the nuns file out, she stands in apprehensive fury looking out specially for her supporters. Anxious to be ladies, even the sewing nuns keep their embarrassed eyes fixed on the ground as they tread forward to their supper of rice and meat-balls, these being made up out of a tinned food for dogs which contains some very wholesome ingredients, quite good enough for them.

When they are gone, and Felicity with them, Mildred says, 'You struck the right note, Alexandra. Novices and nuns alike, they're snobs to the core.'

'Alexandra, you did well,' says Walburga. 'I think Felicity's hold on the defecting nuns will be finished after that.'

'More defective than defecting,' says Alexandra. 'Winifrede, my dear, since you are a lady of higher instincts you may go and put some white wine on ice.' Winifrede, puzzled but very pleased, departs.

Whereupon they join hands, the three black-draped nuns, Walburga, Alexandra and Mildred. They dance in a ring, light-footed; they skip round one way then turn the other way.

Walburga then says, 'Listen!' She turns her ear to the window. 'Someone's whistled,' she says. A second faint whistle comes across the lawn from the distant trees. The three go to the window to watch in the last light of evening small Felicity running along the pathways, keeping well in to the rhododendrons until she disappears into the trees.

'The ground is sopping wet,' says Alexandra.

'They'll arrange something standing up,' Mildred says.

'Or upside down,' says Walburga.

'Not Felicity,' says Alexandra. 'In the words of Alexander Pope:

> Virtue she finds too painful an endeavour,
> Content to dwell in decencies for ever.'

IV

THE DEAF AND ELDERLY ABBOT OF YNCE, who is driven over to the Abbey once a week to hear nuns' confessions, assisted by the good Jesuit fathers Maximilian and Baudouin, has been brought to the Abbey; in company with the two Jesuits he has witnessed the voting ceremony, he has proclaimed Alexandra Abbess of Crewe before the assembled community. The old Abbot has presented the new Abbess with her crozier, has celebrated a solemn Mass, and, helped back into the car, has departed deeply asleep in the recesses of the back seat. Throughout the solemn election Felicity was in bed with influenza. She received from her friend Bathildis the news of Alexandra's landslide victory; her reaction was immediately to stick the thermometer in her mouth; this performance was watched with interest on the closed-circuit television by Alexandra, Mildred and Walburga.

But that is all over now, it is over and past. The leaves are falling and the swallows depart. Felicity has long since risen from her sick bed, has packed her suitcases, has tenderly swathed her sewing-box in sacking, and with these effects has left the convent. She has settled with her Jesuit, Thomas, in London, in a small flat in Earl's Court, and already she has made some extraordinary disclosures.

'If only,' says Walburga, 'the police had brought a charge against those stupid little seminarians who broke into the convent, then she couldn't make public statements while it was under investigation.'

'The law doesn't enter into it,' says the Abbess, now dressed in her splendid white. 'The bothersome people are the press and the bishops. Plainly, the police don't want to interfere in a matter concerning a Catholic establishment; it would be an embarrassment.'

Mildred says, 'It was like this. The two young Jesuits, who have now been expelled from the Order, hearing that there was a nun who – '

'That was Felicity,' says the Abbess.

'It was Felicity,' Walburga says.

'Yes. A nun who was practising sexual rites, or let us even say obsequies, in the convent grounds and preaching her joyless practices within the convent . . . Well, they hear of this nun, and they break into the convent on the chance that Felicity, and maybe one of her friends – '

'Let's say Bathildis,' Walburga says, considering well, with her mind all ears.

'Yes, of course, Felicity and Bathildis, that they might have a romp with those boys.'

'In fact,' says the Abbess, 'they do have a romp.'

'And the students take away the thimble – '

'As a keepsake?' says the Abbess.

'Could it be a sexual symbol?' ventures Mildred.

'I don't see that scenario,' says the Abbess. 'Why would Felicity then make a fuss about the missing thimble the next morning?'

'Well,' says Walburga, 'she would want to draw attention to her sordid little adventure. They like to boast about these things.'

'And why, if I may think aloud,' says the Lady Abbess, 'would she call the police the next night when they come again?'

'They could be blackmailing her,' Walburga says.

'I don't think that will catch on,' says the Abbess. 'I really don't. Those boys – what are their dreadful names?'

'Gregory and Ambrose,' says Mildred.

'I might have known it,' says the Abbess for no apparent reason. They sit in the Abbess's parlour and she touches the Infant of Prague, so besmeared with rich glamour as are its robes.

'According to this week's story in *The Sunday People* they have now named Maximilian, but not yet Baudouin, as having given them the order to move,' Walburga says.

' "According to *The Sunday People*" is of no account. What is to be the story according to us?' says the Abbess.

'Try this one for size,' says Mildred. 'The boys, Gregory and Ambrose – '

'Those names,' says the Abbess, 'they've put me off this scenario already.'

'All right, the two Jesuit novices – they break into the convent the first night to find a couple of nuns, any nuns – '

'Not in my Abbey,' says the Abbess. 'My nuns are above suspicion. All but Felicity and Bathildis who have been expelled. Felicity, indeed, is excommunicated. I won't have it said that my nuns are so notoriously available that a couple of Jesuit youths could conceivably enter these gates with profane intent.'

'They got in by the orchard gate,' says Mildred thoughtlessly, 'that Walburga left open for Father Baudouin.'

'That is a joke,' says the Abbess, pointing to the Infant of Prague wherein resides the parlour's main transmitter.

'Don't worry,' says Walburga, smiling towards the Infant of Prague with her wide smile in her long, tight-skinned face. 'Nobody knows we are bugged except ourselves and Winifrede never quite takes in the whole picture. Don't worry.'

'I worry about Felicity,' says Mildred. 'She might guess.'

Walburga says, 'All she knows is that our electronics laboratory and the labourers therein serve the purpose of setting up contacts with the new missions founded throughout the world by Gertrude. Beyond the green lines to Gertrude, she knows nothing. Don't worry.'

'It is useless to tell me not to worry,' the Abbess says, 'since I never do. Anxiety is for the bourgeoisie and for great artists in those hours when they are neither asleep nor practising their art. An aristocratic soul feels no anxiety nor, I think, do the famine-stricken of the world as they endure the impotent extremities of starvation. I don't know why it is, but I ponder on starvation and the starving. Sisters, let me tell you a secret. I would rather sink fleshless to my death into the dry soil of some African or Indian plain, dead of hunger with the rest of the dying skeletons than go, as I hear Felicity is now doing, to a psychiatrist for an anxiety-cure.'

'She's seeing a psychiatrist?' says Walburga.

'Poor soul, she lost her little silver thimble,' says the Abbess. 'However, she herself announced on the television that she is undergoing psychiatric treatment for a state of anxiety arising from her excommunication for living with Thomas in sin.'

'What can a psychiatrist do?' says Mildred. 'She cannot be more excommunicated than excommunicated, or less.'

'She has to become resigned to the idea,' the Abbess says. 'According to Felicity, that is her justification for employing a psychiatrist. There was more clap-trap, but I switched it off.'

The bell rings for Vespers. Smiling, the Abbess rises and leads the way.

'It's difficult,' says Mildred as she passes through the door after Walburga, 'not to feel anxious with these stories about us circulating in the world.'

The Abbess stops a moment. 'Courage!' she says. 'To the practitioner of courage there is no anxiety that will not melt away under the effect of Grace, however that may be obtained. You recite the Psalms of the Hours, and so do I, frequently giving over, also, to English poetry, my passion. Sisters, be still; to each her own source of Grace.'

Felicity's stall is empty and so is Winifrede's. It is the Vespers of the last autumn Sunday of peace within the Abbey walls. By Wednesday of next week, the police will be protecting the place, patrolling by day and prowling by night with their dogs, seeing that the press, the photographers and the television crews have started to go about like a raging lion seeking whom they may devour.

'Sisters, be sober, be vigilant.'

'Amen.'

Outside in the grounds there is nothing but whispering trees on this last Sunday of October and of peace.

Fortunate is the man who is kind and leads:
who conducts his affairs with justice.
He shall never be moved:
the just shall be in everlasting remembrance.
He shall not fear sad news:
his heart is firm, trusting in the Lord.

The pure cold air of the chapel ebbs, it flows and ebbs, with the Gregorian music, the true voices of the community, trained in daily practice by the Choir Mistress for these moments in their profession. All the community is present except Felicity and Winifrede. The Abbess in her freshly changed robe stands before her high seat while the antiphon rises and falls.

Blessed are the peacemakers, blessed are the clean of heart:
for they shall see God.

Still as an obelisk before them stands Alexandra, to survey what she has made, and the Abbess Hildegarde before her, to find it good and bravely to prophesy. Her lips move as in a film dubbed into a strange language:

> When will you ever, Peace, wild wooddove, shy wings shut,
> Your round me roaming end, and under be my boughs?
> When, when, Peace, will you, Peace? – I'll not play
>   hypocrite
>
> To my own heart: I yield you do come sometimes; but
> That piecemeal peace is poor peace. What pure peace
>   allows
> Alarms of wars, the daunting wars, the death of it?

In the hall, at the foot of the staircase, Mildred says, 'Where is Winifrede?'

The Abbess does not reply until they have reached her parlour and are seated.

'Winifrede has been to the ladies' lavatory on the ground floor at Selfridge's and she has not yet returned.'

Walburga says, 'Where will it all end?'

'How on earth,' says Mildred, 'can those two young men pick up their money in the ladies' room?'

'I expect they will send some girl in to pick it up. Anyway, those were Winifrede's instructions,' says Alexandra.

'The more people who know about it the less I like it,' Walburga says.

'The more money they demand the less I like it,' says the Abbess. 'Actually, I heard about these demands for the first time this morning. It makes me wonder what on earth Baudouin and Maximilian were thinking of to send those boys into the Abbey in the first place.'

'We wanted Felicity's love-letters,' Mildred says.

'We needed her love-letters,' says Walburga.

'If I had known that was all you needed I could have arranged the job internally,' says the Abbess. 'We have the photo-copy machines after all.'

'Felicity was very watchful at that time,' Mildred says. 'We had to have you elected Abbess, Alexandra.'

'I would have been elected anyway,' says the Abbess. 'But, Sisters, I am with you.'

'If they hadn't taken her thimble the first time they broke in, Felicity would never have suspected a thing,' Walburga says.

Mildred says, 'They were out of their minds, touching that damned thimble. They only took it to show Maximilian how easy it was to break in.'

'Such a fuss,' says the Abbess, as she has said before and will say again, with her lyrical and indifferent air, 'over a little silver thimble.'

'Oh, well, we know very little about it,' says Mildred. 'I personally know nothing about it.'

'I haven't the slightest idea what it's all about,' says Walburga. 'I only know that if Baudouin and Maximilian can't continue to find money, then they are in it up to the neck.'

'Winifrede, too, is in it up to the neck,' says the Abbess, as she has said before and will say again.

The telephone rings from the central switchboard. Frowning and tight-skinned, Walburga goes to answer it while Mildred watches with her fair, unseasonably summer-blue eyes. Walburga places her hand over the mouthpiece and says, 'The *Daily Express* wants to know if you can make a statement, Lady Abbess, concerning Felicity's psychiatric treatment.'

'Tell them,' says the Abbess, 'that we have no knowledge of Felicity's activities since she left the convent. Her stall in the chapel is empty and it awaits her return.'

Walburga repeats this slowly to the nun who operates the switchboard, and whose voice quivers as she replies, 'I will give them that message, Sister Walburga.'

'Would you really take her back?' Mildred says. But the telephone rings again. Peace is over.

Walburga answers impatiently and again transmits the message. 'They are very persistent. The reporter wants to know your views on Felicity's defection.'

'Pass me the telephone,' says the Abbess. Then she speaks to the operator. 'Sister, be vigilant, be sober. Get your pencil and pad ready, so that I may dictate a message. It goes as follows:

'The Abbess of Crewe cannot say more than that she would welcome the return of Sister Felicity to the Abbey. As for Sister Felicity's recent escapade, the Abbess is entirely comprehending, and indeed would apply the fine words of John Milton to Sister Felicity's high-spirited action. These words are: "I cannot praise a fugitive and cloistered virtue, unexercised and unbreathed, that never sallies out and sees her adversary, but slinks out of the race . . . " – Repeat that to the reporter, if you please, and if there are any more telephone calls from outside please say we've retired for the night.'

'What will they make of that?' Mildred says. 'It sounds awfully charming.'

'They'll make some sort of a garble,' says the Abbess. 'Garble is what we need, now, Sisters. We are leaving the sphere of history and are about to enter that of mythology. Mythology is nothing more than history garbled; likewise history is mythology garbled and it is nothing more in all the history of man. Who are we to alter the nature of things? So far as we are concerned, my dear Sisters, to look for the truth of the matter will be like looking for the lost limbs, toes and fingernails of a body blown to pieces in an air crash.'

'The English Catholic bishops will be furious at your citing Milton,' says Walburga.

'It's the Roman Cardinals who matter,' says the Abbess, 'and I doubt they have ever heard of him.'

The door opens and Winifrede, tired from her journey, unbending in her carriage, enters and makes a deep curtsey.

'Winifrede, my dear,' says the Abbess.

'I have just changed back into my habit, Lady Abbess,' Winifrede says.

'How did it go?'

'It went well,' says Winifrede. 'I saw the woman immediately.'

'You left the shopping-bag on the wash-basin and went into the lavatory?'

'Yes. It went just like that. I knelt and watched from the space under the door. It was a woman wearing a red coat and blue trousers and she carried a copy of *The Tablet*. She started washing her hands at the basin. Then she picked up the bag and went away. I came out of the lavatory immediately, washed my hands and dried them. Nobody noticed a thing.'

'How many women were in the ladies' room?'

'There were five and one attendant. But our transaction was accomplished very quickly.'

'What was the woman in the red coat like? Describe her.'

'Well,' says Winifrede, 'she looked rather masculine. Heavy-faced. I think she was wearing a black wig.'

'Masculine?'

'Her face. Also, rather bony hands. Big wrists. I didn't see her for long.'

'Do you know what I think?' says the Abbess.

'You think it wasn't a woman at all,' Walburga says.

'One of those student Jesuits dressed as a woman,' Mildred says.

252

'Winifrede, is that possible?' the Abbess says.

'You know,' says Winifrede, 'it's quite possible. Very possible.'

'If so, then I think Baudouin and Maximilian are dangerously stupid,' says the Abbess. 'It is typical of the Jesuit mentality to complicate a simple process. Why choose a ladies' lavatory?'

'It's an easy place for a shopping-bag to change hands,' Walburga says. 'Baudouin is no fool.'

'You should get Baudouin out of your system, Walburga,' says the Abbess.

Winifrede begins to finger her rosary beads very nervously. 'What is the matter, Winifrede?' says the Abbess.

'The ladies' toilet at Selfridge's was my idea,' she laments. 'I thought it was a good idea. It's an easy place to make a meeting.'

'I don't deny,' says the Abbess, 'that by some chance your idea has been successful. The throw of the dice is bound to turn sometimes in your favour. But you are wrong to imagine that any idea of yours is good in itself.'

'Anyway,' says Walburga, 'the young brutes have got the money and that will keep them quiet.'

'For a while,' says the Abbess of Crewe.

'Oh, have I got to do it again?' Winifrede says in her little wailing voice.

'Possibly,' says the Abbess. 'Meantime go and rest before Compline. After Compline we shall all meet here for refreshments and some entertaining scenarios. Think up your best scenarios, Sisters.'

'What are scenarios?' says Winifrede.

'They are an art-form,' says the Abbess of Crewe, 'based on facts. A good scenario is a garble. A bad one is a bungle. They need not be plausible, only hypnotic, like all good art.'

V

'GERTRUDE,' SAYS THE ABBESS into the green telephone, 'have you seen the papers?'

'Yes,' says Gertrude.

'You mean that the news has reached Reykjavik?'

'Czechoslovakia has won the World Title.'

'I mean the news about us, Gertrude, dear.'

'Yes, I saw a bit about you. What was the point of your bugging the convent?'

'How should I know?' says the Abbess. 'I know nothing about anything. I am occupied with the administration of the Abbey, our music, our rites and traditions, and our electronics projects for contacts with our mission fields. Apart from these affairs I only know what I am told appears in the newspapers which I don't read myself. My dear Gertrude, why don't you come home, or at least be nearer to hand, in France, in Belgium, in Holland, somewhere on the Continent, if not in Britain? I'm seriously thinking of dismantling the green line, Gertrude.'

'Not a bad idea,' Gertrude says. 'There's very little you can do about controlling the missions from Crewe, anyway.'

'If you were nearer to hand, Gertrude, say Austria or Italy even – '

'Too near the Vatican,' says Gertrude.

'We need a European mission,' says the Abbess.

'But I don't like Europe,' says Gertrude. 'It's too near to Rome.'

'Ah yes,' says the Abbess. 'Our own dear Rome. But, Gertrude, I'm having trouble from Rome, and I think you might help us. They will be sending a commission sooner or later to look into things here at Crewe, don't you think? So much publicity. How can I cope if you keep away?'

'Eavesdropping,' says Gertrude, 'is immoral.'

'Have you got a cold in the chest, Gertrude?'

'You ought not to have listened-in to the nuns' conversations. You shouldn't have opened their letters and you ought not to have read them. You should have invested their dowries in the convent and you ought to have stopped your Jesuit friends from breaking in to the Abbey.'

'Gertrude,' says the Abbess, 'I know that Felicity had a pile of love-letters.'

'You should have told her to destroy them. You ought to have warned her. You should have let the nuns who wanted to vote for her do so. You ought to have – '

'Gertrude, my devout logician, it is a question upon which I ponder greatly within the umbrageous garden of my thoughts, where you get your "should nots" and your "ought tos" from. They don't arise from the moral systems of the cannibal tribes of the Andes, nor the factions of the deep Congo, nor from the hills of Asia, do they? It seems to me, Gertrude, my love, that your shoulds and your shouldn'ts have been established rather nearer home, let us say the continent of Europe, if you will forgive the expression.'

'The Pope,' says Gertrude, 'should broaden his ecumenical views and he ought to stand by the Second Vatican Council. He should throw the dogmas out of the window there at the Holy See and he ought to let the other religions in by the door and unite.'

The Abbess, at her end of the green line, relaxes in the control-room, glancing at the white cold light which plays on the masses of green ferns she has recently placed about the room, beautifying it and concealing the apparatus.

'Gertrude,' she says. 'I have concluded that there's some gap in your logic. And at the same time I am wondering what to do about Walburga, Mildred and Winifrede.'

'Why, what have they done?'

'My dear, it seems it is they who have bugged the Abbey and arranged a burglary.'

'Then send them away.'

'But Mildred and Walburga are two of the finest nuns I have ever had the privilege to know.'

'This is Reykjavik,' Gertrude says. 'Not Fleet Street. Why don't you go on television? You would have a wonderful presence, Lady Abbess.'

'Do you think so, Gertrude? Do you know, I feel very confident in that respect. But I don't care for publicity. I'm in love with English poetry, and even my devotions take that form, as is perfectly valid in my view. Gertrude, I will give an interview on the television if need be, and I will quote some poetry. Which poet do you think most suitable? Gertrude, are you listening? Shall I express your views about the Holy See on the television?'

Gertrude's voice goes faint as she replies, 'No, they're only for home consumption. Give them to the nuns. I'm afraid there's a snowstorm blowing up. Too much interference on the line . . .'

The Abbess skips happily, all by herself in the control-room, when she has put down the green receiver. Then she folds her white habit about her and goes into her parlour which has been decorated to her own style. Mildred and Walburga stand up as she enters, and she looks neither at one nor the other, but stands without moving, and they with her, like Stonehenge. In a while the Abbess takes her chair, with her buckled shoes set lightly on the new green carpet. Mildred and Walburga take their places.

'Gertrude,' says the Abbess, 'is on her way to the hinterland, far into the sparse wastes of Iceland where she hopes to introduce daily devotions and central heating into the igloos. We had better get tenders from the central-heating firms and arrange a contract quickly, for I fear that something about the scheme may go wrong, such as the breakdown of Eskimo family life. What is all that yelping outside?'

'Police dogs,' says Mildred. 'The reporters are still at the gate.'

'Keep the nuns well removed from the gates,' says the Abbess. 'Do you know, if things become really bad I shall myself make a statement on television. Have you received any further intelligence?'

'Felicity has made up a list of Abbey crimes,' says Walburga. 'She complains they are crimes under English law, not ecclesiastical crimes, and she has complained on the television that the legal authorities are doing nothing about them.'

'The courts would of course prefer the affair to be settled by Rome,' says the Abbess. 'Have you got the list?' She holds out her hand and flutters her fingers impatiently while Walburga brings out of her deep pocket a thick folded list which eventually reaches the Abbess's fingers.

Mildred says, 'She compiled it with the aid of Thomas and Roget's *Thesaurus*, according to her landlady's daughter, who keeps Winifrede informed.'

'We shall be ruined with all this pay-money that we have to pay,' the Abbess says, unfolding the list. She begins to read aloud, in her clearest modulations:

' "*Wrongdoing committed by the Abbess of Crewe*".' She then looks up from the paper and says, 'I do love that word "wrongdoing". It sounds so like the gong of doom, not at all evocative of that fanfare of Wagnerian trumpets we are led to expect, but something that accompanies the smell of boiled beef and cabbage in the back premises of a Mechanics' Institute in Sheffield in the mid-nineteenth century . . . Wrongdoing is moreover something that commercial travellers used to do in the thirties and forties of this century, although now I believe they do the same thing under another name . . . Wrongdoing, wrongdoing . . . In any sense which Felicity could attach to it, the word does not apply to me, dear ladies. Felicity is a lascivious puritan.'

'We could sue for libel,' Walburga says.

'No more does libel apply to me,' says the Abbess, and continues reading aloud: ' "Concealing, hiding, secreting, covering, screening, cloaking, veiling, shrouding, shading, muffling, masking, disguising, ensconcing, eclipsing, keeping in ignorance, blinding, hoodwinking, mystifying, posing, puzzling, perplexing, embarrassing, bewildering, reserving, suppressing, bamboozling, et cetera."

'I pine so much to know,' says the Abbess, looking up from the list at the attentive handsome faces of Mildred and Walburga, 'what the "et cetera" stands for. Surely Felicity had something in mind?'

'Would it be something to do with fraud?' says Mildred.

'Fraud is implied in the next paragraph,' says the Abbess, 'for it goes on: "Defrauding, cheating, imposing upon, practising upon, outreaching, jockeying, doing, cozening, diddling, circumventing, putting upon, decoying, tricking, hoaxing, juggling, trespassing, beguiling, inveigling, luring, liming, swindling, tripping up, bilking, plucking, outwitting, making believe the moon is made of green cheese and deceiving."

'A dazzling indictment,' says the Abbess, looking up once more, 'and, do you know, she has thought not only of the wrongdoings I have committed but also those I have not yet done but am about to perform.'

The bell rings for Vespers and the Abbess lays aside the dazzling pages.

'I think,' says Walburga, as she follows the Abbess from the private parlour, 'we should dismantle the bugs right away.'

'And destroy our tapes?' says Mildred, rather tremorously. Mildred is very attached to the tapes, playing them back frequently with a rare force of concentration.

'Certainly not,' says the Abbess as they pause at the top of the staircase. 'We cannot destroy evidence the existence of which is vital to our story and which can be orchestrated to meet the demands of the Roman inquisitors who are trying to liquidate the convent. We need the tapes to trick, lure, lime, outwit, bamboozle, et cetera. There is one particular tape in which I prove my innocence of the bugging itself. I am walking with Winifrede under the poplars discussing the disguising and ensconcing as early as last summer. It is the tape that begins with the question, "What is wrong, Sister Winifrede, with the tradional keyhole method . . . ?" I replayed and rearranged it the other day, making believe the moon is green cheese with Winifrede's stupid reply which I rightly forget. It is very suitable evidence to present to Rome, if necessary. Sister Winifrede is in it up to the neck. Send her to my parlour after Vespers.'

They descend the stairs with such poise and habitual style that the nuns below, amongst whom already stir like a wind in the rushes the early suspicion and dread of what is to come, are sobered and made vigilant, are collected and composed as they file across the dark lawn, each in her place to Vespers.

High and low come the canticles and the Abbess rises from her tall chair to join the responses. How lyrically move her lips in the tidal sway of the music! . . .

Taking, obtaining, benefiting, procuring, deriving, securing, collecting, reaping, coming in for, stepping into, inheriting, coming by, scraping together, getting hold of, bringing grist to the mill, feathering one's nest . . .

Sisters, be sober, be vigilant, for the devil goeth about as a raging lion seeking whom he may devour.

Gloating, being pleased, deriving pleasure, et cetera, taking delight in, rejoicing in, relishing, liking, enjoying, indulging in, treating oneself, solacing oneself, revelling, luxuriating, being on velvet, being in clover, slaking the appetite, *faisant ses choux gras*, basking in the sunshine, treading on enchanted ground.

Out of the deep have I called unto thee,
O Lord:
Lord hear my voice.

O let thine ears consider well:
the voice of my complaint.
If thou, Lord, will be extreme to mark
what is done amiss:
O Lord, who may abide it?

Happy those early days! when I
Shined in my angel infancy.
Before I understood this place
Appointed for my second race,
Or taught my soul to fancy aught
But a white, celestial thought.

'The point is, Winifrede, that you took a very great risk passing the money to a young Jesuit seminarian who was dressed up as a woman in Selfridge's ladies' lavatory. He could have been arrested as a transvestite. This time you'd better think up something better.'

The Abbess is busy with a pair of little scissors unpicking the tiny threads that attach the frail setting of an emerald to the robes of the Infant of Prague.

'It pains me,' says the Abbess, 'to expend, waste, squander, lavish, dissipate, exhaust and throw down the drain the Sisters' dowries in this fashion. I am hard used by the Jesuits. However, here you are. Take it to the pawn shop and make some arrangement with Fathers Baudouin and Maximilian how the money is to be picked up. But no more ladies' lavatories.'

'Yes, Lady Abbess,' says Winifrede; then she says in a low wail, 'If only Sister Mildred could come with me or Sister Walburga . . . '

'Oh, they know nothing of this affair,' says the Abbess.

'Oh, they know everything!' says Winifrede, the absolute clot.

'As far as I'm concerned I know nothing, either,' says the Abbess. 'That is the scenario. And do you know what I am thinking, Winifrede?'

'What is that, Lady Abbess?'

'I'm thinking,' the Abbess says:

'I am homesick after mine own kind,
Oh, I know that there are folk about me, friendly faces,
But I am homesick after mine own kind.'

'Yes, Lady Abbess,' says Winifrede. She curtsies low and is about to depart when the Abbess, in a swirl of white, lays a hand on her arm to retain her.

'Winifrede,' she says, 'before you go, just in case anything should happen which might tend to embarrass the Abbey, I would like you to sign the confession.'

'Which confession?' says Winifrede, her stout frame heaving with alarm.

'Oh, the usual form of confession.' The Abbess beckons her to the small desk whereon is laid a typed sheet of the Abbey's fine crested paper. The Abbess holds out a pen. 'Sign,' she says.

'May I read it?' Winifrede whines, taking up the papers in her strong hands.

'It's the usual form of confession. But read on, read on, if you have any misgivings.'

Winifrede reads what is typed:

I confess to Almighty God, to blessed Mary ever Virgin, to blessed Michael the archangel, to blessed John the Baptist, to the holy apostles Peter and Paul, and to all the saints, that I have sinned exceedingly in thought, word and deed, through my fault, through my fault, through my most grievous fault.

'Sign,' says the Abbess. 'Just put your name and your designation.'

'I don't really like to commit myself so far,' Winifrede says.

'Well, you know,' says the Abbess, 'since you repeat these words at Mass every morning of your life, I would be quite horrified to think you had been a hypocrite all these years and hadn't meant them. The laity in their hundreds of millions lodge this solemn deposition before the altar every week.' She puts the pen into Winifrede's frightened hand. 'Even the Pope,' says the Abbess, 'offers the very same damaging testimony every morning of his life; he admits quite frankly that he has committed sins exceedingly all through his own grievous fault. Whereupon the altar boy says: "May Almighty God have mercy on you." And all I am saying, Winifrede, is that what's good enough for the Supreme Pontiff is good enough for you. Do you imagine he doesn't mean precisely what he says every morning of his life?'

Winifrede takes the pen and writes under the confession, 'Winifrede, Dame of the Order of the Abbey of Crewe,' in a high and slanting copperplate hand. She pats her habit to see if the emerald is safe in the deep folds of her pocket, and before leaving the parlour she stops at the door to look back warily. The Abbess stands, holding the confession, white in her robes under the lamp and judicious, like blessed Michael the Archangel.

VI

'WE HAVE ENTERED THE REALM of mythology,' says the Abbess of Crewe, 'and of course I won't part with the tapes. I claim the ancient Benefit of Clerks. The confidentiality between the nuns and the Abbess cannot be disrupted. These tapes are as good as under the secret of the confessional, and even Rome cannot demand them.'

The television crew has gone home, full of satisfaction, but news reporters loiter in a large group outside the gates. The police patrol the grounds with the dogs that growl at every dry leaf that stirs on the ground.

It is a month since Sister Winifrede, mindful of the Abbess's warning not to choose a ladies' lavatory for a rendezvous, decided it would show initiative and imagination if she arranged to meet her blackmailer in the gentlemen's lavatory at the British Museum. It was down there in that blind alley that Winifrede was arrested by the Museum guard and the attendants. 'Here's one of them poofs,' said the attendant, and Winifrede, dressed in a dark blue business suit, a white shirt with a faint brown stripe and a blue and red striped tie, emblematic of some university unidentified even by the Sunday press, was taken off to the police station still hugging her plastic bag packed tight with all those thousands.

Winifrede began blurting out her story on the way to the police station and continued it while the policewomen were stripping her of her manly clothes, and went on further with her deposition, dressed in a police-station overall. The evening paper headlines announced, 'Crewe Abbey Scandal: New Revelations', 'Crewe Nun Transvestite Caught in Gents' and 'Crewe Thimble Case – Nun Questioned'.

Winifrede, having told her story, was released without charge on the assurances of the Abbess that it was an internal and ecclesiastical matter, and was being intensively investigated as such. This touchy situation, which the law-enforcement authorities were of a mind to avoid, did not prevent several bishops from paying as many calls to the Abbess Alexandra, whitely robed in her parlour at Crewe, as she would receive, nor did it keep the stories out of the newspapers of the big wide world.

'My Lords,' she told those three of the bishops whom she admitted, 'be vigilant for your own places before you demolish my Abbey. You know of the mower described by Andrew Marvell:

> While thus he drew his elbow round,
> Depopulating all the ground,
> And, with his whistling scythe, does cut
> Each stroke between the earth and root,
> The edged steel, by careless chance,
> Did into his own ankle glance,
> And there among the grass fell down
> By his own scythe the mower mown.'

They left, puzzled and bedazzled, having one by one and in many ways assured her they had no intention whatsoever to discredit her Abbey but merely to find out what on earth was going on.

The Abbess, when she finally appeared on the television, was a complete success while she lasted on the screen. She explained, lifting in her beautiful hand a folded piece of paper, that she already had poor Sister Winifrede's signed confession to the effect that she had been guilty of exceeding wrongdoing, fully owning her culpability. The Abbess further went on to deny rumours of inferior feeding at Crewe. 'I don't deny,' she said, 'that we have our Health Food laboratories in which we examine and experiment with vast quantities of nourishing products.' In the field of applied electronics, the Abbess claimed, the Abbey was well in advance and hoped by the end of the year to produce a new and improved lightning conductor which would minimize the danger of lightning in the British Isles to an even smaller percentage than already existed.

The audiences goggled with awe at this lovely lady. She said that such tapes as existed were confidential recordings of individual conversations between nun and Abbess, and these she would never part with. She smiled sublimely and asked for everyone's prayers for the Abbey of Crewe and for her beloved Sister Gertrude, whose magnificent work abroad had earned universal gratitude.

The cameras have all gone home and the reporters wait outside the gates. Only the rubbish-truck, the Jesuit who comes to say Mass and the post-van are permitted to enter and leave. After these morning affairs are over the gates remain locked. Alexandra has received the bishops, has spoken, and has said she will receive them no more. The bishops, who had left the Abbess with soothed feelings, had experienced, a few hours after leaving the Abbey, a curious sense of being unable to recall precisely what explanation Alexandra had given. Now it is too late.

Who is paying blackmailers, for what purpose, to whom, how much, and with funds from what source? There is no clear answer, neither in the press nor in the hands of the bishops. It is the realm of mythology, and the Abbess explains this to Gertrude in her goodbye call on the green telephone.

'Well,' Gertrude says, 'you may have the public mythology of the press and television, but you won't get the mythological approach from Rome. In Rome, they deal with realities.'

'It's quite absurd that I have been delated to Rome with a view to excommunication,' says the Abbess, 'and of course, Gertrude, dear, I am going there myself to plead my cause. Shall you be there with me? You could then come back to England and take up prison reform or something.'

'I'm afraid my permit in Tibet only lasts a certain time,' Gertrude huskily replies. 'I couldn't get away.'

'In response to popular demand,' says the Abbess, 'I have decided to make selected transcripts of my tapes and publish them. I find some passages are missing and fear that the devil who goes about as a raging lion hath devoured them. There are many film and stage offers, and all these events will help tremendously to further your work in the field and to assist the starved multitudes. Gertrude, you know I am become an object of art, the end of which is to give pleasure.'

'Delete the English poetry from those tapes,' Gertrude says. 'It will look bad for you at Rome. It is the language of Cranmer, of the King James version, the book of Common Prayer. Rome will take anything, but English poetry, no.'

'Well, Gertrude, I do not see how the Cardinals themselves can possibly read the transcripts of the tapes or listen to the tapes if their existence is immoral. Anyway, I have obtained all the nuns' signed confessions, which I shall take with me to Rome. Fifty of them.'

'What have the nuns confessed?'

The Abbess reads in her glowing voice over the green telephone to far-away Gertrude the nuns' *Confiteor*.

'They have all signed that statement?'

'Gertrude, do you have bronchial trouble?'

'I am outraged,' says Gertrude, 'to hear you have all been sinning away there in Crewe, and exceedingly at that, not only in thought and deed but also in word. I have been toiling and spinning while, if that sensational text is to be believed, you have been considering the lilies and sinning exceedingly. You are all at fault, all of you, most grievously at fault.'

'Yes, we have that in the confessions, Gertrude, my trusty love. *O felix culpa*! Maximilian and Baudouin have fled the country to America and are giving seminars respectively in ecclesiastical stage management and demonology. Tell me, Gertrude, should I travel to Rome by air or by land and sea?'

'By sea and land,' says Gertrude. 'Keep them waiting.'

'Yes, the fleecy drift of the sky across the Channel will become me. I hope to leave in about ten days' time. The Infant of Prague is already in the bank – Gertrude, are you there?'

'I didn't catch that,' says Gertrude. 'I dropped a hair-pin and picked it up.'

Mildred and Walburga are absent now, having found it necessary to reorganize the infirmary at the Abbey of Ynce for the ailing and ancient Abbot. Alexandra, already seeing in her mind's eye her own shape on the upper deck of the ship that takes her from Dover to Ostend, and thence by train through the St Gothard the long journey to Rome across the map of Europe, sits at her desk prettily writing to the Cardinal at Rome. O rare Abbess of Crewe!

Your Very Reverend Eminence,

Your Eminence does me the honour to invite me to respond to the Congregational Committee of Investigation into the case of Sister Felicity's little thimble and thimble-related matters . . .

She has given the orders for the selection and orchestration of the transcripts of her tape-recordings. She has gathered her nuns together before Compline. 'Remove the verses that I have uttered. They are proper to myself alone and should not be cast before the public. Put "Poetry deleted". Sedulously expurgate all such trivial fond records and entitle the compilation *The Abbess of Crewe*.'

Our revels now are ended. Be still, be watchful. She sails indeed on the fine day of her desire into waters exceptionally smooth, and stands on the upper deck, straight as a white ship's funnel, marvelling how the wide sea billows from shore to shore like that cornfield of sublimity which never should be reaped nor was ever sown, orient and immortal wheat.

AIDING *and* ABETTING

NOTE TO READERS

The following story, like all those connected with the seventh Earl of Lucan, is based on hypothesis.

The seventh Earl has been missing since the night of 7th November 1974 when his wife was taken to hospital, severely wounded in her head, and the body of his children's nanny was found battered, in a mailsack, in his house. He left two ambiguous letters.

Since then he has been wanted on charges of murder and attempted murder, of which he was found guilty by a coroner's jury. He has not shown up to face trial in the criminal courts.

The seventh Earl was officially declared dead in 1999, his body has never been found, although he has been 'sighted' in numerous parts of the world, predominantly central Africa. The story of his presumed years of clandestine wanderings, his nightmare existence since his disappearance, remains a mystery, and I have no doubt would differ factually and in actual feeling from the story I have told. What we know about 'Lucky' Lucan, his words, his habits, his attitudes to people and to life, from his friends, photographs and police records, I have absorbed creatively, and metamorphosed into what I have written.

The parallel 'story' of a fake stigmatic woman is also based on fact.

M. S.

I

THE RECEPTIONIST LOOKED TINIER than ever as she showed the tall, tall, Englishman into the studio of Dr Hildegard Wolf, the psychiatrist who had come from Bavaria, then Prague, Dresden, Avila, Marseilles, then London, and now settled in Paris.

'I have come to consult you,' he said, 'because I have no peace of mind. Twenty-five years ago I sold my soul to the Devil.' The Englishman spoke in a very foreign French.

'Would you feel easier,' she said, 'if we spoke in English? I am an English speaker of a sort since I was a student.'

'Far easier,' he said, 'although, in a sense, it makes the reality more distressing. What I have to tell you is an English story.'

Dr Wolf's therapeutic methods had been perfected by herself. They had made her virtually the most successful psychiatrist in Paris, or at least the most sought-after. At the same time she was tentatively copied; those who tried to do so generally failed. The method alone did not suffice. Her personality was needed as well.

What she did for the most part was talk about herself throughout the first three sessions, turning only casually on the problems of her patients; then, gradually, in an offhand way she would induce them to begin to discuss themselves. Some patients, angered, did not return after the first or at least second session, conducted on these lines. Others remonstrated, 'Don't you want to hear about *my* problem?'

'No, quite frankly, I don't very much.'

Many, fascinated, returned to her studio and it was they who, so it was widely claimed, reaped their reward. By now her method was famous and even studied in the universities. The Wolf method.

'I sold my soul to the Devil.'

'Once in my life,' she said, 'I had a chance to do that. Only I wasn't offered enough. Let me tell you about it . . . '

He had heard that she would do just this. The friend who had recommended her to him, a priest who had been through her hands during a troubled period, told him, 'She advised me not to try to pray. She advised me to shut up and listen. Read the gospel, she said. Jesus is praying to you for sympathy. You have to see his point of view, what he had to put up with. Listen, don't talk. Read the Bible. Take it in. God is talking, not you.'

Her new patient sat still and listened, luxuriating in the expenditure of money which he would have found impossible only three weeks ago. For twenty-five years, since he was struck down in England by a disaster, he had been a furtive fugitive, always precariously beholden to his friends, his many friends, but still, playing the role of benefactors, their numbers diminishing. Three weeks ago his nickname Lucky had become a solidified fact. He was lucky. He had in fact discovered some money waiting for him on the death of one of his main aiders and abetters. It had been locked in a safe, waiting for him to turn up. He could afford to have a conscience. He could now consult at leisure one of the most expensive and most highly recommended psychiatrists in Paris. 'You have to listen to her, she makes you listen, first of all,' they said – 'they' being at least four people. He sat blissfully in his smart clothes and listened. He sat before her desk in a leather chair with arms; he lounged. It was strange how so many people of the past had been under the impression he had already collected the money left for him in a special account. Even his benefactor's wife had not known about its existence.

He might, in fact, have been anybody. But she arranged for the money to be handed over without a question. His name was Lucky and lucky he was indeed.

But money did not last. He gambled greatly.

The windows of Dr Wolf's consulting rooms on the Boulevard St Germain were double-glazed to allow only a pleasing hum of traffic to penetrate.

'I don't know how it struck you,' said Hildegard (Dr Wolf) to her patient. 'But to me, selling one's soul to the Devil involves murder. Anything less is not worthy of the designation. You can sell your soul to a number of agents, let's face it, but to the Devil there has to be a killing or so involved. In my case, it was many years ago, I was treating a patient who became psychologically dependent on me. A young man, not very nice. His problem was a tendency to suicide. One was tempted to encourage him in his desire. He was simply nasty, simply cruel. His fortune was immense. I was offered a sum of money by his cousin, the next of kin, to slide this awful young man down the slope. But I didn't. I sensed the meanness of the cousin, and doubted whether he would really have parted with the money once my patient was dead. I refused. Perhaps, if I had been offered a substantially larger sum, I would have made that pact with the Devil. Who knows? As it was, I said no, I wouldn't urge the awful young man to take his own life. In fact I encouraged him to live. But to do otherwise would have definitely, I think, led to his death and I would have been guilty of murder.'

'Did he ever take his life, then?'

'No, he is alive today.'

The Englishman was looking at Hildegard in a penetrating way as if to read her true thoughts. Perhaps he wondered if she was in fact trying to tell him that she doubted his story. He wanted to get away from her office, now. He had paid for his first session on demand, a very stiff fee, as he reckoned, of fifteen hundred dollars for three-quarters of an hour. But she talked on. He sat and listened with a large bulging leather brief-case at his feet.

For the rest of the period she told him she had been living in Paris now for over twelve years, and found it congenial to her way of life and her work. She told him she had a great many friends in the fields of medicine, music, religion and art, and although well into her forties, it was just possible she might still marry. 'But I would never give up my profession,' she said. 'I do so love it.'

His time was up, and she had not asked him a single question about himself. She took it for granted he would continue with her. She shook hands and told him to fix his next appointment with the receptionist. Which, in fact, he did.

It was towards the end of that month that Hildegard asked him her first question.

'What can I do for *you*?' she said, as if he was positively intruding on her professional time.

He gave her an arrogant look, sweeping her face. 'First,' he said, 'I have to tell you that I'm wanted by the police on two counts: murder and attempted murder. I have been wanted for over twenty years. I am the missing Lord Lucan.'

Hildegard was almost jolted at this. She was currently treating another patient who claimed, convincingly, to be the long-missing lord. She suspected collusion.

'I suppose,' said the man at present sitting in her office, 'that you know my story.' She did indeed know his story. She knew it as thoroughly as anyone could, except for the police, who naturally would keep some secrets to themselves.

Hildegard had gathered books, and obtained press-cuttings dating from 1974, when the scandal had broken, to the present day. It was a story that was forever cropping up. The man in front of her, aged about sixty-five, looked very like the latest police identikit of Lord Lucan, but so in a different way did the other patient.

The man sitting in front of her had reached down for his brief-case. 'The story is all here,' he said, tapping the bulging bag.

'Tell me about it,' she said.

Yes, in fact, let us all hear about it, once more. Those who were too young or even unborn at the time should be told, too. The Lord Lucan with whom this story is concerned was the seventh Earl of Lucan. He was born on 18th December 1934. He disappeared from the sight of his family and most of his friends on the night of 7th November 1974, under suspicion of having murdered his children's nanny and having attempted to murder his wife. The murder of the girl had been an awful mistake. He had thought, in the darkness of a basement, that she was his wife. The inquest into the death of the nanny, Sandra Rivett, ended in a verdict 'Murder by Lord Lucan' and a warrant for his arrest. As for his wife, Lady Lucan's account of the events of that night fitted in with the findings of the police in all relevant details. However, the police had one very strongly felt complaint: the missing Earl had been aided and abetted in his movements subsequent to the murder. His upper-class friends, said the police, had helped the suspect to get away and cover his tracks. They mocked the police, they stonewalled the enquiries. By the time Lord Lucan's trail had been followed to any likely destination he could have been far away, or dead by his own hand. Many, at the time, believed he had escaped to Africa, where he had friends and resources.

From time to time throughout the intervening years 'sightings' of the missing suspect have been reported. The legend has not been allowed to fade. On 9th July 1994 the *Daily Express* wrote about him and the frightful end of Sandra Rivett by mistaken identity.

> The work, it appeared, of a madman or someone deranged by pressure beyond his control . . . His cheques were bouncing all over smart Belgravia, the school fees had not been paid, he had overdrafted at four banks, borrowed money from a lender (at 18 per cent interest), £7,000 from playboy Taki and £3,000 from another Greek. His mentor, gambler Stephen Raphael, had also lent him £3,000.

On the night of 7th November 1974, the basement of his wife's house was dark. The light-bulb had been removed. Down the stairs came a woman. Lucan struck, not his wife but the nanny. 'When is Sandra's night off?' he had asked one of his daughters very recently. 'Thursday,' she said. But that Thursday Sandra did not take her evening off; instead she went down to the kitchen to make a cup of tea for herself and Lucan's estranged wife. Sandra was bashed and bludgeoned. She was stuffed into a sack. Bashed also was Lucan's wife when she came down to see what was the matter. She was bashed and bloodied. She told how she had at last foiled the attacker whom she named as her husband. She bit him; she had got him by the balls, unmanned him, offered to do a deal of complicity with him and then, when he went to the bathroom to wash away the blood, slipped out of the house and staggered a few yards down the street to a pub into which she burst, covered with blood. 'Murder! . . . the children are still in the house . . . '

He had tried to choke her with a gloved hand and to finish her with the same blunt instrument by which Sandra was killed.

The police arrived at the house. The Earl had fled. He had telephoned his mother telling her to take care of the children, which she did, that very night.

The Earl was known to have been seen briefly by a friend. Then lost. Smuggled out of the country or dead by his own hand?

The good Dr Wolf looked at her patient and let the above facts run through her head. Was this man sitting in front of her, the claimant to be Lord Lucan, in fact the missing murder suspect? He was smiling, smiling away at her thoughtfulness. And what had he to smile about?

She could ring Interpol, but had private reasons not to do so.

She said, 'There is another "Lord Lucan" in Paris at the moment. I wonder which of you is the real one? Anyway, our time is up. I will be away tomorrow. Come on Friday.'

'Another *Lucavi*?'

'I will see you on Friday.'

I I

HILDEGARD WEIGHED UP THE ODDS between the two claimants while she ate her lunch at her favourite bistro in the rue du Dragon. She was eating tripe, their speciality. And what, she wondered, did Lucky mean by a pact with the Devil? She might bring him round to this. Whether he was the real Lord Lucan or not, Hildegard felt he was referring to something genuinely in his past. She would not be at all surprised to find that, as the missing Earl, he was a fake; but she would be astonished if he had not at some earlier time compromised his conscience: 'I sold my soul to the Devil.' That must mean something.

Walker, the name by which her other Lucan patient had asked to be called, had an appointment with Hildegard two days later. Walker was a surname; his first name, Robert, was never used. 'Robert Walker. Please always call me Walker. Nobody must guess that I am the seventh Earl of Lucan. There is a warrant out for my arrest.' Walker was tall, white-haired, white-moustached. From the newspaper photographs dating back twenty-odd years, he might well be the missing Earl, and again, he might not.

'On the whole,' said Hildegard, 'I think he is not Lucan. And neither is the other, most probably.' She was talking to her companion-in-life (as he had been for over five years) Jean-Pierre Roget. They sat in the sitting-room, part of their large flat. It was evening. She sat in a beige leather armchair, and so did he.

'Undoubtedly,' he said, 'the two men are acquainted with each other, working together. It would be too much to ask that they should separately consult you among all the psychiatrists in Paris, two imposters, or one an imposter, one real. I can't believe it.'

'Nor can I,' she said. 'Nor do I.'

'You should try to keep an open mind.'

'What does that mean?' she said.

'At least listen well to what they say.'

'I've listened to Walker. He sounds very troubled.'

'It's taken him a long time to be troubled. What has he been doing all these years not to be troubled before?' Jean-Pierre wondered aloud.

'Escaping from justice. Running away here and there. He had friends.'

'And Interpol? How does he know you won't hand him over?'

'Neither of them knows,' she said. 'That's what I can't understand.'

'Oh,' he said, 'I can. People generally have faith in the discretion of a psychiatrist, as they do with a priest.'

'Professionally, I was quite happy working with Walker,' she said. 'But now, with this new one . . . Sooner or later I'll have to come to grips with him.'

'What does he call himself?'

'Lucan,' she said. 'Just that.'

'What do his friends call him?'

'He says he's called Lucky. His friends have always called him Lucky Lucan. That was in the papers.'

'Which of your two patients,' said Jean-Pierre, 'resembles his photographs most?'

'Both of them,' said Hildegard.

'Hildegard,' he said, 'could either of them have anything on you? Something from your past, anything?'

'Oh, my God,' she said. 'There is always that possibility. Anyone any time could have something in their past. I can't think . . . but it would be unlikely, unbelievable. What would such people want with my past?'

'Perhaps nothing,' he said.

'Perhaps – what do you mean, Jean-Pierre?'

'Well, I don't mean exactly that you yourself might be wanted by Interpol. On the other hand . . . '

'On the other hand, what?' She had become uneasy, menacing. Jean-Pierre decided to back off.

'There is no other hand,' he said, 'since you are not on the wanted list.' He smiled very fetchingly at her. His affection was real. 'If one of these men is the missing Lucan he might feel it safe to confide in you if he knew of something in your past life that you wanted to hide. But as that is not so, since you say it isn't, that theory is ruled out, isn't it?'

'No,' she said. 'If one of them is the real Lucan he might imagine that he had something on me. Anyone might get that idea. They are probably in it together, is all I say.'

III

WALKER KEPT HIS APPOINTMENT with Hildegard.

'I am not really interested in whether you are Lord Lucan or not,' she told him. 'I am interested in you, what you are doing here, why you need a psychiatrist, why your nerve has failed you if that is so. I am interested in a number of important factors, but not greatly in what your name may have been in 1974. You are prompted to see me now, in these weeks. Why?'

'In England,' he said, 'I have been declared officially dead in order to wind up my estate. I have come to think of myself as a dead man. It distresses me.'

'It is believed by some people,' she said, 'that the real Lord Lucan committed suicide shortly after he had murdered a girl over twenty years ago. It is a rational belief.'

'His body was never found,' said Walker. 'Naturally. Because I am Lucan.'

'You are not the only claimant,' she said.

'Really? Who is the other?'

'There could be many others. Several, at least. At what scope or advantage I can't imagine. I should have thought you'd want to keep it quiet.'

'I am keeping it quiet,' said Walker. 'My secret is safe with you.'

'Are you sure?'

'Yes, I'm sure.'

'I have only to ring Interpol.'

'So have I.'

'To give yourself up?' she said.

'No, to give you up, Dr Wolf.'

'Me? What do you mean?' Her voice had changed as if she had difficulty swallowing, as if her mouth was dry.

'You are Beate Pappenheim, the fake stigmatic from Bavaria who was exposed in 1986, who disappeared with so many millions of marks from the Pappenheim Catholic Fund that nobody knew how many, who – '

'What you are saying,' she said, 'means nothing to me. Let's return to your problem, which, as I see it, is one of identity.'

'I know who I am,' he said. 'I have friends. Helpers. People who know who I am.'

'Perhaps, then, you don't need me,' she said, arranging the pens on her desk a little more neatly than they had been.

'Beate Pappenheim,' he said, 'how long does a warrant for arrest last? A whole lifetime?'

'My name is not Pappenheim,' she said, 'and I am not a lawyer. I imagine a warrant for arrest in most countries lasts a lifetime or until the event of an arrest being made, but surely among your friends and helpers there is one who knows or practises criminal law?'

'My friends are getting old and some have died,' said Walker the so-called Lucan. 'None of them has practised the law. They are gentlemen, they are millionaires, but not lawyers.'

'You come here,' said Dr Wolf, 'with your story of being Robert Walker alias the seventh Earl of Lucan, a fugitive from British law, wanted for murder. What proof can you offer that any of this story is true?'

'I don't need to prove anything.'

'If you wish to continue as my patient you do,' she said. 'Especially since I have another patient, Lucan, who also claims that he did the murder; in fact, is almost proud of it.'

'Dr Pappenheim . . .'

'Mr Walker, it's money you want, isn't it?'

'Partly.'

'Bring me proof that you are Lucan and I'll pay you, partly. And now your time is up, for which you pay me. You pay at the desk and no fooling.'

'Next Friday, Dr Pappenheim?'

'Get out.' She glared at him but he smiled at her as he rose, suave, casually dressed, rich, manicured, simply awful.

Hildegard took out of her handbag a small scent-spray which she puffed on either side of her neck. She put the spray back in her bag, thinking, I'm an animal trying to put that man off the scent. Where did he come from, that muck-raker? She phoned Jean-Pierre, knowing confidently of his admiration for her methods and his respect for her fame. 'Yes, I am being threatened,' she said, 'about some past life of mine, something in another world. It's upsetting me. Not rationally, of course. But I don't know quite what to do.'

'We can discuss it tonight, Hildegard. Why are you upset? Don't you expect your patients to be nuts?'

'It's that first Lord Lucan, Walker by name. Who do you suppose Walker really is?'

'A private detective,' said Jean-Pierre. 'Someone making enquiries about the real Lucan, it could be.'

'See you later,' she said.

Jean-Pierre was seven years her junior. Their difference in age was not apparent. Hildegard had a charming face and form, with dark well-cared-for hair, a pale skin and large grey eyes. Jean-Pierre was a man of big build, already grisly-grey with a beard. For over five years now he had shared his life with Hildegard. He could think of no one else, practically nothing else, but Hildegard.

Jean-Pierre was a metal- and wood-worker, with a workshop and foundry where he spent his working days. Jean-Pierre had a genius for making things, such as bells, fire-irons, horse brasses, doors, windows, and especially adjustable bookcases. He also restored objects which had been broken; he made lamps out of vases and mended good china jugs. His workshop was like a junk heap of Europe, a history of antiquity, with its corner cabinets and consoles filled and littered with little boxes, primitive telephones, shells, ancient coins, everything. He used coins for eyes, frequently, when he felt in the mood to make up a mask in wood and iron. He liked wooden shoe-forms. This place of business was in the suburbs, by road (he had a Fiat van) half an hour from the centre outside of the rush hour. He now lived with Hildegard in the rue du Dragon on the left bank.

IV

DO NOT LOSE HOLD OF THE NAME Hildegard Wolf. Her real name, Beate Pappenheim, now comes into this story, but she leads us inevitably to Hildegard. Beate was a young student in Munich in the 'seventies when she suddenly got tired, very, very tired, of being poor. This happens to a great number of impoverished people. Not all can do something about that condition.

Beate, a medical student who hoped to specialize in feminist psychology, was having a very hard time. She attended her university classes in the mornings and early afternoon she studied English. But from four p.m. to eight p.m. she had to work a four-hour shift at the handbag counter of a department store. It was the only way she could make a living, earning enough to pay for her cheap bedsitting room and meagre food. Her parents lived in the country on a pig farm. She went to see them by bus one weekend a month, taking with her an offering of tinned foods, oatmeal, or pickled cucumber. Her studies fascinated her. The job at the handbag department of the store wearied her heart out. She was tired of women who came to buy handbags and who tried the capacity of their purchases by first emptying their own bags to see if the contents would fit into the new one. It was then that Beate Pappenheim would frequently catch sight of the fat, bulging notecases of some of these women. Sometimes the money, solid packets of Deutschmarks, was not even enclosed in a wallet. Beate coveted this money. She would have stolen had she been able to do so without detection. She was tired, tired. Still in her twenties, she felt worn out. Her need for money was continual. Her boy-friend was a theological student, of the Protestant faith. He spoke English fluently, made her speak to him in English so that she could read the English-language textbooks in psychology. He would have loved to be a Catholic, the churches were so much more cheerful than any others, so full of colour and glitter, incense and images.

One day on a Saturday when she was not visiting the farm, her boyfriend, Heinrich, came to visit her. It was three in the afternoon. He had a key. He found her on the bed covered in blood. She was having a menstrual haemorrhage. Blood all over the sheets, the floor, her hands. Heinrich ran for the landlady, who screamed when she saw Beate. Meanwhile the young man located a doctor who came and gave Beate an injection and the landlady orders to clean up the mess. Heinrich took over the job from the trembling woman who was also concerned about her bed sheets and the curtains, for blood had even spread to the windows, somehow.

Much later Beate was able to sit up. The landlady, to Beate's surprise, was now sympathetic and brought her some soup which Heinrich heated up on the spirit stove in the corner of the room. 'You reminded me,' said the landlady, who was a Catholic, 'of a picture I saw as a child of Sister Anastasia of the Five Wounds. She was a stigmatic. She worked miracles, so they said. But the Church never recognized her as a saint. When the Bishop came to visit the churches in the diocese we had to run and put the picture out of sight. But we often had a collection for Sister Anastasia. She was good to the poor.'

This was how Beate got her idea of being a holy stigmatic. She changed her address. Every monthly menstrual cycle she covered herself in blood and bandaged her hands so that blood appeared to seep through. She was stricken every month, as the phenomenon is traditionally represented, with at least one of the five wounds of Christ (a nail-wound on each hand and foot, and a sword wound in the side). In between the cycles she wrote out testimonies to her healing powers, aided and abetted by Heinrich who appeared so much to believe in Beate's claims that possibly, on interrogation, it would have emerged that he truly believed them. The nature of belief is very strange.

Beate had arranged for thousands of leaflets to be printed:

BLESSED BEATE PAPPENHEIM

THE STIGMATIC OF MUNICH

Please repeat the following prayer seven mornings a week for seven weeks. Beate Pappenheim prays and suffers for you.

O Lord, bless us through the good offices of our sister Beate Pappenheim. We beseech Thee to hear her prayer on behalf of our sick/suffering brother/sister [delete as appropriate] N. In the name of the Five Wounds of Jesus Christ Our Lord.

Underneath was a picture of Beate holding up her bloodstained hands.

Below this was printed a brief biography of Beate with emphasis on her church-going persistence from childhood upwards.

The leaflet concluded:

I enclose the sum of .... for the aid of Beate Pappenheim's Poor. Please send what you can afford. No gift is too small.

Heinrich had some friends in the theological college on whom he tried this leaflet. 'She really works miracles.' Nearly all of them laughed it off. But not all. After a while the news of Beate's miracle-working reached the nursing profession and somehow or other got to the shores of Ireland, the great land of believers. There it exploded into a real cult, so that when eventually (it took eight years) she was exposed as a fraud by analysis of her menstrual blood, more money in Irish currency than any other was found to have been placed to her account. Meanwhile, she had escaped, disappeared.

Beate during that time had been able to live in comfort. Every month she took to her bed and bloodily received pilgrims. Miracles did happen, as in fact they sometimes do. When she was finally exposed, a great number of her followers, mainly poor people, refused to believe what the newspapers reported.

Beate herself had fled abroad. She changed her name to Hildegard Wolf. She moved, later, to Paris and set up as a psychiatrist there. With her change of name her personality expanded; it changed considerably. She would have sworn that the Beate Pappenheim of her past was a 'different person' from herself; but she had never for the past twelve years been obliged to consider the question. She had just put Beate out of her mind, destroying her old birth certificate and replacing it with a new one obtained from a lawyer in Marseilles.

She had not been forgotten altogether by the acquaintances, the friends, enemies and hangers-on of her old life, those who had profited by the cult of Blessed Beate Pappenheim. And many a poor and ageing Catholic devotee of France and the British Isles remembered her name, remembered the sacrifices of their youth – the small sums, to them large, sent to Germany each month in the form of postal orders, or simple ten-shilling notes put into an envelope with a prayerful letter.

Because they had sent the money they mostly continued to believe in her, long after the *Catholic Herald* and *The Tablet*, for instance, had published reports of Beate's scientifically proved fraud. 'Beate, you have got to be true. I believe in you because I sent you all my savings and I prayed your Novena' were the words of one typical letter subsequently Returned to Sender, Address Unknown. Heinrich returned to his theological college, keeping quiet.

Walker, the first so-called Lord Lucan, arrived in time for his next appointment, and was shown in. He sat down and lit a cigarette without permission.

'Put it out,' she said.

'I like a cigarette after lunch.'

'But I haven't had my lunch,' said Hildegard firmly. 'I am just about to send down to the brasserie for a sandwich.' She buzzed her secretary. 'Have them send up a ham-and-cheese sandwich and a quarter bottle of red wine,' she ordered.

'To get down to the question of your identity . . . ' Walker began. But Hildegard was defiant. 'If you have come here for a consultation that is what you'll get. On the question of sandwiches, sooner or later we all have to stop for a sandwich or grab a sandwich before the theatre. I always have a sandwich sent up on days like today when one is expecting a boring patient, very boring. Neither in anticipation, nor retrospect, can one's digestion cope with a full meal. It is best to *faire monter* a sandwich. How old are you?'

'Sixty-five next December.'

'You look older.'

'I've had a rough time. I've been on the run. Let me explain – '

'When I've had my sandwich.' Hildegard kept silent till the girl had arrived bearing a tray. She started to eat. Between mouthfuls she spoke on, but every time she took a bite he tried to speak, too. It was quite a battle, and Hildegard won it. 'Sandwiches,' she said, 'like diamonds, are for ever. Children love them. They are the most useful, yet often the most despised of foods.' She was carried away by fantasy. 'My fondest memories from childhood are connected with sandwiches. At children's parties – '

'The most secure way of keeping my identity private is not to reveal it. But if I do have to make it known that I am Lucan, as in the case of consulting a psychiatrist as you see I have decided to do,' he said, 'the only secure way is to know something secret about the psychiatrist equal in criminality to my own case.'

'Murder would be difficult to equal,' she said. 'The sandwich was first invented by the fourth Earl of Sandwich in the eighteenth century who was a gambler like yourself, if in fact you are Lord Lucan. He devised this means of nourishment at odd hours without the necessity of leaving the gaming table for his meals, Mr Walker.'

'But you are still wanted for fraud,' said Mr Walker, 'of a particularly disreputable kind. How many poor housemaids did you rob of their savings when you were Beate Pappenheim?'

'Where you come from, of course,' said Hildegard, 'the sandwiches are spread with butter. Sandwiches of the British Isles differ greatly from German sandwiches.' She poured herself a glass of wine from the small bottle on the tray. There remained another sandwich which she lifted and slowly contemplated, then carefully took a nibble of. 'German sandwiches are much thicker, with some sort of pickles and sausage or cheese inside. Your English sandwiches, on the other hand, are cut thin, thin. They are buttered. They have fillings like chopped egg and tomatoes, sprinkled with cress which hangs in tiny threads, temptingly, out of the sides. They – '

'I know, I know,' said Walker. 'I remember them at the school sports occasions. What I have come here to discuss is the situation, which is, what are you going to do about it? I refer to the situation I described at our last sitting.'

'Oh, you are growing a beard,' Hildegard said, 'and besides,' she said as she sipped and daintily chewed at her leisure, 'there are shrimps, there are lobster and salmon, which make ideal sandwich-fillings. Strawberry sandwiches are great for picnics.

'There was a time,' she continued before Mr Walker could interrupt again, 'when bakers would sell a sandwich loaf already sliced, either white, brown or wholemeal. Probably there remain some bakers who do this. Now, I'm sure that while you sit there you find yourself eagerly desiring one of these delicious sandwiches. Don't they fill you with English nostalgia?' She wiped the corners of her mouth delicately with the pink paper napkin provided by the brasserie, and looked at her watch.

'Goodness – the time!' she said. 'I'm afraid we have to make it an abbreviated session today as I have a most urgent engagement outside the office with a patient too sick to visit me. I must visit her. Please make another appointment at the desk, if you wish to continue. Next Friday?'

'No,' he said.

'Very well,' she said. 'Good-bye.'

'You'll be hearing from me,' said Mr Walker alias Lord Lucan. 'I'll be in touch, Fräulein Pappenheim.'

She had pressed the buzzer on her desk. The petite receptionist appeared at the door.

'The patient wishes to make another appointment,' said Hildegard. She added in a more confiding tone, 'The usual fee.'

V

FROM ALL ACCOUNTS AND POLICE records of the affair of
the seventh Earl of Lucan he was an extremely arrogant
person. Arrogance is incurable. It usually arises from a deep
(sometimes justified) sense of inferiority. Another feature of
this Earl of Lucan, which supposedly he maintained, was a
peculiar eating habit which lasted apparently the whole of
his adult life up to his disappearance. And beyond? He ate
nothing but smoked salmon and lamb chops every day; in
winter the chops were grilled, in summer they were served
en gelée. Dull people found him amusing. Interesting people
thought him desperately dull. His wife was not very popular
with Lucan's gambling set. Lady Lucan was unimaginative
but honest. She protected her children, and in a bitter court
case with Lucan she had won custody of them.

Jean-Pierre had studied the huge pile of press-cuttings
which Hildegard had obtained from London. He said to her,
'The two Lucans are in league, you may be sure of that, if
one of them is trying in some way to blackmail you. Myself, I
think it unlikely that two men should turn up at your studio
at the same time, both claiming to be Lucans.'

'I think the second may be the genuine man,' said
Hildegard, 'the first a friend of his, a helper, making sure I
don't turn the genuine Lucan over to the police.'

'I am not sure of that,' he said.

'Nor am I. Perhaps neither man is Lucan.'

'Beate Pappenheim. Was it really your name?'

'Yes.'

'Beate Pappenheim . . . how lovely.'

'Why,' said Jean-Pierre the following evening, 'did you not tell me before about your exciting early life as a stigmatic?'

'Listen,' she said, 'I caused miracles. I really did cure some people. Strangely enough, I did.'

'I believe you,' said Jean-Pierre. He thought: I do believe her. She is magic. And when he thought of his life previous to meeting Hildegard he wondered how he had managed.

'We could put one of your Lucans to the test by asking him to dinner. Give him smoked salmon followed by lamb chops and see if perhaps he eats them eagerly. It says in all the books about him that he ate just that and only that,' Jean-Pierre said.

'If you prepared the meal he would of course eat it eagerly,' she said. Jean-Pierre was indeed a good cook and sometimes made their dinner on the nights-off of their two *au pair* young men. 'Which one should we invite, Lucan I or Lucan II?' said Hildegard.

'Lucan II alias Lucky.'

'That's what I'll do. Invite Lucky and give him smoked salmon and lamb chops. That diet of his was a detail reported in all the books and articles about him. It would be of some interest to see how he reacts. I'd like to make him nervous. Perhaps I could ask him a question like "Suppose that Death is a male character, what would Death's wife be like?"'

'From what I've read about him, that's too imaginative. He could never grasp such a proposition.'

'Perhaps not,' she said. 'In fact I am sure you're right. Do you know he's reputed to be very, very dull?'

'Yes, I know that. Perhaps I could lace his drink with something – we'll see. I could get you a harmless loquacious pill,' Jean-Pierre suggested. 'Something to last the evening and at the same time make him talk. I know a pharmacist.'

'How clever you are!'

Hildegard thought this over all the next day. The more she thought of it the more she liked the idea of a pill secretly administered to aid the patient to speak out. Unethical, of course. Illegal, no doubt. Neither of the Lords had hitherto bothered Hildegard personally very much, nor did they do so now. She only wondered how she could achieve a good result . . . 'I could get you a loquacious pill . . . ' She really adored Jean-Pierre; he was so very much of her own calibre. If you can comprehend a morality devoid of ethics or civil law, this was really the guiding principle of both people. And in their dealings with Lord Lucan it was on those particular moral grounds that they determined to deal with him heavily. What shocked Hildegard most in the Lucan story was his, and his set's, lack of remorse over the dead nanny, a young girl of twenty-nine, full of prettiness, life, humour. When a relative called at the Lucan home by arrangement to collect her belongings, they were handed over at the door by Lady Lucan herself, stuffed into a paper bag, and that was that.

Hildegard and Jean-Pierre read through all the press-cuttings together. 'What strikes me,' said Jean-Pierre, 'is how Lucan succeeded in antagonizing the police and the press without ever meeting them. This was mainly due, I think, to the attitude of his friends.'

'But he was really an awful man,' said Hildegard. 'For one thing he was sexually violent. He beat his wife with a cane. Very sick, that.'

'He was sick, yes. All big gamblers are sick, anyway. And if he was also a sexual sadist . . . do you recognize any of that in either of your men?'

'I see it in both. The possibility is in both. The evidence in the law suit for his children shattered Lucan. He thought his wife would observe secrecy in the matter of his sexual sadism, but she didn't. He felt betrayed. But as he was trying to make her out to be mad, obviously she had a moral right to reveal his mental condition. Besides, a bad-tempered man looking after children . . .'

'I suppose,' said Jean-Pierre, 'you realize that, unlike most of your patients, the authentic Lord Lucan really is mad?'

'You think so?'

'I'm convinced. On the facts revealed in the inquest and the biographical research over the years, he is insane.'

'But which one is the real one?'

'Hildegard, I don't like your being alone with him. Are you sure you are safe – I mean, physically?'

'I'm sure of nothing.'

'Except that Lucan I, Walker, is trying to threaten you, to obtain your complicity through blackmail. For which,' said Jean-Pierre, 'I will somehow smooth him out, I will solve his problem.'

'Darling, he is very large.'

'And I, too. I am also clever.'

Lucky had consumed his smoked salmon, served as it had been with very fine slices of buttered toast. He was now working his way through the three lamb chops on his plate. The wine was from Bordeaux and he absorbed it like blotting paper.

'What was remarkable,' he said, 'was that there was so much blood. If I had got my wife as I thought I was doing, there would never have been so much blood, so much. But I will never forget the blood that flowed in such quantity from that girl, Sandra Rivett. There must be something about the lower orders, they bleed so. I cannot forget that blood. It got everywhere. Pools of it.'

They had decided to dine in a bistro, to give Jean-Pierre time to focus his full attention on Lucky. All round the walls were signed photographs of old-time actors wearing hats, and actresses greatly be-furred. Hildegard found these reassuring, they pre-dated the memories both of her guest and of herself, and were something solid to be surrounded by in this moment of testing and confessing. 'Blood,' she said, 'is nothing new to me. As you probably know.'

'I should probably know?'

'Yes, your accomplice, the other Lucan, has no doubt informed you that I was the stigmatic of Munich, Beate Pappenheim.'

'I seem to remember the name,' said Lucky. 'But I have no accomplice. Are you crazy? My information comes from the late Reverend Brother Heinrich in whose prayer-hostel I lodged for some months.'

'I was covered with blood, endless blood. And I effected countless cures. I am not crazy. Heinrich was a poor little student. He took my money, plenty of it.'

'There was a scandal, though, I seem to think.'

'You seem to think right. I am wanted for fraud as you are for murder. Heinrich knew that I changed my name.'

'Murder plus attempted murder,' he said. 'My wife didn't bleed so much, you know. It was the nanny. Blood all over the place.'

Hildegard felt almost sympathetic towards him. 'Blood,' she said, 'blood.'

'They say it is purifying,' he said.

She thought, immediately, 'Could he be a religious maniac?'

'It is not purifying,' she said, 'it is sticky. We are never washed by blood.'

'It is said we are washed in the Blood of the Lamb,' he said, sticking his knife into lamb chop number three. 'I sang in the school choir.'

She was exultant in her suspicion. A religious maniac. The possibility consoled her. She had not, after all, found the clear opportunity of slipping Jean-Pierre's talking pill into his wine but still Lucky was talking, talking. She assumed it was the psychological effect on him of his old menu, salmon and lamb, which in fact he must have been deprived of for most of his clandestinity, lest the police should be on the watch for just that clue.

VI

GENERALLY SPEAKING, SCOTSWOMEN who do not dye their
hair have a homogeneous island-born look, a well-born look,
which does not apply in the south. The man who called himself
Lucky Lucan, who was a snob from his deepest guts, sat with
his whisky and water in the lounge of the Golf Hotel at a small
village outside Aberdeen, and greatly admired the young fair
good-boned waitress. He had picked this spot, as he always
picked spots when it was time for him to move on, with a
pin on a map open before him. It had always worked well.
Nobody was looking for him at a place he had picked out with
his eyes shut and a pin in his hand. This time he had, however,
picked from a map of North Britain. He had business there.

'Christina,' she said when he asked the girl her name. 'Do
you want a table for lunch?'

'I do. And I don't suppose,' he said, 'that you have smoked
salmon or lamb chops on the menu?'

'We have both.'

'Good. I like lamb chops.'

He was not really aware of the fact that he was sizing up
the girl in a certain way that related to Hildegard Wolf. She
was younger than Hildegard. Her hair was light gold. She
was decidedly skinnier. Lucky then realized, all of a sudden,
that he was really thinking of Hildegard, and had been all
through his nine holes of golf.

'What is your name?' he said again to the Scottish waitress.

'Christina. They call me Kirsty.'

'Kirsty, I want a double malt whisky. I want smoked salmon to start followed by lamb chops and the trimmings.'

'Your room number?' she said.

'I'll pay the restaurant bill in cash.'

He paid everything in cash, on principle. His source of cash was here in Britain. Nowadays, he came twice a year to collect it personally from his old friend, rich Benny Rolfe, who always, since Lucky's operation to change his features, had a fat package of money ready for him on his visits. Benny on this occasion was abroad, but he had arranged for the package of pounds sterling to be placed in Lucky's hands, as he had done twice a year since 1974 without fail. Most of the cash came out of Benny's own pocket, but there was always a certain amount contributed by Lucan's other old friends and collected by Benny Rolfe.

'Aren't you disgusted, ever, by what I did?' Lucky had asked Benny on one of these occasions. 'Aren't any of you horrified? Because, when I look back on it, I'm horrified myself.'

'No, dear fellow, it was a bungle like any other bungle. You should never let a bungle weigh on your conscience.'

'But if I'd killed my wife?'

'That would not have been a bungle. You would not have been the unlucky one.'

'I think of Nanny Rivett. She had an awful lot of blood. Pints, quarts of it. The blood poured out, all over the place. I was wading in it in the dark. Didn't you read about the blood in the papers?'

'I did, to tell you the truth. Perhaps murdered nannies have more blood to spill than the upper class, do you think?'

'Exactly what I would say,' Lucan had said. He was disappointed that Benny himself was not available on this visit. He ate through his lamb chops. He studied Kirsty and compared her to Hildegard. From the window of the dining room the North Sea spread its great apparent calm. Benny Rolfe was now in his mid-seventies. Nearly all Lucky's old staunch aiders and abetters were over seventy now. Who would provide him with money when his benefactors were gone? So mused Lucky, never letting his mind embrace an obvious fact: one of these days he, too, would be 'gone': a solution to the cash problem. But Lucky did not think along those lines, and he was now filled with nostalgia for Hildegard that dear doctor. 'We are washed in the Blood of the Lamb.' He looked warily over his shoulder at this thought.

After dinner he went for a stroll, stopping at a little arts-and-crafts shop which was open late, precisely for people like Lucky to stop at. Among the hideous Scottish folk-jewellery he found a fine piece of carved crystal, a pendant, for Hildegard, for Hildegard. He waited while the bearded young fellow wrapped it up for Hildegard, paid over the price and tucked the little parcel in his breast pocket.

VII

ALL ALONG THE SHELVES under the three windows of Hildegard's consulting room was placed her collection of miniature cactus plants. It was of such an extreme rarity that Hildegard was quite annoyed when one of her patients innocently presented her with another cactus. It was never of an equally rare status as her own ones, and yet she was obliged to have the new little plant on show at least for a while.

Walker had brought her such a plant; it was good but not quite good enough. She placed it with pleased carefulness on the shelf, quite as if it was of the last rarity.

Hildegard waved Walker to his chair.

'There are two of you,' Hildegard said.

Walker looked put out. 'Oh, there has to be two of us,' said Walker. 'One who committed the crime and one who didn't.'

'And which of the two is the real Lucan?'

'I am,' he said. His eyes shifted from the window to the door as if entrapped.

'Well, you're a liar,' she said.

'I often wonder about that,' said Walker. 'After years of being me, it's difficult, now, to conceive being him. How did you know there was a pretender?'

'A man called Lucky Lucan is one of my clients. He claims to be the seventh Earl.'

'What a sneak, what a rotter!' Walker was really upset. 'The seventh Earl is myself.'

'Sneaks and rotters hack children's nurses to death, you mean?'

'It was a mistake. Nanny Rivett was killed in error.'

'And the hack-and-bash job on Lady Lucan?'

'That was different. She should have died. I was in debt.'

'God, I'd like to turn you over to Interpol,' said Hildegard.

'You won't do that, Beate Pappenheim. Don't forget that I'm a professional gambler. I know when the odds are loaded against me. That's why I'm on the run, that's why I'm here, in fact. All I am asking for, Beate Pappenheim, is free psychiatric treatment. Nothing more. Just that. Your secret, your bloody secret will be safe with me if mine remains safe with you.'

'And Lucky Lucan – my other client?'

'He shouldn't have come to you at all. He's a swine.'

'He looks awfully like the original.' Hildegard opened the file she had already placed on her desk in preparation for the interview. 'See here,' she said, 'Lucan aged thirty-eight on the beach, Lucan in his ermine robes, Lucan in his tennis clothes, Lucan at a dance, and playing cards at the Clermont Club with his notorious friends. And,' she said, 'I have also a photo-kit of what he should look like now, based on computer-devised photos of his parents at your age, and here's another police identikit which allows for plastic adaptations to the jawbone and the nose. Look at it. Look.'

'But look at me.'

'You look the same height. Your eyes are spaced convincingly. Your English voice is very probable. Yes, but you don't convince me. How did you get together with Lucky Lucan?'

'I hired him. There were so many occasions when I was nearly caught, especially when collecting the funds that my friends have put at my disposal, that I thought I would take on a double. He effectively fools my friends when he goes to collect. Strangely enough Lucky, so-called, resembles me when I was in my forties more than he does now. And of course, they hardly want him to linger.'

'And suppose it's the other way round? My other client is Lucan and you are the hired substitute?'

'No,' said Walker.

'Well, I can't take you both on as patients.'

'You won't need to. I'll deal with Lucky, so-called. People like us know how to deal with people like him.'

These last words of that afternoon's conversation hovered over Hildegard's imagination. '*People like us know how to deal ...*' Of course Walker had meant to disturb her. She was aware of that. Once before he had said, when she had asked him why he had not taken the simpler course of giving himself up and standing trial for murder, 'People like us don't go to prison.' He was over-full of his aristocratic qualities, as he supposed them to be, and this was what had led Hildegard to assume he was a fake. 'People like us *know how to deal with people like him.*' Perhaps, after all, he was the real Lord Lucan. '*People like us know how to deal. . .*' Did Lucan have that conviction in mind when he 'dealt' with the woman he thought was his wife, when he 'dealt' with the knowledge of his blunder that he had killed only the children's nurse? People like us . . . people like them . . . It was almost melodramatic, but then, as Hildegard told Jean-Pierre that night, the very situation of Lord Lucan and his disappearance had a melodramatic touch. It was this very naïve approach to his personal drama that had probably confused the police in the days after the murder. They were looking for upper-class sophistication, but they got nothing but cheap show-biz from Lucan's friends. Lucan had been drinking heavily, Lucan was hopelessly in debt. But no, Lucan is a friend of ours, he is one of us and you don't understand that people like us . . . Lucan had sent letters to a friend while he was still so covered in blood that the stains appeared on the envelope. Lucan had turned up in a panic at a friend's house that night of the murder, with a bloodstain on his trousers.

Blood. 'What I'm afraid of,' Hildegard said when she discussed it with her lover, 'is that Walker will murder Lucky. It would be in character.'

'But you say that you believe Lucky to be the real Lucan?'

'There is always a doubt. I could be wrong. But Walker sticks in my mind as an unscrupulous fake.'

Jean-Pierre had been making notes. It was an hour before they would sit down to dinner. Jean-Pierre gave Hildegard her preferred drink, a small quantity of whisky dowsed in water, took one for himself, a dry martini, and got out his notebook. He read:

After twenty-five years of playing the part of the missing Lord Lucan he surely is the part. The operative word is 'missing'. If indeed he has been Lord Lucan in an earlier life he had never gone missing before. After the murder he went without money apparently, without decent clothing, without a passport. He just disappeared.

If he was the real Lord Lucan the clandestine life must have meant a loss of innocence – that he had not known he possessed. The spontaneous pleasure, for instance, of just being in Paris, as so many English people experience. The boulevards, the banks of the Seine, the traffic, the bistros, the graffiti on the walls – all lost in the new life of careful watchfulness. The odds would be against him, as he must have known if he was Lucan the professional gambler. The police were active in those early months of his clandestine flight.

And as the years piled up with nothing achieved but his furtive travels in South America, in Africa, in Asia, between intervals of quick, dangerous trips to Scotland and Paris to pick up his old friends' money, what had he become? Someone untraceable with blood on his hands, in his head, in his memory. Blood . . .

. . . My nature is subdued
To what it works in, like the dyer's hand.

When he disappeared in 1974 he was thirty-nine. The detective assigned to his case, Roy Ranson, died in recent years. Sightings of the seventh Earl are still frequent. Lucan is here, he is there, he is everywhere. In a final message to Lucan, Roy Ranson wrote, 'Keep a watchful eye over your shoulder. There will always be someone looking for Lucan.'

He must have gone through several false passports, several false names.

'Well, Hildegard,' said Jean-Pierre, 'which of your Lucans fits my profile best?'

'Neither,' she said, 'and both.'

'Why,' said Jean-Pierre, 'are the Lucans getting psychiatric therapy?'

'They are sick,' said Hildegard. 'Especially Lucky. Sick, and he knows it.'

'I mean to find out,' said Jean-Pierre, 'why they actually want psychiatric treatment.'

'Perhaps they need money. They want it from me,' said Hildegard. 'It could be that Lucan's source of income is drying up.'

'It could be. I'd like to know,' said Jean-Pierre. 'I read a recent article in which Lucan's friends claim that he is dead beyond the shadow of a doubt. "Shadow of a doubt" were the words. If they never found his body or other evidence there is a shadow, there is a doubt. There is a possibility that he is alive and another possibility that he is dead. There is no "beyond the shadow of a doubt". None whatsoever. That is journalistic talk. There are shadows; there are doubts.'

'That's what I thought when I read it. Not that I care one way or another. Only I have these Lucan patients and I'm under pressure of, well, call it exposure.'

'Yes, I call it exposure, Hildegard. Let's be clear. One gets nowhere by being muddy.'

'Nowhere,' she said, smiling gratefully at him.

Their dinner was prepared and served by the two *au pair* young men who were close friends with each other. It was a convenient arrangement. Dick and Paul were former students at a psychiatric institution where Hildegard lectured. She had found them to be engrossed with each other, anxious to shed their families, and not at all keen to study. They were delighted to show their prowess at cooking (which was not very great) and general housekeeping. They got on well with Hildegard and in a chummy way with the maid Olivia, who came every morning to clean up. Dick and Paul went shopping for the household, and advised Olivia how to shop economically for her sexy clothes. It was a tranquil background for the love affair between Hildegard and Jean-Pierre. Only the facts of blood which hovered over Hildegard's professional life and her memories of the past disturbed her.

The dinner consisted of a mysterious brown fish soup, a mousse of spinach and cream cheese with tiny new potatoes, and a peach ice-cream with cherry sauce. Jean-Pierre and Hildegard ate it appreciatively, half-consciously, happier with the fact of being cooked for and served at all than with the actual dinner. The young men, slim, tall and wiry, cleared the table and brought them coffee in the sitting-room. It had been arranged at first that their status entitled them to join Hildegard and Jean-Pierre at the table for meals, but really they preferred to eat alone together in the kitchen, with occasional friends who had belonged to their student days, rather than with their employers. And this suited Jean-Pierre and Hildegard, too. They could talk more openly, for one thing.

While they dined they discussed that other supper in the bistro with Lucky. He had certainly consumed his smoked salmon followed by lamb chops with obvious satisfaction.

'Well, it was very good smoked salmon; the lamb chops were very well prepared.'

'What did you make of him?'

'From the way he was talking I would say Lucky is Lucan, and his mind is giving up. His conscience is taking over. In his mind, God might tell him to kill again.'

Walker appeared in Jean-Pierre's workshop. There were no customers at that hour, ten-thirty a.m. Jean-Pierre was working on a plastic eye which was intended for a statue.

'My name is Walker.'

'I know who you are.'

'I want to speak to you,' Walker told Jean-Pierre.

'I have no money for you,' said Jean-Pierre.

Walker left the premises.

Hildegard was in her office talking to the patient known as Lucky.

'I'm not supposed to be here,' Lucky told her.

'I know. How long have you known Walker?'

'About ten years.'

'What is your real name?'

'I'm not at liberty to say.'

'What was your profession?'

'A theological instructor.'

'A priest?'

'I am a *défroqué*.'

'How very interesting. Why were you defrocked?'

'I got married,' he said.

'And now? Where is your wife?'

'That would be telling,' he said.

'I think you are Lucan,' Hildegard said.

'No you don't.'

'Have it your own way. There is every sign that you are the wanted man.'

'My job is just to collect from the aiders and abetters. Lucan is a name in the newspapers. He could be dead.'

'Why does Walker send you to collect?'

'Oh, he sometimes collects himself. But I look more like Lucan.'

She studied his face. 'Yes, in a way you do. In a way you don't. It could be you were once a priest, though. You have a touch of that theological look that can never be thrown off. Only a touch. Now look, Lucky, you are going to deal with one question. You knew Heinrich Esk, that theological student at the Protestant college in Munich, let us say about ten, eleven years ago, didn't you?'

'Twelve years ago,' he said.

'As I've told you, I worked some miracles,' said Hildegard. 'And that is the truth.'

'Undoubtedly. But you were a fraud. A fake stigmatic. Heinrich told me everything. He died of leukaemia, you know.'

'What do you want from me?' Hildegard said.

'Advice. I sold my soul to the Devil, as I've already told you.'

'And you want it back?'

'I want it back.'

312

'You must break with Walker for a start,' she said.

'That would be difficult.'

'I know. Well, I can't take you both on as patients.'

'I think you have no choice.' Suddenly, Lucky produced a small package. 'I brought you this from Scotland,' he said, passing the little box to Hildegard.

'You thought of me in Scotland,' she said, opening the little parcel with many exclamations of quite genuine appreciation of the crystal pendant.

'I thought of you all the time,' he said.

'That is a normal reaction towards an analyst. And what were you doing in Scotland, exactly?'

'I'm afraid that's a secret. Your other Lucan is furious because I came to you. In fact, I've been round the world in the past twenty-five years. I've been short of money at times and had to be a salesman of textbooks on Presbyterianism and physiotherapy; I've been a gentleman's gentleman – I did well. I've been a genealogist helping the Mormons to trace their ancestry – that was too dangerous, though – I had to make trips to London. What a pity: it was lucrative.'

'And how did you become a priest?'

'Well, I hid in a monastery for a time.'

'That didn't make you a priest.'

'Well, not quite. I just went around with a dog collar.'

'Most of the money wasted on psychoanalysis,' Hildegard said, 'goes on time spent unravelling the lies of the patient. Your time is up.'

'Am I Lucan?' he said. 'I want you to know that I believe in myself.'

VIII

MARIA TWICKENHAM, SEPARATED from her husband, attracted many men, but did not greatly encourage them. Maria's reputation was not the subject of scandal or gossip. But the police inspectors who called at her house the day after the murder of Lord Lucan's nanny in November 1974 were not to know that. They were unable to exclude from their minds a possibility that the two were lovers, beautiful as she was, handsome as he was.

It was on the morning of the day after Lord Lucan's disappearance that the police were at Maria's door. One in uniform, two in civilian clothes. There was no answer. They returned in the evening. A man of about forty answered the door.

The uniformed man said, 'Good afternoon. Is Mrs Twickenham at home?'

'She is my wife. She's in South Africa. I am Alfred Twickenham.'

'May we have a word with you, sir?'

'What about?'

'I believe you and your wife are close friends of Lord Lucan. We're wondering about his whereabouts in view of the tragedy that occurred at his home last night.'

'What tragedy?' said Alfred.

'I'd have thought you would have heard,' said the policeman. 'The children's nurse was murdered and the wife severely wounded. The news has been on TV and it's all over the papers. Surely you have heard?'

'Oh, vaguely,' said the man.

'He was a friend of yours. May we come in a minute? We're the Metropolitan Police. We'd like to ask a few questions.'

'Oh, I can't help you. He isn't so very close a friend.' They tramped in while he continued, 'I don't know Lucan all that well.'

In the dining room, where he took them, Alfred didn't invite them to sit down. He stood twirling the atlas-globe: his small daughter did her homework in here. 'My wife,' he said, 'knew Lucan better than me.'

' "*Knew*"?'

'Well, she probably still does know him. Remember, though, Lucky Lucan plays baccarat and we both play bridge predominantly. There's a difference.'

'Suppose,' said one of the plain clothes men, 'that I told you a car that he was using was seen parked in this street at eleven or thereabouts last night?'

'I don't know about that. My wife is in South Africa just now. Perhaps she would know more about Lord Lucan.'

'When did you last see Lord Lucan?'

'I can't remember.'

'Roughly speaking?' said one of the men.

'I can't remember. I see so many people. I think I saw him a month ago at the races.'

'And this is the first time you've heard about the murder and the attack on Lady Lucan in Lower Belgrave Street last night?' The man's eyes were wandering over the polished sideboard, the silver, as if he really wasn't expecting a straight answer.

'But I don't follow murders. I have quite enough to do, as you can imagine. I sell milk.'

'Sell milk?'

'Yes, I run a milk concern.'

'Oh, yes.' One of the other policemen had come to the rescue. 'Twickenham's Dairy Products.'

'That's right,' said Alfred.

'But isn't it upsetting for you to hear about a murder in the house of someone you know? We are looking for Lucan. He's disappeared. How does that affect you?'

'It's devastating. But he plays baccarat and poker, and my wife and I don't. We always played bridge.'

'Thank you, sir, for your cooperation.'

'Don't mention it.'

Alfred felt strongly that his house and office phones were already being tapped. Next morning he stopped at the Army and Navy Stores, where he put through a call. 'Have you heard the news?' he said to the man who answered the phone. 'Well, he's on his way to Caithness. Yes, you know where. Right. I'm calling from a box. If he passes by you . . . Of course, do just that. Oh, poor Lucky!'

At four in the afternoon Alfred went to pick up his daughter from day school.

'I wonder,' said the father, 'if anyone asks you did I have a visitor last night, could you tell them to mind their own business? Just that. Mind their own business.'

'Quite right, Daddy,' said the child.

'No one has the right to ask.'

'I know.'

The child was used to her father's friends' appearances. There was a maintenance and alimony case extending from the far-away mother, and the daughter was quite convinced that her parents had every right and reason to keep their private life private. Her best friends at school, five of them, were in roughly the same position.

'Why did I do it?' Alfred asked himself in his more mature years. 'Why did I cover up his whereabouts? Why? And so many of us did it. Why? The police knew very well we were doing so. There was something about Lucan. I wonder if that's really him they've seen, wherever it is. And why, if so, do his friends feel they must protect him, with all that blood, let's face it, on his hands?'

Blood on his hands. Blood all over his clothes that night of the murder. He did not go straight to Caithness after all, but to some other people in the country, and then to some others, and finally to Caithness, while someone else parked the car he had borrowed in Newhaven.

Maria Twickenham had been beautiful in a way which is not accountable, not to be reckoned by separate features. She was tall and gawky, long-legged, knock-kneed; her nose, too long, went very slightly awry; her mouth, a lovely shape, was definitely too wide; her greyish eyes were nicely spaced but dull and too small; her complexion, perfectly smooth, was, however, drab. How all these factors combined to make her into a striking beauty was inexplicable.

On her return to London to finalize her divorce, Maria heard the story of Lucan's visit from her husband. He felt the young daughter was bound to provide a version of Lucan's visit followed by that of the exciting policemen. At the time Maria accepted Alfred's actions as normal.

And now, decades later, Maria Twickenham read in the paper of yet another sighting of the missing seventh Earl. According to this report he was observed reclining in a hammock, in a British fruit merchant's luxurious garden somewhere small and, to Maria, forgettable, in East Africa. He appeared to have been plastically altered but was still, with the help of a computer's identikit system, recognizable. The reporter of this news had returned next day with a photographer but the hounded one, having sensed danger, had gone. At the house nobody could help. 'A white man of about sixty lying in a hammock? You must be mad. People have been turning up here all morning. I'm going to rename my house *Pilgrim's Rest*. Anyway, there's no one here this time of year . . . '

Maria thought back over the years which had done so much to change her life, her personality, her looks, her principles, her everything in a way, little by little. She thought back.

To Maria the memory was like that pill-box veiled hat she had found among her old things, dating from the early 'seventies, last worn at the Derby. She could not wear the hat any more, nor could she again accept her husband's concealment of Lucan. Certainly, she knew that if it were to happen to her, if it were to happen that a Lucan should turn up blood-stained and frantic with a perfectly ridiculous story about passing a basement window and seeing his wife being attacked by a man, Maria, herself, would not clean him up, feed him and pass him on to the next set of good friends. Friendship? Yes, but there can be too severe a strain on friendship. In friendship there is a point of collapse – a murderer revealed, or a traitor – they are people-within-people hitherto unknown.

But what was the difference, Maria wondered, between then and now? More than a quarter of a century was the difference. Alfred had married again, had died. There was something in the air one breathed. Habits change. States of mind change. Collective moods change. The likeable, working-class, murdered young nanny was now the main factor. At the time the centre of the affair was Lucan.

Maria's daughter Lacey, now over thirty, had started in her late teens to influence her mother in a quite natural and unpremeditated way. Having read the most sensible and well-informed of the books on the subject of Lucan, Maria's daughter said, 'How could you ever know such a type? What possessed Daddy to help him to escape? But how could he have been a friend in any case, such a ghastly snob? Anyway, if he could kill once he could kill again, no matter he wasn't tried for murder, the risk of his being a killer is overwhelming. Hadn't anyone any feelings for the poor lovely nurse-girl? Did everyone really believe he could be excused for attempting to kill his wife simply because he didn't like her and didn't want her to have custody of the children? Was Lucan mad?'

In some cases, Lacey reflected, there comes a moment when the best of friends, the most admiring, most affectionate, when faced with a certain person's repeated irrational behaviour, had to admit that the person is more or less mad. 'Mad' covers a whole minefield of mental conditions.

Maria's daughter, now beginning to be free, her children already in their teens, wanted to write a book. People who want to write books do so because they feel it to be the easiest thing they can do. They can read and write, they can afford any of the instruments of book-writing such as pens, paper, computers, tape-recorders, and generally by the time they have reached this decision, they have had a simple education. Lacey's main experience was based on her mother's, which was the fact that she had known the missing, probably the late, Lord Lucan. Lacey took her mother's bundle of press-cuttings, she read all the articles and books about Lucky Lucan that she could lay hands on. Then she started on a series of interviews with some of the living remnants of his life. Not many would consent to see her, and those few who did were mostly convinced that Lucan had committed suicide, either to avoid justice or to avoid injustice, as the case might be. One charming widower, a former acquaintance of the missing Earl as an undergraduate, was more forthcoming. He had retired to a stone house in Perthshire.

'If I had my time again,' he told Lacey, 'I would have looked into the affair with meticulous thoroughness. I would have solved the mystery.'

'Don't you feel that enough was done at the time?' Lacey said.

'I certainly don't. There was a kind of psychological paralysis, almost an unconscious conspiracy to let him get away. It was not only that he was a member of the aristocracy, a prominent upper-class fellow, it was that he had pitched his life and all his living arrangements to that proposition. His proposition was: I am a seventh Earl, I am an aristocrat, therefore I can do what I like, I am untouchable. For a few days after the murder, this attitude over-awed the investigators and his friends alike. Besides, it was not an ordinary murder, not a shooting affair, it was a horrible bloody slaughter; his wife was in hospital with gaping head wounds which she said were inflicted by him. He was seen by friends with blood on his trousers but they couldn't, or in other words didn't want to, believe he had perpetrated all that violence. In those first days, and even first weeks, he managed to get away. He did so on the sheer strength of his own hypnotic act. A similar case, before your time, was the escape of the traitors Maclean and Burgess. Maclean was particularly upper-class-conscious (although he was nothing, really) but it took everyone in, rooted them to the spot when the facts broke in the Foreign Office. They got away purely on the hypnosis of their life-stylish act.'

Lacey listened intently. Before Dr Joseph Murray, as his name was, had finished his meditative discourse, she had started, with hope in her heart, to form a plan.

'You say if you had your time again . . . ' said Lacey.

'Yes, I would have plunged right in. I think I could have nabbed him. The police were slow. The friends who aided and abetted Lucan ran rings around the police. Those police were used to low-life criminals from the streets and from the rooming houses of Mayfair and Soho. Clever sharpsters, they were unnerved by the stonewalling toffs; they were not exactly abject, not at all. But they were hesitant, out of their depth. When one of the friends of Lucan exclaimed when approached, "Oh dear, and good nannies are so scarce!" the police took this for heartless reality instead of a quip in poor taste. That sort of thing. I would have known how to deal with the situation the very night of the murder. I wouldn't, believe me, Lacey, have been overwhelmed.'

'It's not too late,' said Lacey.

'What?'

'Hopefully, you could still find him,' said Lacey with the utmost enthusiasm. 'I want to interview him, only. I wouldn't want necessarily to hand him over. I think he must be alive.'

'Perhaps. Personally, I believe in justice, but . . . '

'How could there be justice in such a case?' said Lacey.

Joseph Murray smiled at her. 'You're quite right, of course. Human justice could never equal the crime. All the books and articles – such piles of them – that have been written on the subject, appear to agree that Lucan, if guilty, was very guilty. Indeed I incline to agree with the theory – you'll find it in Marnham's book – that there was an accomplice, a hit-man. If so, that hit-man is somewhere on the loose. I must say that the theory is highly tenable. If sound, it would explain a number of loose factors, small as that number is.'

'Will you help me to launch a new search?'

'Oh, no. Not now.'

'Oh, yes. *Now*, Dr Murray,' said pretty Lacey. 'Now,' she repeated.

'Call me Joe,' he said.

'Joe,' she said, 'now,' she said.

Joe was the youngest son of a prosperous family. He was now in his sixties, not too tall, fairly slim. He had never married again after his young wife had died while he was teaching at Cambridge. He was a virtual and ardent zoologist and in fact took up a zoologist's interest in many human affairs outside of his personal life. About Lucan he appeared to feel as he spoke, almost zoologically. What species was Lucan? Joe was all the more curious on this score, in that he had been a friend of Lucan's. How he regretted not having had long conversations with Lucan outside of topics such as baccarat, craps, poker, *vingt-et-un*, and the possible winner of the three-thirty. Now that he came to think of it, he had never really thought of Lucan, so that when the scandal broke and Lucan did not step forward to clear himself it did seem to Joe as if Lucan could possibly be, in a way hitherto partly concealed from his acquaintances, bad-tempered to a degree that was outside of human, and was something else. Well, he reflected, that's perhaps another way of saying that poor Lucan was mad. Lucan besides was a silk purse, and it was useless to expect such an object to turn into something so good, so true, as a sow's ear.

'You know,' Joe said then to Lacey, 'I think there must have been an accomplice, a hit-man.'

'Why do you think so?'

'I knew Lucan. Not closely, but enough. When we were undergraduates. He had no imagination, or at least very little. Now, think of what he claimed in his letters and statements to his friends and on the phone to his mother the night of the murder. He said he was passing the house in Lower Belgrave Street where his wife and children were staying, when he saw from the pavement a man in the basement attacking his wife, and went to the rescue, and got all bloodied. It is the question of his seeing a man. To someone of limited imagination it would be a natural excuse – *a man*. The man was most probably, in fact, the man prominent in his mind and memory, the hit-man, the accomplice.'

'The police network failed,' said Lacey, 'to produce any man on the run that night. They found no accomplice. There was no light in the basement, and nothing could be seen, from the street, anyway.'

'The police didn't find Lucan, either. They were slow throughout. If you'd like to leave your notes with me, and any cuttings that are contemporaneous with the crime, I'll give a bit of thought to the subject. Now, my dear, you'll stay for a bite, won't you? My helper puts it ready in the microwave, and there's always more than enough for two.'

Lacey accepted the invitation and made herself at home at the kitchen table. She told Joe how she was separated from her husband, awaiting a divorce; there was no real fault on either side but that was how it was. Joe told her she was good-looking, perhaps even prettier than her mother had been at her age. He remembered Maria Twickenham quite well, she had been around and knew Lucan, 'though not intimately'. But who had known Lucan intimately?

'Lucan – who knew him really?' Joe said.

'His wife? His parents?'

'Only partially – none of them could have known him, fully.'

'He talked previous to the murder about murdering his wife.'

'Yes, well, talk . . . People often talk that way. It doesn't mean anything, necessarily; in fact, quite the opposite. It could be argued that if he intended the murder he wouldn't have talked about it.'

'I want you to come with me and see that priest I mentioned in my letter. Is he still at the same parish?'

'Father Ambrose? I got a Christmas card. Yes.'

'You'll come with me?'

'I don't know about that. And there's Benny Rolfe.'

'Who's he?'

Benny Rolfe, Joe explained, was a prosperous business-man who was once a friend of Lucan's. It was rumoured that he financed Lucan's sojourn abroad. 'You must remember that if Lucan's alive, he may have changed more radically in appearance than the mere passage of years can explain. He would have undergone perhaps extensive plastic surgery.'

'Then how would his friends recognize him?'

'That's the point. They would expect to not quite recognize him immediately; they would expect him to have undergone facial surgery. Which leaves the way wide open for a crook, posing as Lucan, making an understandably rapid visit to a friend, to pass a few general remarks, collect his money and run. Lucan could be dead while the conspiracies to elude the law continue. All I want to say, really, my dear, is that your search for the real Lucan might be fruitless.'

'Could he get away with it?'

'Enough,' said Joe, 'has been written about Lucan to prompt even an amateur actor of feeble intelligence. He would be in a position to know practically every detail of the past. A fake Lucan might be entirely convincing.'

'Obviously,' said Lacey, 'you think Lucan's dead.'

'I think nothing. I think nothing at all on the subject. His friends are divided fifty–fifty on the possibility that he killed himself soon after the murder. I should say fifty–fifty.'

'Would you know if you met him – '

'If he was real or fake? Yes, I think I should. Perhaps . . . '

'Then let's find him,' said Lacey, with so much of the en-thusiasm of the novice that Joe was lost for words; he simply smiled. 'Am I talking a lot of nonsense?' she said.

'Yes and no. I must say that without trying, nobody gets anything, anywhere. And then, of course, the whole Lucan story is thoroughly surrealistic. The only real things about it are a girl's battered body in a mailsack, his wife's head wounds, her testimony that she had been attacked by him, and blood all over the place. Apart from those vital factors – and they are vital, to say the least, aren't they? – the disappearance of Lucan partakes of the realistic-surrealistic. He was ready to disappear to avoid bankruptcy; on the other hand his friends were numerous. They seem to have been faithful in the class-conscious sense. I find very little evidence that any of the friends, the aiders and abetters as they might be, cared a damn for Lucan the man.'

'Mummy found him quite amusing,' said Lacey. 'But do you know, she told me that if she had that time over again she wouldn't like Daddy's covering up for Lucan. Something has happened to her conscience between then and now. Has this happened to other people who were involved at the time?'

'Oh, quite likely. We are not the same people as we were a quarter of a century ago. We are necessarily different in our ideas. In my view it is an economic phenomenon. We cannot afford to be snobs. Since Lucan's day, snobs have been greatly marginalized. Not entirely. Benny Rolfe, who is reputed to be Lucan's benefactor, is an old-fashioned snob. Few people today would take Lucan and his pretensions seriously, as they rather tended to do in the 'seventies. I daresay even Benny Rolfe is tiring of Lucan, if he's still alive.'

IX

ON THE ROAD TO CAITHNESS Joe and Lacey respectively marvelled how they seemed to have 'known each other all our lives'.

'You make me feel young again,' he said.

She liked the sound of that. She was hardly expecting to track down the elusive, the perhaps non-existent Earl; not really. It was the prospect of a chase that excited her, this promising and enjoyable beginning. They were on their way, now, to a house they had merely heard of, right in the far north of Scotland. It was assumed that Benny Rolfe, whose house it was, would very likely be away. He was in any case hardly ever there. It would be all the more convenient perhaps to question the housekeeper and the houseman who Joe knew lived there in perpetuity. If someone like Lucan had been to see Benny, those people would know. Of course they wouldn't talk. Not really talk. But there were ways of talking and talking, and something somehow might trickle through. 'Of course we mustn't ask direct questions,' said Joe.

'Oh, it would be fatal, I agree.'

The great lovely steep hills were all around them. The feeling of northern nature, a whole geography minding very much its own business, cautious, alien, cold and haughty, began here. The sky rolled darkly amid patches of white light. On they drove, north, north.

Yes, there was a light high up there in the turret. The bell, which was an old-fashioned pull-bell which pealed hysterically throughout the house, brought no response for the first ten minutes of their wait in the drive, in the dark.

Joe fetched a torch from his car and started prowling around, while Lacey stood hugging her coat around her, staring up at the light in the Gothic tower. Suddenly she heard a shuffle, and in a moment the door opened to a flood of light.

Joe reappeared very quickly.

'Yes?' said a man's voice.

'This is the residence of Mr Benny Rolfe, isn't it?'

'This is Adanbrae Keep. It was you that rang up?' the speaker said. He was a middle-aged, red-haired and bearded man wearing a handyman's apron. 'I thought you'd come early, gave you up. Well, you know Benny isn't here. Come in, if you will. Come in and sit yourselves down.'

The hall of Adanbrae Keep was welcoming enough, with new-looking chintzes. The man put a click-light to the fire which started to blaze up obediently.

'Benny's in France,' he said. 'Sit yourselves down. Would you like a cup of tea? My name's Gordon.'

'Yes,' said Joe.

'Oh, please,' said Lacey.

'Are you all alone here?' said Joe.

'No, no. There's the stable man, Pat Reilly, there's my garden boy, Jimmie – he's gone off to lend a hand at the golf tavern and make himself a bit extra, there's Mrs Kerr, she is in her room, but she won't be in bed yet, if you'd like to meet her I could get her. I'll just put on the kettle.'

'I'd like to see Mrs Kerr,' said Lacey when he had left the hall.

Joe said, 'We've no right to trouble them. Benny wouldn't like it. He'd think us awfully rude. It's all right just to call in, but we mustn't seem to snoop, or probe, or anything like that.'

'I'd like to probe,' said Lacey.

Just then, down the main staircase came a short dark woman of about forty with a wide lipsticked smile. 'I'm Betty Kerr,' she said. 'I heard you arrive. We just about gave you up. Are you staying anywhere around here?'

She had a pink roller, probably overlooked, still in her hair. She sat down on one of the chintz chairs. Joe told her the hotel they had booked for the night, of which she expressed approval.

'We thought we would just look in,' said Lacey, 'as Mr Rolfe isn't available, we tried everywhere, but we only wanted to sort of trace someone who might have been here recently. An old friend of Dr Murray's – that's my companion here – that we want to get in touch with.'

'What name?' said Betty Kerr.

In came Gordon the Red bearing a tray of tea-cups with the pot and jug.

'Lucan,' said Joe.

'No, I don't know of a Lucan,' said Betty Kerr. She poured out the tea and handed it out to the couple. This was an event, plainly, and she liked it. 'Did he play golf? There was a gentleman here playing golf. But no, he wasn't a Lucan. A wee man with a bag of old clubs like forty years ago. Gordon had to clean his mashie with emery paper.'

'No, the old university friend I'm trying to contact is tall.'

Gordon was hovering around. 'That could be the gentleman who was to dinner about three weeks ago. He spent the night here. He was "John" to Benny, I seem to remember. Just a minute, I'll look at the book.'

The visitors' book on its lectern stood near a closed door which led to the drawing-room. Joe went over to it with

Gordon, and they looked at the open page. 'Nobody here; he didn't sign at all, the man I'm thinking of,' said Gordon. 'There's very few visitors, so it would be on this page.'

Joe, by way of curiosity, turned back a few pages, but although he recognized a few of the names, nothing corresponding to Lucan was there. 'Anyway, Lucan's second name was John and generally applied to him when he was a student. It means nothing, though, John by itself could be anybody.'

'A tall man with white hair, in his sixties, squarish face,' said Gordon helpfully. 'In good form, I would say. I didn't take much notice.'

They had returned to the fireplace. Joe realized that the description would fit Lucan as he might be today.

It was plain to both Joe and Lacey that they had probed enough. They had neither of them desired to go blatantly behind Benny's back. Joe had already told Lacey he intended to drop Benny a line explaining his search for Lucan. 'After all, it's a legitimate search,' he had remarked to Lacey.

Now he said, 'Well, thank you, Gordon, and you, too, Mrs Kerr.'

'I hope,' said Lacey, 'we haven't disturbed you.'

'Mind how you go. Take your time,' said Betty Kerr. 'You could have stayed for a meal, but we don't have much in the house. Not like when that gentleman was here. Smoked salmon and lamb cutlets two days running.'

'Smoked salmon and lamb chops . . .'

'That's right. Benny ordered them specially for him. His preference.'

Next morning on their way still further north Joe was truly optimistic. They had already celebrated the final words of the Adanbrae Keep domestics, but Joe could not keep off the subject. It was like winning a bet at long odds.

' "Smoked salmon and lamb chops served two meals run-ning . . . " Benny knows Lucan's preferences. What a fool Lucan is to allow himself to be trapped by that characteristic of his; that eccentric taste for smoked salmon and cutlets day in, day out for years on end. It had to be Lucan.'

'Or someone like him, who has studied his ways from the press accounts,' said astute Lacey. 'And Benny Rolfe would expect him to have had his face fixed.'

The landscape was bleak and flat, below a pearly sky. They seemed to be driving into the sky. St Columba's monas-tery, lately established, was some way out of a silent, almost deserted but well-kept stone village.

A young bespectacled lay brother bade them wait a minute. Joe had telephoned in advance. Sure enough, Father Ambrose appeared as if by magic with his black habit float-ing wide around him. You could not see if he was thin or fat. He had the shape of a billowing pyramid with his small white-haired head at the apex as if some enemy had hoisted it there as a trophy of war. From under his habit pro-truded an enormous pair of dark-blue track shoes on which he lumbered towards them. As he careered along the cold cloister he read what was evidently his Office of the day; his lips moved; plainly, he didn't believe in wasting time and did believe in letting the world know it. When he came abreast of Lacey and Joe he snapped shut his book and beamed at them.

'Joe,' he said.

'Ambrose, how are you? And how goes it in your new abode? This is Lacey, daughter of Maria Twickenham. Remember Maria?'

'Well, well. How do you do? How's Maria?'

They followed him into a polished parlour; it smelt keenly of cleanliness.

It will be seen that the above description of Ambrose applies to a man very convinced of himself. Calling or no calling, Ambrose had arranged his life so that there was no challenge, no fear of any but the most shallow pitfalls. He could hardly err, there was no scope for it. He was good at raising funds.

'You want to know about Lucan,' said Ambrose.

'Yes, we're looking for him.'

'People have been looking for him this quarter-century. I brought down the press-cuttings for you. I'll have to go shortly but you can stay and look through them.' He had lumbered over to an open glass-fronted cabinet and now placed a very thick package on the table before them. In the meantime the young lay brother came in with a tray of milky coffee with dry sweet biscuits. He placed them on the table and withdrew, almost disintegrated, so shadowy was he.

Exactly above the parlour where Joe and Lacey set about their perusal of the press-cuttings was a bedroom, a simple monk's cell, eight by seven feet with a mullioned window open to the vast northern plain in which St Columba's monastery had been put up, not very long ago.

There was a tap on the door and without waiting for a reply the tapper, Ambrose, floated silently in. His finger was laid on his lips.

'Say nothing,' said Ambrose. 'Make no sound. Lucan, you have to go.'

'Why, what's wrong?'

'Lower your voice. A couple of people are intensely looking for you. I say intensely. They're here in the monastery, in the parlour just underneath.'

'Here? Oh, my God, have they got a warrant?'

'They're not the police, Lucan, they are worse. They are Joe Murray with the daughter of, guess who? – Maria

Twickenham. Her name's Lacey. Yes, Maria's daughter and the image of her mother. They have apparently nothing to do but hunt you down. Lacey is writing a book about you, of course.'

'Maria's daughter. Oh, my God.'

Ambrose placed his finger once more to his lips. 'Silence is your only hope.' He explained that he was keeping the couple occupied with a large file of press-cuttings.

'About me?'

'Of course about you. I don't want them to suspect anything. I gave them my whole collection to look at.'

'That will help them, Ambrose.'

'Meantime, though, you can be on your way.'

'Where to?'

'Keep to the east, Lucan, and I'll direct them south-west somehow. You'll find a bed-and-breakfast at Kirkwall. They'll never think of tracing you to that little hole.'

Some twenty minutes later the lay brother was observed by Lacey escorting a black-robed monk with a bulging hold-all to a light-coloured station-wagon. They shook hands and the car departed. Lacey looked back at her copy of the London paper which held a not-very-revealing article about Lucan. She said, suddenly, 'You know, this would be a good place for Lucan to hide. Are you getting anything out of these cuttings? I'm not, I seem to have seen them all.'

'They're fairly new to me,' said Joe. 'I wouldn't mind another half-hour's go at them, if that's all right by you, Lacey, dear.'

'Yes of course it's all right.' She felt how strongly he was attracted by her, and began to consider to herself that the idea of a love affair between them might not be a bad idea, even if it was only an idea.

The door opened and in wafted Ambrose.

'How are you getting on?' He fingered one of the press-cutting piles. 'How strange it must be,' he said, 'to be Lucan, if he is still alive. From what I knew of him his thoughts will be entirely on evading capture, all the time; every day, every move, every contact with the world, all his acquaintances – all, all, revolving around that one proposition, that he must avoid capture.'

'He must be haunted by what he did,' said Lacey.

'Not him,' said Joe.

Ambrose joined in with a conviction that almost betrayed him. 'Oh no, he doesn't think of the murder,' he said. 'Wherever he is, whoever he is now, he thinks of nothing but escape.'

'Do you see him ever?' said Joe.

'Not for sure. He has pretenders.'

'Not much of a cause to pretend to,' said Lacey.

'Now, what . . . ' said Ambrose. He seated himself as comfortably as he could at the central table, which was at present covered with newspaper pages and cuttings. 'What, Lacey, brings you to this manhunt?'

'I'm going to write a book.'

'And you think you'll find him where everyone else has failed? – the journalists, the police and others – who knows? There have been sightings, no findings, for a quarter-century.'

'What a fascinating subject it is,' said Joe. 'I want to help Lacey all I can.'

'Would you tip off the police if you found him?' said Ambrose.

'Yes,' said Lacey. 'No,' said Joe, simultaneously.

They laughed. 'I think he must have had a lot of hardships,' Joe said. 'He made a blunder.'

'Oh, but he fully intended to kill his wife,' said Lacey. 'The intention was there. Which one he killed is basically irrelevant. He had been talking about murdering his wife.'

'People talk, they talk,' said Ambrose. 'It was a dreadful, frightful affair, there's no doubt about that.'

'Why is it,' said Lacey, 'that most people – those who didn't know him as well as his friends and acquaintances – didn't at all believe he would take his own life? He was driving round the very night of the murder seeing friends of his and phoning his mother, and he also wrote some letters to his friends. Instructions about his overdrafts, garbled explanations, a declaration that he was going to lie low, but no good-byes, no hint that he might end his life, and no remorse, not a word of sorrow about the death of young Sandra, poor young Sandra. Yes, if I located him tomorrow I would tip off the police.'

'And you, Ambrose?' said Joe.

'Oh, in my trade you know how it is,' said the priest, and left it at that.

They were on their way south, gladly leaving behind them the flatlands of the north, the pearl-grey skies full of watery foreboding and squawking seafowl.

Lacey had with her a pile of press-cuttings – there would be about thirty – which Ambrose had arranged to be photocopied for her. He had been anxious to get rid of the couple, had not even offered to show them round the fairly new monastery.

'The man we are looking for is stupid but cunning, not clever,' she said.

'That's very true. One would think you'd known him, Lacey, as I did. He was stupid and boring. You had to draw him out. Sometimes, if you succeeded in drawing him out, he could be quite amusing though.'

'But not clever.'

'Oh no, not clever. He had a flair for gambling. Always lost in the end but he had a physical presence, so that a gaming house would find him an asset, egging on the novices and so on.'

'Are you sure you'd recognize him?' said Lacey.

'No. I don't think I would. At least, not face-on because I'd bet that he's had facial surgery. But you know, I might recognize him from the back. His shape, his movements, the way he walked. Now, if you find him, what are you going to do?'

'Arrange an interview.'

'He'd never agree to that.'

'Perhaps he would have to agree,' said Lacey. 'Or face exposure.'

Joe did not reply. Plainly, he thought, she has it both romantically and practically worked out. Why doesn't she just write the book? A book about Lucan. Why bother with Lucan himself?

Lacey went on, 'You see, I'll do a deal with him.'

'I was under the impression,' said Joe, 'that you wanted to get him arrested and tried.'

'In a way,' she said. 'Because I think he is guilty.'

'Oh, you could never be sure. As I remember him he was an unpredictable fellow. Although I didn't care for him much to begin with, well, as I say, he rather grew on me.'

They were silent for a good while. Then suddenly Lacey said, 'Oh my God!'

'What's the matter?' He was driving, and slowed down.

'Did you see from the window that monk getting into a station-wagon? He was saying goodbye to that lay brother. Then he drove off.'

'Yes, I did look out just then. I saw you were looking.'

'That couldn't be Lucan, could it?'

Joe thought for a moment. 'I only saw him from the back. It could have been Lucan, yes. From the height it could have been. But so could anyone that height and, I suppose, age, look like Lucan.'

'Wouldn't it have been natural for him to have come straight to Ambrose from Benny Rolfe's? He left early from Adanbrae Keep. Wouldn't he have come straight on to Ambrose, his old gambling friend?'

'Very likely,' said Joe. 'And now I come to think of it, that man could have been Lucan.'

'We shouldn't jump to conclusions,' she said. 'Be cautious, Joe. Dozens of men, from the back, could be Lucan.'

'It was a station-wagon,' he said, in a stunned way.

'Was it a Ford?' she said.

'Well, of course I don't know. It might have been a Ford but I couldn't swear.'

'Nor could I.'

'He could have stopped over at St Columba's. Almost certainly he would do that.'

'But Father Ambrose didn't know his whereabouts,' said Lacey.

'Ambrose is a liar. Always very shifty. All obsessed gamblers are liars.'

'The Prior of a monastery?'

'I think it possible,' said Joe, 'for a man to be a holy person and a glib liar at the same time. He might be trying to protect a man.'

They were now well into Easter Ross. Traffic began to appear as if out of the scenery, and they pulled up at a small lakeside hotel called The Potted Heid.

The Lucan who had been seen off at St Columba's by the lay brother was the one called Lucky. Having been directed east, he decided to go south. If Joe Murray and Maria Twickenham's daughter were tracking him he wanted to keep an eye on them.

To the south, to the south. Lucky Lucan was heading for the airport.

But he was not at all sure how far he could trust Ambrose. Had he put the couple on his trail? Had they recognized him while he hurried across the courtyard to the hired station-wagon, so wretchedly noticeable? The couple had been in the parlour engrossed, Ambrose had said, in newspaper cuttings. They were writing a book about him. Why did Ambrose keep newspaper cuttings about the Lucan case? Benny Rolfe, mused Lucan, was inconsiderate, was scared. He should have arranged the money payments by transfer instead of forcing him to come and collect in this eccentric way. But Benny was scared of being caught as an accomplice. No guts. Lucan decided to find a road-house somewhere near Inverness. They would probably have to pass that way. He would wait the next morning, get another car, and if possible, follow them.

As it fell out, Joe and Lacey delayed their departure from The Potted Heid to make love. It was after ten in the morning that they dumped their bags downstairs, and looked into the breakfast room. The high-priced and unjovial hotel produced some inscrutable coffee. Breakfast was definitely over. On the table where they were served the coffee which slopped over the saucer was a half-filled ashtray. Lacey, in great high spirits, pointed this out to the sullen houseman who totally ignored her. They went to pay the bill and were told that Joe's credit card didn't work. Then Lacey's didn't work. Joe said, 'Let's see,' and adjusted the card machine on a workable flat surface. His card then worked. They felt good to be on their way. They felt very good, anyway, at the grand beginning of a love affair, free and full of enterprise, without any mess of impediments.

The hills, glens, lochs, wrapped themselves around the lovers' mood. The weather was good, with alternating cloud and sun-breaks, making spectacular effects.

They stopped beyond Inverness for lunch at a good pub, Muir's Cairn, this time a lucky find. Could Lucan have gone ahead of them? About ten cars were parked outside the pub, two of them white, a medium-sized Renault and a family Ford. Inside, it was warm, there was a good crowd of people at the tables and at the bar. They were given a table by the window with a fine view.

'Now,' said Lacey, 'let's look at the clients.' Joe was already looking over the top of the menu.

There was no sign of a single man vaguely resembling the monk who had been seen into the station-wagon. From where they sat it was difficult to see everyone around the bar which stretched away into a more public salon.

Lacey glanced out of the window behind her. It was raining, now. Two or three people and a couple were making towards their cars. One man in particular drew her attention. He was putting on a dark-green waterproof short jacket, and got into a white car. He was not the man they were looking for but it now occurred to Lacey that it was quite possible the suspect Lucan had changed cars. It would be possible to do so between Caithness and Inverness, and certainly not difficult for a man of Lucan's resources. She remarked on this to Joe. He, in turn, observed that the further south they went the less likely were they to find their man.

'And besides, he might have gone directly south after leaving Benny's place,' said Joe.

'But you know Betty Kerr said he was going north. That might mean the monastery. He was very close to Ambrose in his younger days, according to my mother,' Lacey said.

Smoked salmon was on the menu and so were lamb cutlets. Joe pointed this out. 'Sounds delicious,' said Lacey. 'That's my choice.' Around them people at the other tables were being served mainly fish and chips or large salads piled with eatables covered with mayonnaise.

Joe, too, chose smoked salmon followed by lamb cutlets, mainly out of love for Lacey. He was in fact so taken with this charming young woman now in his life that he didn't care very much what he ate. He didn't care very much about finding Lucan, except to make Lacey happy.

In the quite authentic glow of their new love affair they did not focus their full attention on the comings and goings of the other customers. However, when they were served their second course of cutlets with green peas, Joe said to the waitress, 'Is the smoked salmon followed by lamb in great demand today?'

'Oh, yes,' she said, 'it's always a good combine.'

Driving south, maddeningly slow on the road, was a white Ford, quite unusual enough a car in those parts. It was driven by a whitish-haired man who, from behind, might have been their man. They were aware that the amusement of guessing the possibilities of tracing Lucan rather outweighed the possibilities themselves. There were many alternative routes to the south of Caithness. But it was definitely fun. The new lovers were in the mood for fun. Still, the car driving so slowly (why slowly?) in front of them was an exciting fact. The driver wanted them to pass, and in spite of numerous bends and dips that made passing inadvisable, they could sometimes have done so. But Lacey, who was at the wheel that afternoon, didn't do so. She kept doggedly behind the white Ford which kept doggedly at its almost funereal pace, much to the fury of the traffic behind them, which passed both cars as best it could.

'Whoever's in that Ford knows we're positively following him,' said Lacey.

They were approaching a tall wall surrounding a large house. Ahead were a number of people dressed in their best clothes for a wedding. The Ford slowed down even more. It glided towards the huge gates with heraldic designs picked out in gold surmounted by a pair of legendary creatures in stone. The white car caused a few young giggling men and women to make way for it as it swung into the drive. As Joe and Lacey passed they could see on the lawn in front of the house a huge marquee. Loud voices and soft music completed the scene of the wedding. Joe and Lacey drove on.

The tall, white-haired stranger made his way over the lawn to the thronging mass of joyful guests, the men in their formal clothes, and occasionally kilts, the women in their smart outfits with big black hats, at least five hundred people. At the far end of the marquee the bride and groom could be seen with their young friends, doubled up with laughter. A quintet was playing softly, to suit the two main generations represented. By instinct, the stranger noticed a tall, dove-grey-clad woman and her equally tall and greyly distinguished husband standing apart. He went over to them. 'How do you do? Congratulations. I'm Walker,' he said. 'I'm afraid I hadn't time to change but they knew I wouldn't. Glad to be here, anyway.' Having said this and shaken hands with the couple, he helped himself to a glass of champagne from a tray that was wafted before him.

'Oh, don't worry about your clothes,' the woman said nervously. The stranger looked down on his dark-grey suit and then beamed up at them. 'So glad you could come, Mr Walker. I don't know half my new son-in-law's friends, I'm afraid.'

'Hundreds of them,' said her husband. 'And hundreds we hardly know on my daughter's side.'

'Well, I'll go and say a word to the happy couple,' said the stranger.

It would have been difficult for him to reach the couple even if he had wanted to. The marquee was very warm both from human heat and from the side-stoves carefully placed along the edges of the tent. The stranger found a spot to stand, and before long was approached by a good-looking middle-aged woman. 'I'm sure we've met somewhere, but I can't place you.'

'Walker,' he said.

'Walker? I don't recall.' She spoke with a strong Scottish accent. 'But I know your face. I'm Bessie Lang.'

'Bessie!' he said. 'Of course. How the years fly!' He took another glass of champagne. She refused one. 'I must remind Bobbie,' said the stranger, 'to give me the guest list. So many people I know here. But of course, the young people, especially on her side, are more or less unknown to me. Oh, there's Bobbie over there' – the stranger waved to the other side of the tent – 'Excuse me, won't you? I have to make myself useful over there. Let's keep in touch.' Then he was gone, lost in another crowd, mingling, smiling, exchanging pleasantries. He shook hands finally with the bridegroom's mother and kilted, lace-shirted father, who were as short, it seemed, as the bride's parents were tall; then, having judged that a good forty minutes had passed, he made his way through the chattering concentration of the Scottish privileged, back to his white Ford.

True enough, on the road, his pursuers had disappeared. Maria Twickenham's daughter and Joe Murray, the latter's name only dimly remembered by Lucan, both of them on the hunt for him. He remembered Maria Twickenham well and felt a great nostalgia for her. If it had been Maria, he might even have revealed himself for twenty minutes. But the daughter . . . And Joe . . . Oh, no, you don't write any book about me, you don't. Ambrose had suspected they were having an affair. 'I know by the way they look over each other's shoulders while they're perusing the press-cuttings,' Ambrose had said. 'There's something about lovers and their slop, I always know it.'

And the girl's name is Lacey, thought Lucan. Very ridiculous. Imagine if I were to put in twelve to fifteen years in a prison cell just to satisfy a girl called Lacey . . .

Anyway he had thrown them at the wedding. Any subsequent enquiries would result in a man called Walker having put in an appearance at the invitation of a man whose name no one remembered.

X

HILDEGARD HAD COME FROM PARIS by train through the tunnel. She had brought two bulging zip-bags full of documents, a small suitcase, her handbag-briefcase, and what she stood up in. She got a taxi and went to the Manderville Hotel at Queen's Gate, where she had booked a room. In the taxi she put her watch one hour back. It would be one-fifteen in Paris, it was twelve-fifteen here. In Paris Jean-Pierre would be on the phone trying vainly, as he had tried for the past half-hour, to reach her and arrange, as usual, where they would eat lunch. This was the first of the hard and difficult aspects of what Hildegard had set out to do. That was, to disappear without trace. She had in fact decided on this course without fully realizing it herself, from the day, the hour, the moment she realized that the Lucan claimants knew about her past.

Jean-Pierre would go round to her office. Ring the bell. No reply. Her secretary – Jean-Pierre would ring her up at home, he would go down to the bar and ring her up. But perhaps no – did Jean-Pierre know her secretary's surname? No, he wouldn't. At three-thirty a young patient beset with unnecessary fears was due to arrive for a session. Dominique, the secretary-receptionist, would by now have let herself in, and would be puzzled by Hildegard's non-arrival. 'Will you take a seat? Dr Wolf will be here any minute,' she would say to the girl. In the meantime, four o'clock having struck, she

343

would ring Jean-Pierre's flat in vain, and then the workshop. 'M. Roget? This is Dominique, Dr Wolf's receptionist. No, there is no sign of Dr Wolf. A patient is waiting. Perhaps you should – yes, please come here. Something must have happened. Please come at once.'

They would ring the hospitals, possibly the police stations. Jean-Pierre would send the patient away with his polite apologies. Eventually, perhaps tomorrow, he might make a statement to the police. Dr Wolf is missing. The police would search her office, the flat she shared with Jean-Pierre. He would be interrogated closely. 'When did you last see Mme Wolf? What was her state of mind?'

He would probably guess her state of mind. He would of course not elaborate on this to the police. He would know she had gone into hiding.

He would wait for a message. About that, she would have to decide. On no account must anyone trace her whereabouts. She had disappeared, perhaps for ever. The Lucans would disappear too, go back to where they had come from; Hildegard thought of them as 'The Lucans', without a thought that only one of them was probably real, and the other a fake.

In Paris, the course of events that Hildegard had imagined more or less took place, except that Jean-Pierre did not report her disappearance to the police.

She had paid up the rent on her office and given notice. She had left the office furniture, but taken her laptop computer and many of the current files, including the Lucan papers. Dominique checked through, wearing her coat and wool cap, ready to go off into her own life, while Jean-Pierre watched. Dominique looked at all the files that were left. 'From my memory,' she said, 'and from my appointments book, the files here belong only to patients who had finished their course. The current files are gone.'

'Who were the current clients?'

'Well, there was Walker, there was Lucky Lucan. There was Mrs Maisie Round, Karl K. Jacobs, and just a minute . . . ' She consulted her diary: 'There was Dr Oscar Hertz. Dr Wolf did like Dr Hertz so very much. There was Ruth Ciampino. Mrs William Hane-Busby, also.'

'No French clients?'

'At the moment, none.'

Jean-Pierre was struck by a stab of jealousy. 'Who was Dr Hertz?'

'Dr Oscar Hertz is a recent widower. He has problems of grief and so on.'

'Do you know the addresses and telephone numbers of all the clients whose files are missing?'

She sat down in her coat and typed, with the aid of her appointments book, what little she knew about the list of names she had just given. 'Dr Wolf spoke seldom about her clients. She was friendly, talkative, very nice to me, but she didn't say much about the patients who came to consult her. Now, I'll leave you my office keys. This is the front door. These are the office door – there are two safety-locks.'

'I know,' he said. 'I have copies of the keys.'

'And the keys to the filing cabinet. The keys to Dr Wolf's desk.'

'I don't have those. Leave them with me.'

'Do you want me to make a statement to the police, M. Roget?'

'There's no need to tell the police.'

'Would it not be correct?'

'There is no need.'

'No?'

'No.'

'Suppose,' she said, 'that Dr Wolf has met with an accident?'

'I don't suppose. You do not take half your office archives with you to have an accident.'

Dominique left, a small figure, wrapped in her coat and scarf, her woolly cap, her pay-cheque in her bag, provided by Jean-Pierre, her blonde hair half-covering her pink cheeks.

She closed the door behind her, but immediately he opened it to call her back.

'Leave me your telephone number and your address.'

'It's in my file,' said Dominique, 'but I'm not sure how long I'll be staying in Paris.'

'No?'

'No.'

He asked her, 'Are you in touch with Dr Wolf?'

'Why should I be in touch with Dr Wolf?'

'I mean no offence, Dominique. But if she gets in touch with you, will you let me know?'

'Yes, I will do that, M. Roget. I will certainly tell you.'

Hildegard had long felt that sentimentality was a luxury she could not afford. Perhaps she had always felt it, right back to the time when the family had a pig farm, and the little pigs squealed pitifully, and bled. These things had to be.

She had fourteen brothers and sisters, some old enough to be her mother or father. Someone washed and dressed her, took her to school, fed her: a brother, a mother, a sister, a father, whosoever. She grew up on the pig farm. The sisters and brothers eventually married and went to live each in a house not far away. They continued in the pig business. Hildegard (then Beate) grew up, with all of them around, among the pigs. She went to school, was clever. She fought herself free from her home. She found Heinrich. She made blood-money.

And now she was supposed to ask herself about her loyalty and love for Jean-Pierre in Paris. She knew very well he would be frantically looking for her. She couldn't afford such sweetness. He would expect some sign of her affection. It was too much to ask. And yet the question asked itself. Oh, Jean-Pierre, what else, what else could I have done?

XI

JEAN-PIERRE HAD PACKED a small bag and set it aside. He was ready to leave Paris any time, at a moment's notice. Hildegard had been missing over a week and no message from her had reached him. He was more worried by this fact than by her absence, for he was convinced that she was safely settled somewhere of her own choice. She had left her car in the garage, paid up three months in advance. The garage owner could give no explanation, no clue. Jean-Pierre was not anxious for her safety. He brooded only over the fact that she hadn't rung him at his business number or on his mobile telephone.

He made a decision to find her and follow. He began with the list of her patients that Dominique had given him. Only Lucan and Walker had no phone numbers against their names.

'Mrs Maisie Round?' Jean-Pierre spoke in English, and quite well.

'Yes, speaking. Who is it?'

'Jean-Pierre Roget. I am a friend of Dr Hildegard Wolf. I – '

'Where is Dr Wolf? It is shameful that she has left in the middle of my treatment. Her secretary just rang and told me she had left Paris, that was all.'

'I was wondering if you had any clue where she was, Madame.'

The woman started to speak again, shrieking, and did not leave off shrieks until she had come to the point in her discourse where Jean-Pierre broke her off. She shrieked:

'It is nothing short of criminal to leave a patient hamstrung in a sitting in the middle of a course just as I was getting to the heart of the matter and she knew that I was arriving at that point of no return so I am now in deep shock and my psyche is severely damaged and at the end of the day the bottom line is I am going to have my attorney issue a writ against Hildegard Wolf and also have her definitely struck off because it looks like here in Paris she was never registered at all with any school or any institute of psychiatry but I paid her over a period of eight months only to find myself neither divorcing from him or engaging with Thomas and I am in a preposterous dilemma that she should have spared me as it was her responsibility to address the problem right from . . . '

At this point Jean-Pierre quietly hung up. He fixed himself a vodka-tonic and rang the next patient.

A woman answered in French.

'May I speak to Dr Karl Jacobs?'

'Dr Jacobs is on holiday. Can I take a message?'

'Well, perhaps you can tell me yourself if Dr Jacobs had any idea of the whereabouts of his analyst, Dr Hildegard Wolf? When will Dr Jacobs be back?'

'He's expected to return in about ten days. I can leave a message for him, but I don't think I can help. A gentleman called Walker has been asking how to get hold of Dr Wolf. He saw Dr Jacobs' name on the desk of the receptionist, I believe, as he was one of Dr Wolf's patients himself. Dr Wolf left suddenly, it seems.'

'Is Dr Jacobs upset?'

'Oh, no, he was very relieved. He said he'd had enough of her.'

Jean-Pierre left his phone number.

The next patient, Dr Oscar Hertz, was the one that Dominique had mentioned that Hildegard had liked. A widower, she had said; his problem, grief.

From Dr Oscar Hertz there was no reply. Jean-Pierre rang Mrs William Hane-Busby's number.

'Yes, speaking,' said the lady in the English tongue.

'I'm a friend of Dr Hildegard Wolf, and I have your name as one of her friends. You see I'm trying to find out where she is.'

'Yes, I would like to know, too. I esteem Dr Wolf greatly. A very distinguished mind. You know she is discussed in the universities and their publications. She must have had some very urgent reason for going off like that. Do you know her well?'

'She's my girl-friend,' Jean-Pierre felt it right to say. He liked this woman's tone.

'She often spoke to me of places she stayed in different parts, you know in Madrid she stayed at a lovely little hotel, the Paradiso, and at Zürich there was a gem of a place she loved, Seelach Gasthof, just a boarding-house really. She loved to stay in places like that, but perhaps she's with friends.'

'Where else did she mention, Madame? London? Brussels?'

'There was a place in London at Queen's Gate, and Brussels I don't know the name, it was a run-down part. She ate at a restaurant called La Moule Parquée, whatever that means. Oh, I do hope you can find her. I very much miss Hildegard. Why ever did she go off just like that?'

'Look,' said Jean-Pierre, 'I'll keep in touch. If she gets hold of you at all will you let me know?' He left his number.

He rang Dick and Paul. Dick answered. 'We were devastated when we got her message. Just a few lines enclosing a cheque and, although we're fully paid up, it kind of hurts.

Do you know when she's coming back, Jean-Pierre? Did she leave any message with Olivia?'

Olivia, the maid whom Jean-Pierre and Hildegard had shared, was still working in the flat. She had already expressed herself as bewildered as everyone else by Hildegard's disappearance.

Jean-Pierre looked at the piece of paper where he had jotted down Mrs William Hane-Busby's information. She had been the only one to furnish any sort of clue as to where Hildegard might be. She had obviously been a confidante as much as a patient. Jean-Pierre put a cross against the Hotel Paradiso, Madrid, and a query against Hotel—, Queen's Gate, London. Maybe Brussels, though. He tried Dr Oscar Hertz's number again. This time he was more successful. A woman answered in guttural English, 'Dr Hertz? – I think he's just come in. Hold on.' A rendering of *Greensleeves* filled in the gap. It was cut off, not before time, by a click and a man's voice. 'Here is Dr Hertz.'

'I'm Jean-Pierre Roget, Hildegard Wolf's companion. I suppose you know she has disappeared.'

'I myself am very anxious about that.'

'If you're so anxious why didn't you telephone me? You know we lived together. You know that.'

'The secretary, Dominique, informed me. There is nothing we can do?'

'Dr Hertz, she had a special friendship with you. She – '

'Oh, yes, I was not a patient.'

'No?'

'No. I was a colleague.'

'You're a psychiatrist?'

'A psychologist, rather. Hildegard was not herself a theorist, she was essentially a practitioner.'

'You speak of her in the past tense.'

'Yes, I speak in the past tense.'

'Oh, God, what do you think has happened to her?'

'Nothing. She wasn't a person to whom things happen. She did all the happenings.'

'You think she's committed suicide on us?'

'I daresay.'

'Well, I daresay you're wrong. I know her better than you do.'

'She was being blackmailed.'

'That I know. And her disappearance is no doubt the result. But she has gone somewhere. Have you any idea where?'

'From a psychological point of view, if she remains alive she would be expected to have gone back to the place of her origin, to the countryside of Nuremberg. There, the most successful psychiatrist would be safe from detection.'

'Thank you, Dr Hertz.'

Jean-Pierre poured himself another drink. 'Cold bastard,' he reflected. He thought of Hertz's words: *From a psychological point of view . . . she would be expected . . .* As if Hildegard herself would not know what she might be expected to do, and avoid just that course of action. Jean-Pierre studied the few scribbles he had made on the telephone pad during his conversations. Certainly the cross he had made against Mrs William Hane-Busby's remarks was the most sensible, although he reserved suspicions about Dr Hertz. The houseboys, Dick and Paul, were probably reticent. Dr Jacobs, whoever he was, perhaps knew more than he would say if he were available. In the meantime Jean-Pierre busied himself in finding out the phone number of Hotel Paradiso, Madrid, the names of hotels, large and small, in Brussels, and in the Queen's Gate area of London.

Hildegard lay on top of her hotel bed aware of the pouring rain of London, which was somehow much worse than the equivalent rain of Paris. Her mind, with the passing of the years, had become ever more studious. It was not only because she feared the Lucan pair, but because she was fascinated by them, that she had brought, in her bulging zip-bags, the Lucan files comprising her notes and three published books on the subject of Lucan the killer, his habits of life, his *milieu*, his friends.

The documents were spread on the bed beside her, that double bed in which Hildegard had felt, every night she had spent in the Manderville Hotel, decidedly alone. Her lover had been replaced by her clinical notes.

She kept in touch with her *au pair* helpers in Paris, Dick and Paul. Yes, Jean-Pierre rang every day to find out if either one of them had heard from her. 'No, don't worry, we haven't said a word.' 'Once, that Mr Walker called. No one by name of Lucan.' 'Jean-Pierre is really frantic, though, Hildegard, why don't you call him?'

'I will,' Hildegard said, 'oh, yes, I will.' Eventually . . . she said to herself.

'Walker-Lucan', as she thought of him, had said to her, 'You know I am officially dead in England, although that leaves a big doubt as to the reality of my death. The House of Lords cannot recognize my death. Sometimes I'm tempted to go back, though, and challenge the courts. I would plead that, as a dead man, I couldn't be tried.'

'It wouldn't work,' said Hildegard. 'You would be tried for murder if you are indeed Lord Lucan.'

'Are you sure?'

'Yes, I am. And you would be found guilty on the evidence.'

'And you, Dr Wolf? On the evidence against you, could you still be tried for fraud?'

'Yes,' said Hildegard.

'All those years ago?'

'In both cases,' Hildegard said, 'all those years ago.'

Conversations like these led Hildegard to wonder if, after all, Walker was the real Lucan. He seemed to have been there at the kill.

But so, in a sense, through immersing herself in the subject, did she. And what interested her even more was the whole world of feelings that preceded Lucan's decision – apparently a good month before the event – to kill his wife. Hildegard opened one of her notebooks and read:

He detested his wife. She had defeated his law suit for the custody of his children, leaving him with a large legal debt and the mortification of being exposed by her as a sexual sadist, a wife-caner. In his eyes, his wife, Veronica, was expendable.

It was, according to the testimony, early in October 1974 that he actually told a friend of his decision to murder his wife, and of his carefully planned precautions. 'I would never be caught,' he told his friend (according to Chief Superintendent Ranson who conducted the investigation into the crime).

Twenty years later Ranson wrote, 'I believe that, rather than the much-quoted love of his children, it is his lack of money, all of it lost through uncontrollable gambling, that provides the key to this case.'

'I believe,' Hildegard had noted, 'that this is very much to the point, if not altogether true. Another motive is spite.'

'Walker,' Hildegard had also put in her notes, 'could be a hit-man hired by Lucan, and Lucky is Lucan himself. Or it could be the other way round. But the evidence is all against this theory.'

Lucky, by Walker's account, genuinely needed treatment by a psychiatrist. Not long after Walker started consulting Hildegard he had said, 'I hear voices.'

By this he probably meant that Lucky 'heard' voices, and equally he was covering the personage of Lord Lucan for a possible confrontation with the law. Establish the 'voices' and Lucan could be found not fit to plead.

But was he fit to plead? Lucky, more so than Walker, Hildegard felt. But there was no doubt that in the weeks before the murder a certain madness had set in. 'Uncontrollable gambling', as the worthy policeman had cited as the main cause of his action, was in itself only a symptom. His hatred of his wife had been an obsession aggravated by the continual dunning letters from the banks to which he owed money.

Hildegard turned the pages of the Chief Superintendent's account. A year before the murder, letters from the bank managers were moving in on Lucan daily. These letters sounded like the phrases of a popular music-hall song:

23rd October 1973

Dear Lord Lucan,
I am extremely disappointed that I cannot trace a reply from you to my letter of the 10th October regarding the borrowing on your account . . .

And in December 1973, as his thirty-ninth birthday approached:

Dear Lord Lucan,
You will know from my recent letters how disappointed I am that you have not been in touch before this to let me know what arrangements are being made to adjust your overdraft here . . .

Lucan put the family silver up to auction at Christie's. He took recourse to money-lenders. Where, demanded Hildegard, did he say goodbye to reality? That he did just that is the only certainty in the case. For even if his plan had come off, even if he had succeeded in killing his wife and not the nanny, he could not have escaped detection. Was it the approach of his fortieth birthday combined with the shock of being a failure in life, irretrievably on the point of bankruptcy, that had removed him from reality? In the second half of the twentieth century, in any case, an inherited earldom was not very real. While it was a social fact, it did not relate to any other social fact of significance, especially in his case where there was little family property, no house with its land, no money. In reality, he belonged to a middle-class environment with upper-class claims in his conscious mind.

'He should have had a trade, a profession,' Hildegard said to herself. 'The calling of a gambler is madness. Being an earl, full stop, is madness. Yes, he needed the help of a psychiatrist. He still needs one. He needs me.'

Hildegard's notebooks were based on the published facts in the first place, and what Lucky had told her in the second.

Lucan had been married eleven years when the murder of the nanny and the savage attack on his wife took place that night at Lower Belgrave Street. He was separated from his wife. He had lost custody of his children. One way and another he had lost his mind. The jury at the dead girl's inquest pronounced her cause of death as 'Murder by Lord Lucan'. This was not itself a trial verdict, but it is impossible to conceive any other jury, on the known evidence, failing to convict him of murder. It is difficult to believe that his friends and family objectively believed his innocence, on the basis of the facts. To protest his innocence in public was the easiest thing he could have done. He had only to step forward and present his case. Surely there would have been some factors in his favour unknown to the investigators if he had not committed the crimes. His wife, covered with blood, had escaped to the nearby pub, from where she was taken to hospital with head injuries. They were inflicted, she said, by Lord Lucan, and the police believed her. They had every reason, with so much corroborative evidence, to believe her.

If Hildegard had only read about Lucan, and never met the probable man himself, she would have assumed that he was, like many obsessive gamblers, block-stupid.

The Lucky Lucan she knew, the Walker-Lucan she knew, were not stupid. Lucan's mind must anyway have been sharpened by constant evasion. Hildegard was conscious that Lucky Lucan, however, had a mental problem. Walker, to her, was probably a plain criminal. She remembered Lucan's loud laugh when he had made one of his jocular remarks. It was a laugh that filled the whole room. At her little jokes he merely gave a smile as if he were anxious about a waste of his time. Although he wore a smile, Walker seldom laughed, and if he did, it was a short, sharp, cynical 'huh'.

Walker had said he 'heard' voices.

What did they say?

'That Lucky is plotting to kill me.'

'But you didn't believe the voices, or you would not have come to consult me.'

'In fact there was only one voice.'

'Male or female?'

'A female voice. I think it was the murdered girl, Sandra Rivett, who spoke.'

In the margin of the page where she had transcribed her recording of this interview, Hildegard had noted: 'It is possible there is no "voice". It is poss. that Walker intends to kill Lucky and is establishing a cover-up of insanity in case he is caught. It is possible – but anything is poss.'

Hildegard added: 'Who is supporting these men? Who aided Lucan in the first place? Who aids and abets him now? He has friends somewhere.'

In the matter of the seventh Lord Lucan's disappearance the public was more mystified than outraged. The more he was described, and his way of life outlined, by his friends, the less he was understood. The case of the seventh Earl is only secondarily one of an evasion of justice, it is primarily that of a mystery. And it is not only the question of how did he get away, where did he go, how has he been living, is he in fact alive? The mystery is even more in the question of what was he like, how did he feel, what went on in his mind that led him to believe he could get away with his plan? What detective stories had he been reading? What dream-like, immature culture was he influenced by? For, surely, he had thought his plan to kill his wife was watertight. Whereas, even if the nanny had taken her night off, even if he had murdered the countess, the plot leaked at every seam as truly as did the blood-oozing mailbag into which the body of Sandra Rivett was packed.

XII

AS HILDEGARD KNEW FROM HER OWN experienceasastigmat-ic fraud, blood, once let loose, gets all over the place. It sticks, it flows, it garishly advertises itself or accumulates in dark thick puddles. Once it gets going, there is no stopping blood.

It was a description by Lucky, finally, of the blood all over his trousers, of the blood oozing from the mailbag, that had inclined Hildegard to believe that he was indeed the Lucan who was wanted for homicide. Walker, on the other hand, was reluctant to describe the murder. He had now told Hildegard that, yes, he had 'performed the deed', and he had even gone into some of the already well-publicized details. Walker sometimes sounded like a printed column out of a tabloid Sunday edition. 'I thought it convenient at that stage to rid myself of a wife that I had come to loathe. She had custody of my children. A ridiculous member of your profession, Dr Wolf, gave evidence in her favour in a court of law. I lost my children. I was allowed to see them twice a month – imagine! I could have sold the house at Lower Belgrave Street to pay off some of my debts. She was mad, but the court would not recognize it.'

'Tell me about the murder.'

'Oh, I suppose it was a murder like any other murder.'

Perhaps these were the words of a hit-man. Perhaps and maybe. But, Hildegard noted, they were hardly a killer's words. And yet, their coldness might fit in with the Lucan known to the public, his mad-cold calculative mind.

But behind it all, at this stage, was blackmail. Blackmail between Lucan and Walker, with Walker the probable blackmailer, and now blackmail of herself: they needed money. What else did they need? Probably a psychiatrist's counselling and comfort? – Yes, probably that, too. And perhaps a sympathetic psychiatrist to testify in the event of a court case.

The last witness to see Lucan after the murder gave evidence at the inquest on the death of Sandra Rivett that Lucan had told her how an unknown intruder had attacked his wife and presumably killed the nanny, he himself having passed the house by chance and intervened. According to the witness, she had the impression that he 'felt rather squeamish about the blood and did not want to look too closely at the sack'.

All right, Lucky was squeamish. Hildegard's story, also dripping in blood, had evidently given him further reason for his squeams. 'You covered your hands, side and feet with your menstrual blood, Dr Wolf.' He had found the courage to come out with that statement, squeamish or not. He had said it in an almost confidential way: we're both in this blood-business together, he seemed to say. Walker, however, had merely referred to 'Your past, Hildegard Wolf or should I say Beate Pappenheim?'

When Lucky had first walked into her office, Hildegard was immediately taken with his resemblance to her prior Lucan patient, Walker. They were not indistinguishable, but they might have been brothers. And certainly, both were white-haired, ageing photos of the thirty-nine-year-old Lucan which looked out of the pages of the quantity of books and press articles written about him from year to year since his disappearance in 1974. Was the real Lucan dead, as numerous people claimed? If he wasn't, how did he materially survive? Walker himself had never claimed that he presented himself to Lucan's friends. It was usually Lucky who periodically collected sums of money, deposited at certain places, with certain people, by rich friends. Friends – how could they be deceived if they had once known Lucan? 'Easy,' Walker had explained. 'They expect Lucan to have undergone surgical modifications to his features. They are right. Your other Lucan patient is a fraud, Dr Wolf. He also goes collecting, as you can imagine.'

'But you work together.'

'Of course. If one of us were caught, it would always be the other, the absent Lucan who would be the real one.'

'And your voices? Don't your friends suspect from the voice?'

'Lucan is known to be musical. We have coordinated our voices. Besides, people might assume that voices change.'

Years ago, there had been an arrest. Lucan is found in Australia! Indeed the suspect turned out to be a very-much-wanted missing man; but he wasn't Lucan. And as far as Hildegard was concerned, neither, as yet, were quite proved to be either Walker or Lucky. She had a naturally objective set of wits. The men were each, to her, 'a mere anatomy, a mountebank . . . a living-dead man', as Shakespeare had put it long ago.

In manners, in speech, Hildegard had written, both Lucky and Walker could have based themselves on the Lucan of the historical case. Their methods of copying would have been fairly easy for the reason that Lucan himself had been a perfect bore, a cut-to-measure gentleman with a pack of memories very, very like that of many another man of his class and education. He does not appear to have had one original idea, ever, beyond that of attempting and planning to murder his wife. He was extremely average of mind. He could have been anybody. With a smattering of information about the past life and schooling of a man like Lucan, given the height and shape, it would not have been difficult to assume a personality that would convince his acquaintances of his identity. Oh, Lucan, Lucan, you hot potato.

The rain had stopped. Hildegard put away her notes. She felt a great longing for Jean-Pierre and regretted not being connected even by e-mail. Surely he would be looking for her, might even find her. But she didn't trust his tact in evading the Lucans. Jean-Pierre lacked duplicity whereas they were altogether a double proposition. Sooner or later she would phone him.

XIII

WALKER HAD A VERY FIXED IDEA of what a gentleman should be. He had studied Lucky Lucan diligently for ten of the years since Lucan had been a wanted man on the loose. He had got most of his ideas about a hundred years out of date, as were the convictions and attitudes of Lucan himself, for Lucan's conceptions of a gentleman were greatly distorted. This had been noted by his fellow guardsmen in the Coldstream regiment, where Lucan played the Earl from start to finish, outdoing the other earls in the practice of earldom.

Walker's notion of a gentleman was further distorted by the reality of Lucan's character. Lucan was, in fact, bent, a natural felon, a failed person. He was self-centred as a man, self-occupied as a nobleman; the mask of the upstart, strangely, was Lord Lucan's favourite mode of self-expression. 'Virtue and honour': his family specifically claimed that these were guiding features of their fugitive kinsman. However, they were obviously not remotely attributes of his; they were the façade which Walker in his role of freelance gentleman had assiduously copied and assumed. Yes, he was now ideally Lucan's doppelgänger, his other self.

Walker's physical resemblance to Lucan had grown over those years since they had met in Mexico. Its initial advantage was the two men's precisely identical height of six-foot-plus and the curious melon-like shape of their heads. Lucan's head was described by an acquaintance as 'bony', and so was Walker's. Their dark colouring had been more or less the same. Only their separate features had differed. This had been attended to gradually in the more recent years by plastic surgery, so that it was now fairly difficult to tell the two men apart.

Lucan, however, had a certain charm, not a great deal of it, but enough to be all the more charming. Walker had none and was always at a loss how to achieve it; was transparent, which at times was in itself quite appealing. Where they resembled each other most in character was in their aptitude for cold indifference; on that level they never failed to be in harmony.

Walker had come to Lucan's notice on a ranch in Mexico, one of Lucan's many places of refuge in the years following his disappearance. His host had been a small spare man, nut-brown, a horse-racing old-time friend; the hostess had been an actress from Bolivia, now retired into a life of retaining her wonderful looks day by day, and keeping her clothes, which she changed frequently, fresh and ironed all the time.

'It's remarkable,' she said, 'how much Walker resembles you. I thought he was you last night when he walked across the lawn to the house.'

'So strange,' said the host, 'I thought so too.'

After two months it was nearly time for Lucan to move on to his next aiders and abetters.

'I will give you Walker,' said the kindly Mexican. 'You may take Walker with you. He'll come in useful.'

Walker was a butler-keeper and head groom (for the establishment was constituted on hierarchical lines).

'I don't know,' said his wife, 'if I can manage without Walker.'

'I give him to Lucan,' said the man, very casually, as if he was presenting the Earl with a silver dish.

'What should I do with him?' said Lucan the comparative blockhead.

'You can use him a thousand ways,' said the all-knowing, all-experienced host. 'He could be arrested in your place, if necessary. You must train him up a bit, make him more your double, teach him your voice.'

'He is very intelligent,' said the wife.

'If he was very intelligent,' said the sage brown fellow, 'he wouldn't be working for us. However, he will do as I say. Besides,' he said wearily, 'I will of course make it worth his while. I give him to Lucan. Get his chin modified, Lucan, and his nose straightened a bit. He's the very image.'

That had been ten years ago. Walker had not needed to make frequent trips to Mexico to collect his former employer's bounty. Unlike Lucan, he was safe with bank transfers. As Walker, no one was looking for him, although as Lucan he had several times fallen under suspicion. As Lucan he had been 'sighted' on the beaches of the world, in cafés. He had been a temporary secretary of a sports club in Sydney, and sighted there. He had been a riding instructor at a school at Lausanne, from where he had to flee from a 'sighting'. Interpol never caught up with him, and if they had, he was, after all, Walker, with Walker's passport, Walker's birth certificate, Walker's own blood group. Lucan, meanwhile, was always elsewhere, in and out of jobs, or lounging in hotel gardens. He painfully avoided the casinos, where he knew he would be looked for.

The Mexican was not his only patron, but he was the richest. When he died in 1998, Lucan was left with only two firm friends of the past, the actress-wife having cut off Walker's allowance and Lucan's hand-outs without explanation. Walker and Lucan went to Paris.

Lucan was always anxious about Walker's voice. Walker had adopted the slightly plummy full-fruited accents of Lucan's speech, but still it was not quite right. Lucan knew that although Walker's looks could pass for a twenty-year-later Lucan with his old friends, the voice, perhaps, could not. So far, he preferred to go 'collecting' by himself.

But money was getting short for both of them. Walker made it plain to Lucan that they were not, ever, to separate. By the time they hit on Hildegard and her past, they needed her more for genuine psychiatric help than for what she could yield through blackmail.

Lucan, in Scotland for his latest collecting venture, received a phone call from Walker.

'Don't think,' said Walker, 'don't so much as let it cross your mind to fail to return to Paris. I need you here.'

Lucan said, 'I'm coming to Paris.' In fact he had nowhere else to go. He hated Walker, but there was no escape from him. And now he had begun to find out more about Walker, who knew so much, so very much, about him, if only through those books and articles that had probed every aspect of his past life.

Walker and Lucan, Lucan and Walker, they were bound together.

Walker, for his part, could hardly bear to look at Lucan's melon-shaped head, exactly like his own.

There was one enormous difference between them, however, and both knew it. Lucan was a killer and Walker was not.

Lucky Lucan believed in destiny. By virtue of destiny he was an earl. His wife had been destined to die, according to his mad calculation. It was the madness of a gambler. During the last two months before the attempt on his wife, Lucan had behaved with comparative civility towards her; even, it was reported, with tenderness. He understood she was destined to die and did not for one moment reflect that this destiny arose merely from his own calculations and plans. His 'needs' dictated fate itself. He had 'needed' the money that would have derived from the sale of the house she occupied, he 'needed' his wife dead, and it was destiny.

It was also now his destiny to share his life with Walker. But an overriding 'need' had arisen. Old friends were dying or dropping off. Lucan needed to rid himself of Walker, and soon; before Walker decided that Lucan must die, it was Walker's destiny to die.

On the plane to Paris, Lucan began to work out the mechanics of Walker's death. Walker was a card to be played in this gambling-den of life; not an ace card, merely a card. It was a situation in which Lucan felt confident, with the sort of confidence with which he had felt he could kill his wife with impunity. His feelings were those of a gambler. His confidence was a card-player's. His sense of destiny obliterated the constant, well-known fact that the gambler loses and the bookie, the croupier or whoever, always wins in the end. Walker was a card to be played, and there was no intention in Lucan's mind generously to share his latest 'collected' windfall with his look-alike. This latest bundle of luck might well be the last, these days being these days.

Walker must go. The stewardess brought him a glass, a half-bottle of flat Vichy water and a miniature Johnnie Walker which Lucan twirled in his fingers with some scorn, before opening and pouring. Presently she returned, offering him a plastic meal which he refused.

Walker must go, die, disintegrate. By habit Lucan wore tinted glasses; they had no special lens: his contact lenses, a messy brown colour, disguising his blue eyes, were made for his natural vision. He was in business class and sat in the aisle seat, which he always preferred. It gave him the feeling of a quick getaway, even on a plane. Twenty-five years had not settled his jitters. No years would do that. If he had remained at home and faced his trial and certain conviction, under the two charges against him, he would by now have been a free man for at least ten years, a fact which he appreciated but did not ponder. There had been no question of his standing trial. He was the seventh Earl of Lucan. He had never got used to, or understood, the casual treatment, often contempt, that had been slung his way in the press by his peers. Not one of the other earls, even those of his schooldays or his regimental years, had spoken up for him. Besides most of his immediate family, which was understandable, only his gambling friends and his less nobly born friends had expressed horror at his plight; they had done their best.

By habit Lucan scrutinized, with more than usual passenger-curiosity, the other travellers. Beside him was a girl with long streaky hair, reading *Newsweek* while picking into her tray of food. She, yes, could be a detective. Had they stopped looking for him? He could never be sure. This trip to England would have to be his last. With modern technology collecting was becoming too dangerous and the collection itself too meagre. He took out his book, a detective paperback. For twenty-five years he had been taking out paperbacks on planes and buses, remembering always to turn the pages regularly, even when his glances were elsewhere. His jitters at all times: he felt he did not deserve such a fate. He hadn't killed his wife, after all. Only the girl with all that blood. He turned a page and sighed. His neighbour read and picked on.

Across the aisle, on his left, were a couple of men, one older than the other. They, too, were busy with their drinks, talking together quite softly but audibly. Lucan disliked homosexuals; what he disliked most about them was what he claimed to be their sentimentality. No ruthlessness; no sense of destiny; no idea that what had to be done had to be done, like the murder. It was a blunder but it was destiny, it was the throw of the dice. The couple beside him across the aisle were a man of about fifty and one of about twenty-five. The older man had shoulder-length hair. The younger had a close-cropped head and was bedecked with worked-silver earrings. They were discussing a film. (Gone were the days when it happened to Lucan that he would overhear people at the next table, in a bus or a waiting-room, discussing him.)

'It was all too obvious,' said the older man. 'All you had to do after the half-way mark, more or less, was sit through it to the end.'

'I thought the sex scenes kind of cool,' observed the younger man.

'Did you? I thought they looked contrived. They did it in their underpants.'

The hostess came along with their trays and they started to eat in the silence due to the task.

Suddenly, from the seat in front of them, the seat diagonally in front of Lucan's to the left, came the electric word 'Lucan', quite discernible amongst the patchy fuzz of their conversation. A bald man of about sixty with a pretty fair-haired woman in her thirties. Lucan released his seatbelt; he stood up and out into the aisle to see them more clearly from the height of his 6' 2". They had a large quantity of newspaper cuttings on the table in front of them. Yes, indeed, they were all old cuttings, some from the long past, all about him.

LUCAN DISAPPEARS
BODY FOUND IN US MAIL SACK
WHO KILLED SANDRA RIVETT?
COUNTESS BLEEDING IN HOSPITAL
LUCAN AT LARGE

Lucan went to the lavatory, came back and settled in his seat. By this time the couple had put away their papers and were eating their meal with a good deal of appetite.

Good God, it is Joe Murray – or is it? Yes, he would be about that age now. Clearly it was Joe, who had been at St Columba's monastery with his girlfriend, Maria Twickenham's daughter, snooping into his whereabouts. It was Joe and this girl who had trailed him down from the north up to the gates of the house with that fortuitous wedding. Yes, it was them. Ambrose had said he'd given them cuttings, bloody fool. Lucan now applied himself to his book, turning pages at due intervals.

Lucan had brought only hand-luggage. As soon as the plane stopped and the passengers were allowed to shuffle out, he reached up into the baggage compartment and fetched down his bag. He hastened.

'Funny,' said Joe to Lacey, as they followed the tall dark-spectacled fellow to the exit, 'how, if you concentrate on a subject, you seem to see examples of it all over the place. I could have sworn that the man along there, three people in front, resembled Lucan. But of course . . . '

Lacey had to tiptoe to see the indicated passenger. So many of the people now pushing up to the exit or reaching for their luggage in the upper compartments were, it seemed to her, excessively big, blocking her view of the possible Lucan. What she managed to see were hefty people, men and women. One of the men was wearing dark glasses, but as soon as he had pulled down his bag he took them off and put them in his breast pocket; hardly the gesture of a Lucan wishing to hide himself.

Lucan was already on the Paris Centre-bound bus by the time Joe and Lacey retrieved their luggage from the roundabout. It was only then that Joe, standing still, said, 'Lacey, you know I believe that man in the plane was Lucan. He caught my eye very rapidly, you know; I think he recognized me; and yes, I recognized him, I really did. But too late; what an old fool I am.'

'We could have had him stopped, even arrested, right there on the plane,' said Lacey. 'The captain has the power to do that.'

'I wouldn't really have cared to call the captain,' said Joe. 'Suppose we'd been mistaken?'

'But aren't you sure?'

'In fact, yes, I'm sure. It's difficult to say what one would do.'

'Oh, Joe,' she said, lifting her luggage and ready to move off with it, 'I thought you wanted to help me.'

'Yes, I do.' He looked round the crowded hall. 'He's gone, of course. Gone. We'll find him in Paris, maybe, though. At least we're almost sure he's in Paris, now.'

'Oh, Paris,' said Lacey. 'Come on, let's get a taxi.'

XIV

JEAN-PIERRE, IN HIS AMPLE, CLUTTERED workshop, was restoring a gramophone of the 1920s for someone with more money than sense, when a tall black young man came to the glass door and rang. Jean-Pierre sometimes kept this door locked even when he was inside, with the shutters up; the area was a rough one.

Jean-Pierre opened the door to this decidedly tranquil customer.

'We've been on the phone,' said the man in English. 'I'm Dr Karl K. Jacobs, patient of Dr Hildegard Wolf.'

'Come in.'

'You rang me up.'

'Yes, I know. You said you were fed up with Hildegard; something like that. Have you any news of her?' Jean-Pierre moved a pile of old magazines and catalogues off a chair, and pushed it with a foot towards Dr Jacobs. 'Sit down.' He himself sat opposite on a rickety work-stool.

'I had enough,' said Jacobs. 'She was always talking about herself, enquiring about the voodoo cults of the Congo, the medicine-men. I had enough interrogation. The concierge at the rue du Dragon told me where your shop is.'

'*Enough*, but you've come for more?' said Jean-Pierre.

'What do you want to know?'

'What do *you* want to know?'

372

'Where she is,' said Karl Jacobs. 'I was recommended to consult her but all she has done is consult me. Then – off.'

'That's her way.'

'She not only consults, she insults. She wants to needle me, reminding me always of my background as she thinks it is. I come from the centre of Africa but I haven't just walked out of the jungle. What about the voodoos, the witch doctors? she wanted to know. How should I know about the medicine-men, all those frauds? I am a qualified MD.'

'Where do you work?' said Jean-Pierre.

'I'm at a private nursing-home north of Versailles, I live near the Marais. I get in and out by autobus, sometimes I use the metro and change. What have I got to do with jungle magic and blood rites?'

'Blood rites?'

'Yes, blood is important in these activities. Why does she worry me?'

'That's something between you and her,' said Jean-Pierre. 'I can offer you a cup of instant coffee or a glass of wine.'

'Wine.'

'I know,' said Jean-Pierre as he poured two glasses of red wine, 'that Hildegard is interested in superstitions.'

'Yes, but why should she be interested at my expense? I paid her for those sessions. I have my own problems.'

'Psychiatrists have their methods, you know,' said Jean-Pierre.

'But I paid her for her advice.'

'Women are expensive,' said Jean-Pierre. 'Look – I'm try-ing to trace her whereabouts, I don't deny. Do you have any clue where she might be?'

'London.'

'Why do you say London?'

'It's where I'd go if I wanted to hide.'

'How do you know she wants to hide?'

Karl Jacobs was neatly dressed in a dark business suit, a blue shirt with a white collar, and a grey striped tie with dark-blue dots. He sat with his long legs stretched forth. An effortlessly athletic man. Jean-Pierre repeated his question, 'Why should she hide?'

'Her interest in voodoo, in blood cults and fraudulent mystifications was very genuine. I think it was probably personal. She could be connected with someone like that.'

'Do you know anything, Dr Jacobs, about these practices?'

'Call me Karl. My name is Karl Kanzia Jacobs. My father was a judge, he's dead. My mother is alive. She is a very important citizen of Kanzia.'

'And Kanzia is where?'

'It's an independent entity of central Africa, slightly north of the equator.'

'But certainly they wouldn't have any witchery and magic there, I imagine,' ventured Jean-Pierre.

'Oh, indirectly, I know something. My grandfather Delihu is still a paramount head man. My uncle was a voodoo chap, he died. He was definitely what you would call in your terms a witch doctor. He performed great good, especially with rites and totems and herbs and of course the terror of beliefs. Beliefs are essential. I can confirm as a medical man that these witch men can cure, but there is also a lot of mumbo-jumbo, like you say. It's a question of cutting a fine line, Jean-Pierre, and Dr Wolf was interested in that aspect, the question of responsibility on the part of the self-styled healer. Myself, I feel it is a treachery to scientific practices to agree with her. And yet . . . She said, if a cure is effected does it matter whether or not there was an actual miracle to cause it? Why should the healer be prosecuted, or at least blamed, if in fact he heals? She put that very question to me. I told her no. I told her there should be no blame, but all this was at the expense of my pocket. I paid for those sessions.'

'Perhaps I can reimburse you on her behalf?'

'Certainly not.'

'But surely,' said Jean-Pierre, 'it is always worthwhile conversing with Hildegard? If it isn't, what are you doing here?'

'She is very fascinating,' said Karl Jacobs, gloomily.

Jean-Pierre asked if they might keep in touch, and assured Karl that once Hildegard returned, as surely she would, he would see to it that she would give him the full sessions he was due. 'If you have any other brainwaves or intuitions about where she has gone,' said Jean-Pierre, 'call me at once. I intend to have her back. She's my girlfriend and my life-companion of more than five years and I can't live without her. London might well be the place. I'll work on that.'

When Karl had gone, Jean-Pierre took out of his pocket the sheet of paper on which he had made notes of all the replies to his enquiries of Hildegard's patients. He scribbled the word 'promising' beside the name of Dr Karl K. Jacobs. Then he studied the list again. Only one name, of course, was equally promising: that of Mrs William Hane-Busby.

Madrid – The Paradiso – he had already called there without success.

Seelach Gasthof – there were so many guest-houses which could fit that description. However, none of them had yielded Hildegard. Then London. 'London is where I'd hide,' Jacobs had said with a quite definite tone. 'London at Queen's Gate . . .' Mrs Hane-Busby had mused.

Jean-Pierre decided to hunt up in the directories all the hotels and boarding-houses at Queen's Gate, London. It was only five-thirty in the afternoon, but he shut up shop.

XV

HILDEGARD LAY IN HER BATH trying to trace back the source of a slightly disconsolate and disagreeable sensation that lingered over from the day. It was six-thirty p.m. The best feature of the hotel was its constant, really hot water; Hildegard profited by it frequently before dinner: the soothing power of a hot bath. What was her feeling of uneasiness due to? She had left the hotel that morning at ten and taken a bus to Marble Arch. From there she went to several department stores in a leisurely way all along Oxford Street. Hildegard had brought few clothes with her, and now she was beginning to need a change. Gradually, that morning, she had acquired a woollen jacket, a pair of suede boots, four pairs of nylon tights, a pair of brown jeans, a brown cotton shirt and a bottle of English toilet spray called *Amours de Boudoir*. It was here that Hildegard's pondering in the bath was arrested. Walking along the ground-floor aisles of the shops that afternoon, she was reminded of her days as a student, earning a poor living from a part-time job at the handbag counter of a department store in Munich. At the cosmetics counter, Hildegard had stopped to try the toilet-water samples being offered by a young woman. It seemed to Hildegard that this woman looked away, and looked again and looked away. Hildegard was taken back to the store of her youth. It was the cosmetics girl who had unwittingly given her the idea of assuming the false stigmata. The cosmetics girl,

Ursula, could make up and transform the most ordinary faces. Hildegard had been fascinated. Ursula did a romantic scar, one day, on the left cheek of a young man who happily said he was going to pose as having been involved in a duel.

Ursula, when the time came, made a deep, false indentation in the palm of Hildegard's hand. Hildegard, then Beate Pappenheim at the height of her success, would get Ursula to come around each month at the time of her menstruation and put the touches of reality on her 'five wounds' so that they could be photographed.

Could that young woman in the department store in Oxford Street be really Ursula? She looked so like Ursula, it was incredible, and then her furtive glances at Hildegard, her look, her look away, her look again, her look away . . . Did she recognize me? Hildegard asked herself.

And then she realized how perfectly ridiculous her idea had been. Ursula twelve years ago must have already been over thirty. Now she would be in her mid-forties, much older than the young woman in the department store of today. Hildegard, pulling her thoughts together, apprehended how she herself must have looked strangely at the girl in order to provoke the strange looks she returned. Hildegard had allowed herself to be sprayed by the scent, had bought some and left. *Amours de Boudoir* – oh, well . . .

All the same, Hildegard was aware that she could still be discovered, exposed. She felt more vulnerable in London than she had ever felt in Paris, perhaps because she looked very French with her dark short-cut hair clinging to her egg-shaped head? She had lost her German look simply by living in France, eating French food, breathing French air. Her skin was still pale, but her waistline small, which had not been so much the case when she had first fled from Munich. She mingled well in Paris, but in London?

'If you want to hide a pebble the best place is the beach'
– an old and true maxim. Hildegard – or as she was, Beate –
when the scandal broke took eventual refuge in Spain, at Avila,
birthplace of two famous Catholic visionaries, St Theresa of
Jesus and St John of the Cross. Nobody thought of looking
for her in that atmosphere of heated romantic ecstasy. She was
considered to be a fraud. Nobody was looking for her at Avila
where a truly holy stigmatic would be likely to linger. In fact
she stayed in a convent at Avila for six months, impressing
the nuns with her devotion and goodness, her daily visits to
the cathedral, to the house of St Theresa, to the birthplace
of St Theresa, and with her meditative walks in the shadow
of Avila's great and ancient walls. After all, she had mused
then (and, in her bath in her London hotel, mused now), I did
apparently effect a number of cures, perhaps by the power
of suggestion, it's true. But people were cured by me in my
stigmatic days. I felt the part.

She wondered, then, if she would change her hair to fair.
If one of the Lucans in fact caught up with her, she had better
disguise herself a little.

Among the names of Lucan's friends published in newspapers in those days after the murder were those of Maria and
Alfred Twickenham. Maria's interview with the police in
South Africa, where she was at the time, was one of many;
it obtained prominence largely through Maria's glamour
and beauty. Her picture was a good accompaniment to the
sensational articles. All the articles were by the nature of the
case sensational. A peer was wanted for a brutal murder.
He had bashed his children's nanny to death with a length
of lead piping, specially prepared to deaden the thuds. Had
there been a relationship with the nanny? No, there hadn't.
Far from it, he had meant those thuds for his wife. Having

removed the light-bulb on the basement staircase, he had mistaken the young nanny descending the stairs for his young wife. On discovering his blunder, he then attacked the wife, reported the papers. She was now in hospital with severe head wounds.

That night Lucan, in a panic, visited some of his friends. The main one in London was the late Alfred Twickenham. His ex-wife was probably still alive. Hildegard knew that all Lucan's other friends were either still in the country and no doubt not accessible to enquirers, or dead.

Hildegard in her anxiety to defend herself from Lucan and Walker with their threatening knowledge, and in an increasingly neurotic state from her confinement to a small London hotel, had still plenty of courage to take a decision. Apart from having her hair dyed a mild beige colour, she wanted to do more than just hide. Looking through the books that had been written on the Lucan case, she noted that all of them were generously illustrated by photographs: Lucan at Eton, Lucan's engagement portrait, Lucan with his friends in his favourite gaming clubs: oh, look at these people, look close. Hildegard was looking close: Doris McGuire, said the subtitle, Charles McGuire – Maria Twickenham. Yes, it was Maria Twickenham, who, according to the telephone directory, still lived in the same house in Lennox Gardens as her husband had occupied at the time of the murder.

Hildegard, with her talent for summoning up new fighting energy, was already on the offensive. She would hunt Lucan, threaten him if absolutely necessary; not he her.

She would chase Lucan, she would hunt him down, confront him, challenge him, dare him to reveal her secret. 'You are charged with the crime of murder and attempted murder,' she could say, 'and I am not. You haven't a chance, given the state of the evidence; you have no extenuating arguments to support you; I have.' And she thought: not to speak of my personal documents so carefully prepared in Marseilles.

It was a question, perhaps, of getting to know Maria Twickenham. That for a start.

Hildegard had now sat in her hired car near the house in Lennox Gardens frequently enough to realize that it was no longer the smart one-family residence of twenty-five years ago. It was still verging on smartness but it was broken up into flats. There had been a coming and going of men and women in their thirties, business-like and attractively dressed; they largely left home around nine a.m. and returned around six p.m. Some passed in and out about lunch time. A white-haired, large woman of about sixty, who might well have been an older version of Maria's photograph, dressed in a woolly jacket and trousers, emerged every morning and returned with at least one full shopping bag. She must be Maria Twickenham, thought Hildegard. But no, on following her with some difficulty to the nearby supermarket, Hildegard managed to squint at the name on her credit card. It wasn't Twickenham, Maria's name, the name in the phone book. It was Louise B. Wilson.

At least this waiting and watching and surreptitious stalking was more to Hildegard's taste than the boring, very boring, daily brood in her hotel room. She set forth once again to sit near the white front door of the Twickenham house with its shining brass door-plates. It was Hildegard's fifth wait when a taxi pulled up, and a tall, thin woman in her sixties emerged from the house under the evening lamplight. She stepped into the cab. Hildegard followed as best she could, but lost it at a traffic-light. She felt sure it contained Maria.

Next morning, about eleven a.m., out stepped the large white-haired Louise B. Wilson again. Hildegard leapt out of her car and approached her. 'Excuse me,' she said. 'I wonder if you can tell me, are there any rooms or flats available in this house?'

'I wouldn't know really,' said the woman. 'I'm just the home-help for Mrs Twickenham. You'd have to ask her.'

'Is she in now?'

'Well, if you have any references. Do you have a reference – who sent you, I mean?'

'Yes, of course. I got the name and address from someone in Paris, where I live. I'm only here doing a university course for some months.'

The ground-floor flat had been reserved for Maria's own use, and Hildegard was asked in to wait while Louise B. Wilson went to make enquiries. In a warm, upholstered sitting-room Hildegard thought she saw in the large mirror over the mantelpiece another woman behind her. But on looking back, there was nobody. Of course, my blonde hair, Hildegard remembered. But this fragmentary episode put Hildegard in an ever more guarded and inventive frame of mind, so that when tall Maria came smiling into the room, Hildegard was ready with her plausible tongue.

'I was given your name by an old schoolfriend of yours in Paris.'

This is a tactic in the con-business that usually works. The mention of a schoolfriend one doesn't remember generally gives rise to a slight feeling of guilt rather than suspicion. Instead of a reaction like: 'This person is probably a fake. I don't know or remember any such schoolfriend,' it is more likely to be: 'My God, have I become so forgetful? Or so grand? Or so detached from my youth? Don't I remember who got married? Well, I don't really care about their fate.'

Maria said, in fact, 'I vaguely remember the name. What was her maiden name?'

'I think it was Singleton, but maybe not. She got married as you probably know into Carters' Publications, tall, brown-haired, extremely athletic. After her divorce, of course, she married someone else, I think. She remembered you so well and knows all about you here in London braving it out as you do. I'm sure you can recall . . . '

Hildegard had an address in Paris ready on her tongue, but it wasn't necessary. 'Yes, of course,' said Maria. 'Of course I remember her. And you'll have some coffee, won't you? I'm about to make some. Let's go into the kitchen.'

There she told Hildegard, yes, there would be a two-room flat on the fourth floor available from the week after next. The tenant was out at his job at the moment, and wouldn't mind her showing it to Hildegard. 'Will you be staying long in London?'

'I have to complete some research. I'm a psychiatrist.'

'How fascinating!' (They always said that.)

Like most people, Maria was intrigued by the thought of having a psychiatrist at hand to talk to, without actually taking the plunge of consulting one. There was nothing wrong with Maria, but she herself thought there was; in reality her problem was boredom.

This problem was about to be solved. Maria, although she really had quite a number of friends, had not for many years met anyone quite like Dr Wolf. Hildegard Wolf was the name on her passport and her fake birth certificate. She had not changed it while hiding in London, so that she would not appear to be hiding, if discovered. And it was much easier to deal with people under a name to which she was accustomed. So she was Dr Wolf ('call me Hildegard') to the enchanted landlady, Maria.

As they talked, Maria almost felt she could recall Hildegard's apocryphal Fay Singleton, so like was she, in any case, to the girls of her day.

'And, of course,' said Hildegard boldly, as the morning wore on, 'you knew Lucan, didn't you? Fay told me. It must have been a shock to find that someone you knew so well was wanted for murder.'

By now, they were in Maria's living room, drinks in hand. 'At one time, well, we couldn't believe it. Of course, I was away at the time. My late ex-husband and I believed it, yes, and yet we didn't. Now that we know more . . . And, after all, times have changed, and after all, Lucky Lucan failed to show up, which was really lowering our standards, we all feel different. Or nearly all of us who knew him of old. Most of my friends who knew Lucan now have a poor opinion of him. He might at least have stood trial. And we all feel, now, for poor Sandra Rivett's son, who was deprived of her so tragically without ever knowing her as a mother; she was supposed to be a sister. Poor girl. Of course, you know Lucky Lucan was a very great bore. I was too young to notice that he was a bore, if you know what I mean. He was just one of the chaps. Very good-looking. But I know someone who was at school with him, at Eton. He sat beside him in the choir. My dear, what a bore he thought Lucan was. And the same in the Guards.'

'Is he alive?' said Hildegard.

'I think so. Personally, I think so. Very few people do. But my daughter, Lacey, is actually trying to trace him. She's going to write a book. She's in Paris just now with Lucky's old friend, Joe Murray – he's the zoologist you've probably heard of – trying to track him down.' She took up a photograph and handed it to Hildegard. 'That's Lacey,' she said.

'How lovely,' said Hildegard quite justly.

'And intelligent, too,' said Maria.

XVI

JEAN-PIERRE'S WORKSHOP WAS becoming a place of pilgrimage for Hildegard's abandoned patients.

Dr Hertz, a thin man in his mid-forties, of medium height and wearing tinted glasses, darkened the doors of Jean-Pierre's place two days after their conversation on the phone. He rang the bell, and Jean-Pierre opened the door.

'I'm Hertz.'

'Come in.'

'Have you heard from Hildegard?'

'Well, what if I have heard?'

'I want to know. I must know what has happened to her. I had a fixed appointment for this afternoon.'

'At her office?'

'Yes, of course.'

'Then you are a patient, after all.'

'You might say patient, you might say colleague. She confided in me. We speak in German.'

Jean-Pierre could have knifed him at that point, but in reality would not have done. He said, 'What do you know about Hildegard's youth?'

'Everything vital. I know she posed as a stigmatic. That I admire. I don't blame her for doing something constructive with her own blood. What else should a woman of imagination do with her menstrual blood? I am a psychologist. I

384

see that now comes this Lucan with blood on his hands in a manner much worse, and his money supply is getting shaky, and his friends are no more, nearly all, and he has heard of Hildegard's activities. So he will expose her for her old crime.'

'And his old crime?' said Jean-Pierre.

'Lucan is elusive. Do you know Hildegard never knew his address in Paris? And in the end, he would turn out to be not Lucan but the other, that man Walker. They had lived on that evasive principle till a few years ago, my friend. Now we have DNA identification, it is more difficult for Lucan, and he is even more slippery.'

'What do you want with Hildegard?' Jean-Pierre said.

'I need her consolation. I am weeping over my dead wife, these three months.'

'I, too, need her consolation.'

'But I will marry her. You will not.'

'How do you know?'

'Because you haven't done so.'

'We've been together more than five years. She doesn't want marriage.'

'If I knew where she was I would go and find her. She could marry me. We have a profession in common.' Hertz looked round the workshop. Jean-Pierre had on his workbench a wooden model of Milan's ornate cathedral, inset with ivory. It was a very elaborate affair. Jean-Pierre was restoring it. The tiny pincers and pieces of ivory lay ready beside the model edifice. Jean-Pierre knew what Hertz was saying with his look: 'She can't be satisfied fully with a companion who is merely an artisan. I am her equal, a professional man.'

'But she hasn't taken refuge with you,' said Jean-Pierre.

'No, but she has left you,' said Hertz. 'I hoped you would know where she has gone.'

'Why not try Nuremberg, as you suggested? Her birthplace?'

'I will try. I feel sure she thinks of me.'
'I don't.'

Hildegard was not thinking of Dr Hertz. She hadn't given him a thought since her flight from Paris.

What she thought of now was her project of pursuing Lucan rather than being pursued. From her successful infiltration into Maria Twickenham's house Hildegard was alive to the possibilities of combining with Lacey and Joe Murray in their search.

Hildegard was to move into Maria's flat the following Monday. She had paid a deposit. None the less, she had now no intention of occupying the flat. She meant to return to Paris and as soon as possible make Lacey and Joe serve her turn. 'Maria,' she said on the phone. 'This is Hildegard Wolf. Maria, I've been called back to Paris.'

'Oh no! That means you won't be moving in here.'

'Unfortunately no. I – '

'Your deposit . . . '

'The deposit – don't think of it.'

Maria, who needed money these days, was quite happy not to think of it. But she said, 'I'm terribly disappointed,' and meant it. She had felt the force of Hildegard's company.

'Oh, I'll be back. Let's keep in touch. You know, Maria, I think I can help Lacey with her book. I have friends who might be able to help her trace Lucan. I know he's been heard of recently around Paris. If you could give me Lacey's address or phone number in Paris I'll get in touch with her. And with Dr Murray.'

'Do you know what? I heard only last night from Lacey. They've been having a wonderful time, but they keep missing Lucan. They thought they saw him the last day of the season at Longchamp, but they were too late. It would be so thrilling for Lacey if she could locate him. Really, Hildegard, she doesn't want – neither of them wants to turn him in. She just wants an interview, anonymously, the story of his wanderings over the past twenty-five years. You need not have any fears about their turning over Lucky Lucan to the police.'

Hildegard, well insulated from such fears, took down the name and phone number of the hotel in Paris where Joe and Lacey were staying.

'Tell her,' said Maria, 'to remember that we didn't know Lucan all that closely. He played blackjack, craps, mini-bac. We played bridge.'

'I'll keep in touch with you, Maria.'

'Oh, Hildegard, yes, please do.'

Lucan had paid his cheque into the bank under the name of Walker, and had cashed a large part of it. He lost all of that at the races next day; it was a day further beclouded by rain, and disturbed by the clear, sudden sight of his two pursuers, Joe Murray and the Twickenham daughter. He thought she caught his eye, that she was very startled. He didn't wait to see how else she looked, but cleared off among the crowds which were dispersing in search of their cars or the shelter of a bar.

He was wary all the time, now, far more than in the past when he had been able to conceal his existence in one or another of Africa's vast, lesser-known territories. There, his aiders and abetters, the politicians, the heads of tribes, were sick, dead, changed or changing. Democracy was rearing its threatening head in nearly all the comfortable corners of that land. Even the simple trick of alternating his identity with that of Walker could now more easily fall foul of the law. DNA profiles and other new scientific perforations of bland surfaces were the enemy now.

Lucan, in the crumby room off the Place Vendôme which he had moved into on his return to Paris, rang the number of his former flat.

'Who's there?' It was Walker's voice. Lucky put down the phone. Walker would have to go. There was no place left for him in life's arrangements, no money to go round.

Gamblers always lose eventually, and if they can't afford to lose it is symptomatic of the situation that the wife should increasingly be blamed for the gambler's 'bad luck', and that she, in turn, should ever more display her dissatisfaction with her reduced domestic life. No household could stand firm in such circumstances. Lucan's children were not the issue; Lucan had come to detest the symbol of his bad luck: his wife and her substantial legal dues awarded by the courts, and had determined to eliminate her. He bungled.

Now Walker was taking her place. Once more, Lucan had come to the end of a cycle of fortune. Old friendships were falling off; people were dead or dying, or they were always somewhere else doing something else. Lucan was still alive? Who cared? Walker was now a liability.

Lucan remembered vividly the horror of his botched murderous attacks. In his frantic telephone calls on that night in 1974 he had reportedly muttered incoherent phrases among which the words 'mess' and 'blood' were distinguished. He now decreed to himself that there should be no blood, no mess, in the disposal of Walker.

In the meantime, having lost heavily at Longchamp, he thought he might as well call on Jean-Pierre Roget, lover of Hildegard Wolf the ex-stigmatic of Munich, to see if there was any news of her, and maybe something to collect in exchange for his dangerous knowledge.

Jean-Pierre was completing a new intricate inlay job on a chest of drawers for a museum of antique furniture, when the door of his workshop opened and in walked a good-looking, dark-haired woman of about thirty-five who seemed obviously, to

Jean-Pierre's sharp mind, one of Hildegard's patients. He was right.

'I'm Mrs Maisie Round, and I've come to dialogue with you,' she declared.

'Oh, I thought you said you were going to sue for damages, Mrs Round. Has your lawyer advised against?'

'My guru suggests eyeball to eyeball, M. Roget. She's usually right.'

'You know,' said Jean-Pierre, 'I'm not in touch with Hildegard.'

'I have to dialogue. I have come to this venue to address the problem that Dr Wolf has left me traumatically in mid-air. At the end of the day, instead of being cured I'm a worse wreck than before. I missed out on a marriage proposal. I want to stipulate that if this situation perpetuates I will need to have recourse to help in a private assisted-living facility.'

'Can't your guru assist you in this – '

A tall man had entered the shop. That melon-shaped head . . . Walker? – No, Lucky Lucan. He had entered before he could see Maisie Round standing behind Jean-Pierre at his workbench.

'Lord Lucan,' said Jean-Pierre, 'may I present Mrs Maisie Round, another of Dr Wolf's patients?'

'Lord Lucan!' she said.

Lord Lucan had turned and walked swiftly out of the workshop. He could be seen hailing a taxi at the end of the street.

'He'll be back,' said Jean-Pierre. 'He's looking for money.'

'Am I crazy or is that the Lucan who murdered the nanny years ago?'

'You are right on both counts. Now I have to close shop, I'm afraid. I am late for a lunch date, hence the confusion.'

Walker was crossing Paris in a taxi. He had seemed to spend a great deal of his life crossing cities in taxis. Lima, Rio, Boston, Glasgow, London, not to speak of Bulawayo, Lagos, Nairobi. All to get from one point to another in aid of Lucan. Now it was Paris, north-east to south, from a Banque Suisse to a Credit Lyonnais and this time with no hope whatsoever in his heart. The account in the first bank had been closed, all the assets withdrawn in two operations, one day following the other, and this was, again, a day after a large deposit had been made in the name of Walker. Lucan must have returned to Paris, he must have gone to some gambling place (or, let's think, yes, the last week of Longchamp) and cleaned out the Scottish connection loot. Now, if there was nothing deposited in the Lyonnais, Walker was practically penniless, alone in a rented apartment, the rent of which had been owing for eight weeks. Shortly, he would be homeless.

And shortly, having discovered that his account in the French bank was also empty, he was on his way, in the Metro, to Jean-Pierre's workshop.

'No,' said Jean-Pierre, when Walker made directly plain his need for 'a loan'. 'Walker,' said Jean-Pierre, 'you are Lucan, in which case you are wanted for murder and attempted murder, or you are Lucan's double, guilty of the offence of aiding and abetting a criminal in his long-term evasion of the law; in other words you are a couple of criminals and you can kindly step out of my workshop.'

'The story of Beate Pappenheim is not very pretty. The old warrant for her arrest has not been lifted.'

'Don't waste my time. It works both ways.'

'We are more elusive than Hildegard.'

A man came in, and got Jean-Pierre's immediate attention. Walker said, 'I'll be back later,' and left. The man was looking for an antique fire-guard, two of which Jean-Pierre was able to produce. There was a good deal of discussion and measuring. Finally the customer chose one, paid, and carried it away under his arm. As he left the shop another man stood in the doorway. The new arrival now entered. He was the African, Dr Jacobs.

'Do you have news?' said Dr Jacobs.

'I do. I've tracked her down to a hotel in London, where she's booked in under her own name, Dr Wolf. She doesn't know it, but I'm leaving tonight for London, where I'll join her.'

'Tell her I've been anxious. I want to resume our sessions.'

'If you really want Hildegard back, you can help me to rid her of a couple of nuisances. Two old men. They are making her life a hell, and she's on the run from them, only from them.'

'How can I help?'

'Africa,' said Jean-Pierre. 'They have been in Africa before, and to Africa they should return.' Jean-Pierre had poured wine for them both and he now pulled round a second chair from the other side of his workbench. They sat talking for two hours, at the end of which Jean-Pierre said, 'Karl Jacobs, you are a true friend.'

'Yes, I think so, Jean-Pierre Roget. I think, always, that I have that talent, to be a true friend.'

When Jean-Pierre entered the lobby of the hotel at Queen's Gate where Hildegard was staying, there was only a young student-like man sitting in a chair reading the *Evening Standard*, and a blonde woman in a black-and-white suit at the desk. By the door were some small pieces of luggage. It was nearly nine-thirty. Jean-Pierre went over to the desk to ask for Hildegard. The woman had paid her bill and now folded it away in her bag. She started towards the door.

'Hildegard!' He was so astonished to see her with her newly fair head of hair that he didn't know quite what to say. He said, 'Will you marry me?'

'What should I do that for?' she said, not knowing, either, exactly what to say.

'Your convalescent widower, Hertz, wants to marry you.'

'I'll have to consult my assistant, Dominique. She's been married twice. What brings you here?'

'You,' he said.

'Well, we're going right back. I'm the pursuer now, and I have the address of a couple of people who are on Lucan's trail in Paris. They've seen him, he keeps evading them but they've seen him.'

XVII

TALL WALKER, HAVING OBTAINED A temporary job as a Père Nöel in a Paris department store, could count on a modest pay for a few weeks ahead. He rather liked the job and fancied he suited it well.

But Walker was weary. The furnished flat comprised two rooms, a kitchen and a bathroom. Lucky normally occupied the bedroom, while Walker slept on a divan in the sitting-room. The place had been decorated by someone with a mania for stripes, pale stripes on the wallpaper, louder ones on the upholstery throughout the apartment. The bathroom tiles formed red stripes punctuated by little bunches of cherries and rosebuds. The towels were striped. The stripes in the sitting-room were green and white. The wall-to-wall stuff on the floor, discernible as a yellowish green by origin, was now a matted and stained old brown. A tap in the bathroom dripped incessantly but Walker didn't feel like approaching the concierge about it; there was the question of the overdue rent which the husband of the concierge ferociously wanted.

Now Walker was idly practising his part before a mirror above the mantelpiece; it seemed to him that he had been attitudinizing most of his life. He had been the perfect English butler in Mexico, he had been Lucky Lucan for over ten years in Central Africa, and recently in Paris; and now Father Christmas at the Bon Marché.

A key in the lock of the front door. Lucky Lucan walked in, not a hair out of place. He held a white carrier bag from which he extracted a bottle of whisky. He put it down on a side table with a thud.

'Where have you been?'

Lucan, on his return from the kitchen with two glasses and a bowl of ice, said, 'Where have I been and what have I done with the money? I might just as well have stayed with my wife. Well, I've had a run of bad luck.'

'I know we're absolutely broke.'

'No,' said Lucan, 'I've just come back from Roget's junk shop. I didn't expect him to let me in, but do you know, he did willingly. I had a long talk with him. We're in business again, we have to go back to Africa.'

'Oh, God! Impossible!'

'Can't be helped. It's inevitable. It's a question of one of these tribal chiefs wanting an English tutor for his children. Two English tutors would be even more acceptable. The utmost discretion about us. His grandson is a Dr Karl Jacobs – here's his card – lives in Paris. There are three sons. No further questions asked. He wants them to grow up like English lords. That's where I fit the bill.'

'Do you trust Jacobs?'

'I shouldn't think so. I haven't met him. But we've nothing much to lose. We've no option, in fact.'

'And Roget?'

'I don't trust him. He's a swine, besides. He makes it a condition that we take this job in Africa. A condition. Otherwise he'll expose us.'

'But Hildegard . . . '

'He tells me Hildegard is well protected. She has the means to defend herself, we don't. And that's maybe the truth. Roget tried to follow me here in a taxi. Some hope! He failed.'

'How much did you get in Scotland?'

'Mind your own business.'

'Haven't you any other old friends?'

'Plenty. One of them has a daughter who wants to get at me. She wants an interview. Writing a book. She's going around with an old gambling friend of mine, Joe Murray. Her mother was Maria Twickenham. They even got on the same plane to Paris as I did. It was touch and go. They half recognized me and half didn't, and then it was too late, you know how it is.'

'I can get a job as a butler again, any time, Lucky. You can count me out of Africa.'

'Oh no I can't. I can make trouble for you and you know it.'

'Not so much as I could make for you.'

'Try it, then.'

It occurred to Walker that much the same conversation had been repeated between them for years; for years on end. He would go to Africa because Lucky Lucan said so.

'I hope,' he said, 'that it will be a comfortable job.'

'Very comfortable. Every comfort,' said Lucan.

'What part exactly?'

'It's a small independent tribal state, north of the Congo, called Kanzia.'

'I've heard of it. A small diamond mine, but extra-large diamonds,' said Walker.

'That's it. And some copper. They do well. They import most things, including equipment for their very decent-sized army.'

'Too hot,' said Walker.

'The Chief's residence has air-conditioning.'

'The Chief?'

'His name's Kanzia, like the place. He calls himself the Paramount Chief. He has a jacuzzi bath,' Lucan said.

'I could swear,' said Lacey, 'that I even saw him dressed as Santa Claus in a department store. Something about his shape, and very tall, no kidding.'

This gave rise to another explosion of laughter all round. There were Lacey, Joe, Jean-Pierre, Hildegard, Dominique, Paul and Dick, with the help of Olivia, all dining together in Hildegard's flat. It was a remarkably happy evening. Lacey, now due home for her children's holidays, had decided to give up her quest. She was recounting with much merriment the number of occasions on which they had missed Lucan by a hair's breadth, and the other occasions on which Joe was either too late or completely mistaken.

'We did really see him on the plane. At Longchamp almost surely. But then Joe had a sighting at a lecture at the British Council. Now, if there is one place Lucan would not be, it would be a lecture at the British Council. A lecture on Ford Madox Ford.'

'And then, you say he was Father Christmas . . . ' said Hildegard.

'That takes the biscuit,' said Joe.

'Well, we've had a good time, Joe and I,' said Lacey. 'It's a pity we never caught up with him after all this effort.'

'He would never have let you interview him.'

'You think not? Even for old friends like Joe and my mother?'

'I don't know,' said Hildegard. They had not been told about Lucan's double. It would be too much for them to take in with all these breaths of happiness they were experiencing. Even a simple manhunt had been so peripheral to their love affair that they had let him slip time and again, and enjoyed it.

'I daresay he'll go back to Africa,' said Jean-Pierre. 'That's where he always feels most secure, I imagine.'

'Oh, surely,' said Hildegard.

'I'm looking forward to getting back to normal, actually,' said Lacey.

'Me, too,' said Hildegard. 'I'm opening my office again next week.'

XVIII

KANZIA WAS A THICKLY FORESTED TERRITORY of about thirty square kilometres, within which was a clearing on a rocky plateau of about five square kilometres. It was bounded by a wide, reedy swamp in the north, a tributary river in the east, a lake in the south and an enemy in the west. That hostile neighbour kept the considerable armed forces of Kanzia constantly on the alert, and was generally useful when the Chief, old Delihu Kanzia, wanted to pick a fight to divert his people's cravings for such indigestible ideas as democracy. As the Chief's grandson, Karl Jacobs, had told Jean-Pierre, the tiny state was renowned for its having extracted over the years an exceptional number of extra-large diamond lumps, from a mine that as yet showed no signs of petering out.

The Chief was supremely happy when his grandson, Karl, in Paris, sent him word by fax that a couple of English earls had been engaged to tutor his three sons, aged thirteen, fifteen and eighteen. He had other small children, but they could benefit from the prestigious village school of Kanzia in the meantime.

For the last lap of their journey Lucky and Walker were borne each on a slung couch attached to four poles. They had left the jeep at the edge of the forest; the rest of the way was a footpath.

'Flies, flies again,' said Lucan. 'People who don't know Africa don't know how thick with flies the air is everywhere. Nobody writes about the flies. Flies, mosquitoes, flying ants, there's no end to them.' He flourished a fly swat that one of his bearers had handed to him. They passed a woman with a child on her back, its eyes and mouth black with crawling flies. In Africa there was nothing to be done, ever, about the flies.

Lucan's four men sweated under their burden. They talked loudly all the way, shouting back also to Walker's bearers.

The Chief was impatient for their arrival. 'What are two English earls doing here in these parts? They have committed crimes?' the wily fellow had asked one of his henchmen.

'Well, one of them is a nanny-basher.'

'What is a nanny?'

'I think it's some kind of an enemy.'

'Then he's a brave man, no?'

'These are Christians. They might bring us a holy scripture and a string of beads. Take no notice.'

'Oh Christians worship the Lamb, unlike the Hindus who worship the Cow. They wash in the blood of a lamb.'

'I don't know about that. I should think it was a sticky way to be washed.'

'They say it makes them white, the blood of the lamb.'

'They're inscrutable, these people, but Karl says they are noblemen.'

Delihu had sent his strongest bearers with their litters and arranged for a long strip of red carpet to be spread down the front steps of his large dwelling.

XIX

HILDEGARD'S BUSINESS FLOURISHED over the following months. She disposed of most of the patients she had left behind when she went to London, for she did not believe in long-term therapy. New patients abounded; she seemed to have the healing touch. She now also returned to her domestic life with Jean-Pierre, untroubled and unmarried as always.

One day in the cold early spring of the following year, Dominique rang through to Hildegard while she was with a patient; this was an unusual procedure.

'Dr Karl Jacobs is here to see you personally.'

'Good. Tell him to wait.'

When his turn came round she greeted him warmly. 'We're in your debt, Dr Jacobs. It's wonderful in Paris these days without the Lucan menace. I hope . . . '

'I bring you information.'

'About them?'

Karl Jacobs began his story:

'You know, my grandfather believed they were both English earls. No matter, let him believe. The three sons did very well under their tuition. They learnt to jump their horses over fences, they learnt to cheat at poker and so on, in the best tradition of a gentleman. The only difficulty was between the two lords. Lord Lucan was hearing voices, and Lord Walker was also assailed by unaccountable fears which I can assure you are peculiar to white people in central Africa.

'My grandfather Delihu was convinced Walker was bewitched, which is always possible in that land. Walker complained that the sun went down too quickly and the long starry nights chilled his soul. Lucan wanted to poison Walker; his voices recommended it. But Chief Delihu Kanzia objected. If you poison a man, you see, Dr Wolf, you can't eat him. My grandfather thought it over, and was advised by the good people of our medicinal miracles that the boys would benefit by consuming an earl; they would become, in effect, Earl Walkers if they should eat Walker. Which is logical – no?'

'Yes,' said Hildegard. 'That's very logical. We become in some measure what we eat, not to mention what we see, hear and smell. The only difficulty is, as you know, Walker is not an earl. Lucan is the earl.'

'No matter,' said Jacobs, 'there was a mistake. Two strong men were set to wait for Walker one night when he was returning from his walk to the Palace Paramount where he had a fine apartment for himself – my grandfather was very benevolent towards him. The men clubbed him to death, only it wasn't Walker, it was Lucan. Such a quantity of blood, my grandfather said . . . The lords were practically identical, except that Lucan was a better teacher. Walker did not have much to teach except fear of the stars.'

'Lucan is dead and buried, then?'

'Lucan is dead, not buried. He was roasted and consumed by all the male children of Delihu. Some of them were rather unwell after the feast, but they are all partly little Lord Lucans now.'

'And Walker?'

'My grandfather discerned that Walker had been spared by unseen spirits of destiny. He has gone to Mexico. My kind grandfather paid his fare. I travelled to Kanzia myself to escort him to an airport. The tribespeople did not care for him at all. They preferred Lucan. But Walker got away. I even helped him to pack his few poor things, and I gave him some of my grandfather's dollars to help him out.'

'It's good of you to come and tell me this, Dr Jacobs.'

'Oh, but I like you so much, Dr Wolf. You've given me such courage to work here in Paris. What I especially came for was to bring you a message that Walker gave me with instructions to send it by e-mail to the German and French consuls in Chad.'

He handed over to Hildegard a handwritten sheet of blue Basildon Bond writing paper. On it was written:

Pappenheim Beate, fraudulent stigmatic of Munich, year 1978 forward, is now a successful psychiatrist in Paris under the false name of Dr Hildegard Wolf. Her sumptuous offices are in the Boulevard St Germain.

'You promised to send this?' said Hildegard.

'Of course. But again, of course, I didn't. In any case the consuls would have thought it mad.'

Hildegard said, 'I appreciate your kindness,' but she obviously meant much more.

'Tear it up,' said Karl K. Jacobs.

She did just that. She looked round the office. It looked cleaner than usual.

Muriel Spark (1918–2006) was born in Edinburgh in 1918 and educated in Scotland. A poet, essayist and novelist, she is most well-known for *The Prime of Miss Jean Brodie* and her writing is widely celebrated for its biting wit and satire. Muriel Spark has garnered international praise and many awards, including the David Cohen Prize for Literature, the Ingersoll T.S. Eliot Award, the James Tait Black Memorial Prize, the Boccaccio Prize for European Literature and the Golden PEN Award for a Lifetime's Service to Literature. She became an Officer of the Order of the British Empire in 1967 and Dame Commander of the Order of the British Empire in 1993, in recognition of her services to literature. *The Times* placed her eighth in its list of the '50 greatest British writers since 1945'. She died in 2006.

SPARK'S EUROPE

A stunning new collection celebrating Spark's European novels

From the grimly gothic *Do Not Disturb* to the razor sharp dissection of manners *The Takeover* and the mordantly brilliant *The Only Problem*, in a panoramic sweep taking in the shores of the Italian lakes to the castles of Geneva and the remote roads of the French countryside, Muriel Spark casts her luminous and searching gaze over the Continent and onto some of the odder specimens of human nature found in its darker recesses.

By turns savage, witty and profound, *Spark's Europe* reaffirms Muriel Spark as one of the most important novelists of the twentieth century.

'My admiration for Spark's contribution to world literature knows no bounds. She was peerless, sparkling, inventive and intelligent – the crème de la crème' Ian Rankin

www.canongate.tv

THE BACHELORS

'I am dazzled by *The Bachelors*. It is the cleverest and most elegant of all Spark's clever and elegant books' Evelyn Waugh

The Bachelors displays the best of Sparkian satire, placing her at the heart of a great literary tradition alongside Waugh and Trollope, Wilde and Wodehouse. It demands rediscovery.

'It's easy to see why Waugh admired *The Bachelors*. On one level, it is a blithely carnivorous satire in the Waugh mould. The bachelors of the title – almost the only men we meet in the narrative – are the thirty-something male barristers, teachers, journalists and museum attendants of a small patch of West London. They lead inturned, doddery, superannuated lives, pottering between grocers, coffee-houses, bedsits and the houses of their mothers and aunts. But the comedy here is serious in a way that Waugh's satanically energetic comedies of misery rarely are . . . comedies of English manners have seldom been darker' *Daily Telegraph*

'My admiration for Spark's contribution to world literature knows no bounds. She was peerless, sparkling, inventive and intelligent – the crème de la crème' Ian Rankin

'Muriel Spark's novels linger in the mind as brilliant shards, decisive as a smashed glass is decisive' John Updike, *New Yorker*

THE FINISHING SCHOOL

In *The Finishing School* Muriel Spark is once again at her biting, satirical best. On the edge of Lake Geneva in Switzerland, a would-be novelist and his wife run a finishing school of questionable reputation to keep the funds flowing. When a seventeen-year-old student's writing career begins to show great promise, jealousy and tensions run high.

A keen portrait of devouring regret, psychological unravelling and the glittering promise of youth, *The Finishing School* is the perfect partner to Muriel Spark's most famous novel *The Prime of Miss Jean Brodie*.

'One of her funniest novels . . . Spark at her sharpest, her purest and her most merciful' Ali Smith

'An eloquent, subtle, poetic exploration of what words are and what they do to us. Enchanting, devastiting, genius' Helen Dunmore, *The Times*

www.canongate.tv

THE PRIME OF
MISS JEAN BRODIE

The Prime of Miss Jean Brodie is Muriel Spark's most significant and celebrated novel, and remains as dazzling as when it was first published in 1961. Now available as an ebook.

Miss Jean Brodie is a teacher unlike any other, proud and cultured, enigmatic and free-thinking; a romantic, with progressive, sometimes shocking ideas and aspirations for the girls in her charge. At the Marcia Blaine Academy she takes a select group of girls under her wing. Spellbound by Miss Brodie's unconventional teaching, these devoted pupils form the Brodie set. But as the girls enter their teenage years and they become increasingly drawn in by Miss Brodie's personal life, her ambitions for them take a startling and dark turn with devastating consequences.

'Muriel Spark's most celebrated novel . . . This ruthlessly and destructively romantic school ma'am is one of the giants of post-war fiction' *Independent*

'A brilliantly psychological fugue' *Observer*

www.canongate.tv